The Prosperity Paradigm

New beliefs that can help you make a greater living by making a greater difference

Steve D'Annunzio

This book is not intended to be considered as financial, medical, legal or any other professional advice or service. The information provided is not a substitute for professional advice or care. If you desire or require financial, medical, legal, or any other expert assistance, you should seek the services of a competent licensed and registered professional. The author, the publisher and their employees and agents are not liable for any damages arising from, or in connection with, the use of or reliance on any information contained in this book.

ISBN 978-1-60402-209-4
First Edition June, 2006
Second Edition September, 2006
Third Edition June, 2007
White Light Press
P.O. Box 23
Hewlett, NY 11557

Printed by Mercury Print
Cover design by Alisha Provostgaard
Printed in the U.S.A.

For ordering go to:
www.theprosperityparadigm.com

Dedication

To the family that make this life beautiful everyday—Anathea, Jenna, Alicia, and Colin. No words can describe the joy you bring, and the understanding you showed during the writing of this work.

To Mom, Dad, Chris and Nancy for always being there with love, no matter what.

To Jeff Locker for the awakening to the world of prosperity, and for unconditional friendship along the way.

To Fred Johnson for being a living example that God is always here, now. I am honored to have you as my teacher and my friend.

To the members of Christ Church Unity in Rochester, and to all members of the mentoring group. You asked the greatest questions that created the perfect context for the '*I*' to express Itself—you are so great—Thank You.

To Garrett Gunderson, Greg Blackbourn, Carl Lutz, and the whole team at The Prosperity Paradigm. My friends, my brothers, our hope for the future...

To the enlightened masters, Sri Bhagavan Ciranjiva Roy, and Dr. David Hawkins, whose religion is kindness and Truth, and whose lives are a living scripture.

To you, with Love...

Table of Contents

Introduction

Every being on Earth is on a journey—a quest, if you will. A quest to find meaning in life for some, a quest to find riches for others, while for others happiness and peace are the goal. Unfortunately, many others struggle to find any direction in life. Why is the goal of life so elusive? Because human beings are schizophrenic. We are constantly listening to, and acting on, one of two dialogues in the mind. Think of one as 'me', and the other as 'I'.

Think about a time you were unhappy with your own behavior. You might say, "I'm disappointed in myself". Now ask, who is the 'I' that is disappointed with the 'myself?' Or think about a time you hit a bad golf or tennis shot, or performed some task in a way that was not as good as you had hoped. Then you involuntarily began berating yourself, possibly saying things like, "You idiot, what's wrong with you?!" Who is berating whom? Can you see that in this kind of situation there appear to be two beings present – one who is belittling and the other who is being belittled? Who is this perfectionist for whom your best is never good enough? Isn't it odd that we act like two beings and no one notices it? Again, one being can be thought of as 'me', and the other as 'I'.

For this author, *'me'* was first a little boy, then a football player, then a musician, then a salesman, then a husband, then a father, then a minister—and on and on. But while 'my' labels shifted throughout life, the essence of who 'I' was never changed. This unchangeable essence was always present, watching all the changes. This will be an important realization for you to make as well. While you have had many different aspects to who you've perceived yourself to be (*me*), your essence *('I')* throughout all those permutations has never changed. This is the real authentic Self that must be discovered for you to attain true prosperity.

'*Me*' can be (and certainly has been in my case) ignorant and extremely limited—while ***'I'*** is brilliant and magnificent. Me is a kind of false or lower self filled with fear and doubt. ***'I'*** is the True You—a higher self filled with much greater power and awareness.

The first remembered awareness of this sense that the true self exists occurred while taking off an uncomfortable Halloween mask, saying, "I'm not wearing this mask!" Even then, ***'I'*** craved authenticity, would not tolerate being masked, and sought to be real and known. While going to sleep that night and fearful of the dark, ***'I'*** again emerged, revealing that darkness wasn't real. (Modern science has now proved this fact) The little 'me' then began to look for light particles in the darkness, and could see them, was reassured, and fell asleep easily. The Infinite ***'I'*** had manifested and been experienced, and the little 'me' took notice of that specific event as a reminder of Truth.

But Truth was elusive because '*me*' was filled with so many fears and desires. ***'I'*** was patient and always present, emerging at certain times with powerful effects. An act of courage to defend younger kids against a schoolyard bully who appeared to be unbeatable…feeling the presence of God so powerfully while alone in nature, that the instant I thanked Him the wind blew me off my bike unhurt…feeling the hollowness of organized religion while making my Catholic communion and confirmation. It was then that the observation occurred that an innate Knowledge of scripture existed within. There was nothing in this lifetime that could logically account for that Knowledge. With little fanfare this observation was simply noticed and discarded, as it did not fit into my life at that time in any way. '*I*' was a Higher Self filled with Love and Courage, and 'me' was a lower self filled with fear and uncertainty. Being raised by parents who were unaware of the Higher Self, '*I*' soon dissipated, and by the age of fourteen was a forgotten memory.

Around most adults, a process of adulteration would happen, which the immaturity of my being was unable to stop. My brain was so easily programmed by older authority figures that, over the next four years, this physical form survived only due to the grace of God. I felt totally lost. The death of several friends due to drug overdose, suicide, and motor vehicle accidents magnified this feeling of lost-ness to an unbearable point. Serious discontent, combined with the seeming possibility of my own non-existence, caused me to pray to God for help. Shortly thereafter (at age eighteen) an enlightened master from India appeared as an answer to my prayer.

Descriptions of my experiences of studying with this being would strain credulity and could be a book unto itself. The high points for your edification are as follows. He effortlessly was One with the '*I*'—and an extraordinary discourse on Truth flowed from him in a way in which the miraculous happened every moment we were together. Whatever served raising the love and expansion for the Highest Good of All was expressed in a refreshingly easy-going, non-dogmatic manner. He quoted the teachings of Jesus Christ when it served, then the Buddha at other times, then Krishna when that context served the highest good. He didn't read or recite these teachings. He revealed them as if he was there when they were uttered, as if aware of every nuance and hand gesture with which they were originally expressed.

He spoke to things that only the '*I*' within me could have known about my own life. When asked how he knew these things, he said, *"the '**I**' within us is the same being and knows all. I know your life because I am you."* He spoke to us with a personal knowledge of our lives because of this fact, doing so in a hilarious, revelatory style. He began and ended every conversation by gleefully proclaiming, "Bam Shankar Bholenath!" (in the ancient language called Sanskrit it translates: *May we recognize God in each other, and His Divine activity in* *all we say and do!)* He repeatedly stressed that he was not a guru, but simply a man who had realized the most natural state of human existence: unity and oneness with God. He had broken through to achieve the enlightened state—he had become one with the *'I'*. The *'me'* is ego—a lower-self fear animal, and within this man the ego was dead. 'I' is the God-Self Higher Mind, and to this master—born Chiranjiva Roy, but we called him Father—**It** was all that existed. The relevant point is that he put spiritual teachings into context for us, bringing them to life as an experiential practical reality in service to the world. Where so many others proselytized about religion, he made the spiritual value of 'prosperity consciousness' knowable and duplicable.

In 1981 he announced he would soon be 'leaving his physical form," and did so a year later. Shortly thereafter, as is the tendency with we humans, everything was forgotten by me. 'Me' had immersed myself in pursuit of the so-called American Dream, but instead had created an ego nightmare, and found myself facing a throat tumor that appeared to threaten my life. I told no one, but it was quite apparent that the lower-self ego had again overtaken me, and the infinite *'I'* was often spoken about, but rarely used. I had become an ignorant hypocrite—spouting spiritual stories when it served my ego as witty cocktail party banter, but not using Spiritual Truth when life difficulties arose and it was time to 'walk the talk.'

'Me' appeared to be dying, and *'I'* made the authentic observation that fear was on the back end of every thought. I was able to make the critical realization that fear was killing me. Recognizing that the tumor was mainly a physical expression of fear, I thought to myself, "what if I begin to ***love*** the tumor—could it possibly shrink? My innate knowledge of scripture reminded me that 'with God all things were possible.' So I began doing the unthinkable—I began thanking God for the tumor, chanting to it with gratitude, singing healing songs to it. I began doing this discipline every day. At first it felt stupid and insincerely futile, as if there was some inner thing that wanted 'me' to die. This Truth then flashed through my consciousness exactly like an inner lightning bolt—a flash of Truth. 'Me' **must** die—it is the ego—IT is what's threatening the body. Either it dies, or the

physical form dies—which would it be?

Whole stories of my existence began to be surrendered, along with a series of 'poor me' myths about why my life wasn't better. As those once-cherished illusions crumbled, a new energy and power began coursing through this body. In direct proportion to the shrinking of the ego, so did the tumor shrink. Within a fairly short time period, it dissipated into the nothingness from whence it came, and the body was healed. From that time period on, it became customary to begin every day with hours of study, prayer, and meditation. In becoming somewhat of a recluse, all my old friends disappeared. Any thing having to do with relieving suffering in the world was voraciously studied in inspired isolation. It was as if my own suffering had made me acutely sensitive to the need to help alleviate suffering in others. Understandably, my family thought I had gone off the deep end, especially when they learned that I quit my successful career in the corporate sales world. To their way of thinking I was doing nothing. But something quite extraordinary was happening—the lower fear-based aspect of 'me' had all but disappeared, only to be replaced by the God-Self of the 'I'.

It was as if the whole world had been transformed, for I was seeing it with new eyes. People I had once held grudges against were easily forgiven and appreciated with humorous amazement. Instead of viewing past hurts with my former righteous indignation, they were seen as important rites of passage that were necessary to create who ***'I'*** currently am. Negative people and events no longer happened, for they were not allowed to be viewed as anything other than perfect and meaningful. It's not that things always went 'my way'. The difference was that when events occurred differently from that which I preferred, I viewed them as 'thy way'—as if they were meant to be that way. Apparent slights were always interesting and valuable lessons, and what was once considered to be miraculous became the norm.

This process of self-discovery had connected the inner awareness to a place of infinite wisdom. As first it was a little odd, but as I continued to move forward, I *experienced* a personal intimate relationship with Infinite Intelligence itself. In difficult situations I would simply relax and remember God—and the right words flowed, not from me, but through me. This 'flow' not only contained the right words, but they came in the perfect sequence, with the right intonation and attitude, using the perfect analogies and anecdotes for the given circumstance. Others didn't know this, because they heard the words come from my mouth. Little by little it became a regular occurrence, and I began to trust that this infinite creativity was always there.

The lifelong love of music began to express itself through this body in all new ways. A new musical scale was discovered, which was first utilized in a set of tuning forks (D'Annunzio, 1994). This new musical scale contained a higher frequency of vibration in which a uniquely healing effect was experienced by those who used them. It became the *Music For Healing* tape/CD series which has since been studied and often results in therapeutic healing benefits in the listener (Denmeade, 1997). Unique ideas to do seminars, write books, and serve the personal development of others became the main thrust of life.

It appeared that 'I' had discovered Soul Purpose, to which all true credit goes to God, who revealed it. Enigmatic scriptures that were once puzzling were made known. It became apparent that when Jesus Christ said that "I am the way, I am the life," etc—and yet these things I have done, ye shall do, and greater" (John 14:12)—he was revealing the inner ***'I'*** that exists as an innate potential inside us all. ***'I'*** is the infinite being of Love within each of us, and this is the possibility to which Jesus referred.

At times, the flow of energy through this physical form became so intense that at one point it appeared as if the body was experiencing a stroke or brain hemorrhage. Much like putting too much electrical voltage through a circuit would blow the breaker, these profound shifts in consciousness were often physically painful. After that event, it was noticed that dizziness was often experienced when passing certain people on the street. I eventually came to realize this was due to the negativity of whatever life situation they were experiencing and thus projecting. Once this was recognized, prayer for the person resulted in a physical rebalancing and the dizziness would stop. In this manner it was simply accepted that prayer for all people was required by the *'I'*. Passing ambulances were prayed for, as were terrible drivers, as were those who were deemed hopeless cases by society. From that point forward, being around any negative energy—whether it was a movie, song, event, or person—had a similarly noticeable effect on the body.

Certain people followed the vibration of love that was flowing through this form, and were thus guided to the work. In one case, a woman who had been crushed in a car accident with a concrete truck—resulting in a seemingly hopeless life, was brought by her friend. All standard allopathic medical treatments had been tried to little or no avail. *'Me'* had nothing to do with her recovery, but *'I'* appeared to behave as a conduit for some sort of healing energy to flow. It first expressed itself in the form of musical toning, then specific visualizations she was guided to do as well as individual meditations and prayers. She recovered, but not all did. Some had miraculous healings and others did not, apparently in perfect accord with the Divine Will of the Infinite Intelligence.

The Higher Self of the *'I'* suggested a spiritual ordination was appropriate to enhance credibility in the eyes of the outside world, and this suggestion was complied with. The *'I'* within laughed at this exercise, which was thoroughly enjoyable. This process took place first through ordination as a Christian minister (Order of Melchizedek), then later as a Hindu monk (Kriya Yoga). Shortly thereafter, the minister of a local non-denominational church, where I had been doing workshops, resigned. The congregation asked that I replace her, and the ordination process consequently made perfect sense. Every guidance from the inner 'I' continued to prove meaningful in much the same way, having been verified over time to be trustworthy beyond ordinary understanding.

Interesting hidden potentials continued to reveal themselves. Someone would supply a word, and a delightful spontaneous song using that word flowed through. The songs were often amazing in their beauty, relevance, and perfection. This quality existed independent of me, and flowed of its own. At times it was so strong as to be unmistakable to all present. At other times it was almost despairing when it was asked to present itself, but for whatever reason was seemingly absent.

While the old group of friends disappeared, high-quality new relationships showed up out of the blue to assist in the expansion of the work in ways almost too perfect to be believed. The wife of the president of a major well-known corporation called to order music for healing tapes. I answered, and eventually—through a series of synchronicities—wound up doing workshops for the Fortune 100 Company her husband represented. The vice-president of a major performing arts center began to support the work, and to introduce it on an international level. A nurse at a famous medical center requested a music therapy workshop to be done there, and the resulting credibility from that work propelled the teachings into many other hospitals. The new career was growing effortlessly, while the only efforts I expended were focused on awareness, study, and doing daily spiritual disciplines. The work had primarily taken on the form of a healing thought-field therapy, and was consistently being offered at hospitals, wellness centers, and churches.

Then, a shift occurred sometime in early spring of 1997. In meditation one morning of that year, the guidance came through loud and clear that I was being sent back into the world of business. Having experienced such a feeling of liberation when I left the old business world, this came as a surprise. I came to understand that the world of business was going to become a new field of spiritual expression because everyone on Earth has their hand in business. In short, it appears that many people were/are turned off by religion, but turned on by business—so the Infinite Intelligence was sending me back into it with a new mission. This mission is to uplift the business world by using non-denominational spiritual principles in the context of productivity training. In the wake of the seeming failure of organized religion to produce a more peaceful world in which to live, business is evidently providing a new playing field for humanity to peacefully grow and evolve.

Empowered by this guidance, I watched for the entrée into this new field to reveal itself. Shortly afterward, the only old friend still present from the previous life called on the telephone. He asked for help in writing a curriculum for a financial services company he was training. The rest fell into place, and the work has now transformed into a Business Ministry. The essence of that curriculum is contained herein. It has been successfully used, over thousands of applications, to create favorable conditions for prosperity to occur in the life of the user.

This work is far from the only one existing on the topic of prosperity. Many others are very valuable, and several of the authors are cited throughout this work. It *is unique* though, in that it deals with prosperity as an effect, revealing that the only true cause is a choice you make every moment. That is the choice between the ego-self lower mind (*me*), and the God-Self higher mind (‘***I***’). It also reveals an aspect of prosperity that is rarely discussed by any other text. That is, the greatest possible wealth a human being can aspire to—Unity and Oneness with God, or Enlightenment. I am not enlightened, but I am a being whose physical form has been taken over by Love itself. As such, the ability to choose love over fear uniquely qualifies this author to write about such an expansive topic.

My promise to you, dear reader, is that when you learn to fully listen to, and act on, the inner ‘***I***’—you will experience true prosperity beyond your wildest imagination. Bॐm Shankar Bholenath!

Steve D’Annunzio
Rochester, NY 2006

Foreword

If you had the opportunity to have a Council of Masters acting as life success teachers for you for free, would you be open to receive their guidance and, most importantly, to act on it? And what if these teachers were the greatest thinkers, philosophers, artists, doctors, business leaders, inventors, saints, sages, and Savior the world has ever known? Would that get you to sit up and heed their proven wisdom even more? Having a brief discussion with any one of them would have indelibly changed your life for the better, had you been able to.

This curriculum is written by them, through me.

The Council of Masters

Scientists/Thinkers	Doctors	Philosophers	Enlightened Masters
Albert Einstein	Wayne Dyer	Socrates	Buddha
David Bohm	Sigmund Freud	Patanjali	Krishna
Isaac Newton	Herbert Benson	Ram Dass	Chiranjiva Roy
Brandon Carter	Larry Dossey	Thoreau	Ramesh Balsekar
Stephen Hawking	Carl Jung	Lao Tzu	David Hawkins
Richard Feynman			
Nicolas Copernicus			
Hans Jenny			

Business Coaches	Economists	Savior
Zig Ziglar	Solomon S. Huebner	Jesus Christ
Brian Tracy	Milton Friedman	
Warren Buffet		

To maximize the value you can receive from reading this work, I strongly suggest for you to realize and implement the following:

1. Have two different color highlighters handy as you read. Everything you find powerful, highlight in yellow—anything you do not understand or agree with, highlight in pink. The pink highlights are the truly important points for you to understand, and they will hence be easy to spot later on for referencing.

2. The intention of this work is to increase joy and success, and nothing else. To this end, please understand that words are symbols, with the same word having different meanings to different people. Controversial words like money, love, God, and others are given specific definitions to facilitate clearer understanding. If some words evoke strong disagreement, remember that words are symbols, and that you are most likely giving a distinctly different meaning than may be herein intended. Or, you have a limiting belief you just came face-to-face with, and the ego within is causing upset. Please read on either way. Much like a map is never the actual terrain, words paint pictures around that which must be experienced to become reality. Therefore,

as best possible, suspend negative judgment and disbelief. Everything written in this curriculum has been personally experienced by this author, except where otherwise noted.

3. The pronouns ***he*** and ***his*** are often used throughout this work when examples are given to illustrate a point. This practice is for simplicity only, considering English language customs, and not meant to be gender-biased. Please read these passages with this understanding.

4. Repetition of key ideas is intentionally used throughout. Conscious intelligence will increase within you as you read this work, so a point you may've struggled with earlier in the text may be encountered later on with a great *Aha!* This is due to the intentional use of spaced repetition.

5. The curriculum is designed for the serious seeker of prosperity via the path of Truth Consciousness. The ego within us all is intrinsically stubborn and prideful. It does not welcome having its cherished beliefs revealed as the illusions of misperception they often are. If you are reading this text with the hidden agenda of confirming that which you already believe, this work may result in paradigm shock—and is probably better bypassed.

6. Remember that you can make an enormously positive difference in a world that desperately needs it, and you are dearly loved.

7. Realize that this curriculum is less about learning, and more about ***unlearning***. Success will reveal itself when its obstacles are removed. By unlearning the obstacles to success, success will reveal itself. If you remove the clouds the sun is always shining. Prosperity is your Truthful birthright, and through the *removal of untruth* your inherent prosperity will shine unimpeded.

Chapter One

Paradigms of Reality

One hundred fifty years ago the great American philosopher Henry David Thoreau said, "most men lead lives of quiet desperation and go to the grave with the song still in them." I have been blessed to earn a living speaking to thousands of people about life success, and I can tell you that most people still live that way. My purpose in writing this book is to offer a possibility for change, by sharing a curriculum for prosperity that can help you become happier, healthier, and wealthier. And, hopefully, to inspire you to discover 'the song'—which I call ***Soul Purpose***—to which Thoreau refers.

It has been said that one's quality of life is the sum total of all choices and decisions one makes. What compels you to make those choices and decisions? You, and every other human being on Earth, live your life by a set of rules and beliefs called a paradigm.

Your paradigm is a cultural rulebook that is stored in the subconscious mind, and forms your version of reality. It contains rules of conduct in every area of life—what to like/not like, how to dress, what to eat, how we heal, how to earn, where to live, what a 'good or bad' job is, what is or isn't socially acceptable behavior, etc. It also contains hidden guidelines about what is possible for you to achieve in the world in which you were raised, *not the world in which you live.*

Most people don't freely choose or decide these things—their cultural programming does. While you *think* you are consciously making choices, the programmed paradigm stored in your subconscious mind is telling you what to do.

These paradigms serve as maps of reality. Your paradigm constitutes your total world-view belief system. It is your beliefs that determine your behavior, and behavior determines results. If the results you are experiencing in any area of your life are not acceptable, where must the change occur? Beliefs! **It is your beliefs that determine your behavior, and behavior determines results**. Each person's paradigm map is a belief system that guides them through life's journey, and that belief system is, for the most part, 'input' by their culture, rather than arrived at by themselves.

After doing well over ten thousand coaching sessions in the area of increased prosperity, I conclusively discovered a hidden truth.

The great majority of human beings are following a paradigm map that guides them to experience money problems and unhappiness. And worse yet, these same people believe that this negativity is their destiny and unchangeable. *Nothing could be farther from the truth.* If you are one of these people, as I was, you are simply following a faulty map. **It is not your <u>fault</u>, but it is your <u>responsibility</u> to make a shift, and shift <u>you can</u>.**

You are responsible for discovering that 'huge possibility' within you—which *you know* is there. By following the guidance of the aforementioned Council of Masters I found mine, and then studied the great success figures in history who also found theirs. While the details of our life stories were quite different, the principles of success were remarkably similar. These principles will be reiterated throughout this curriculum, so that you can re-program yourself to experience **True Wealth**.

From this curriculum you will clearly learn:

- That one of two paradigms—scarcity or Prosperity—will determine your wealth, health and happiness no matter what
- How and why approximately eighty percent of people settle for a life of negativity (Hawkins, 2005)

- The enormous difference between having money and being wealthy (explaining why some miserable people have money—but are not truly wealthy)
- How to reconcile spiritual wealth with material wealth, instead of viewing them as mutually exclusive
- What money is, and how to create a greater flow of it in your life with the highest integrity, respect, and fun
- Understanding Soul Purpose—and a means to not only discover yours, but to live it every moment
- How to experience greater health and happiness by *prioritizing and balancing* the most important aspects of life—family, spirituality, career, and money
- Understand Prosperity Economics, which, if understood and applied, will allow you to create permanent wealth with certainty
- The hidden mission of every being on Earth, and the obstacles that prevent most people from realizing and achieving it
- Most importantly, you will discover the supreme goal of human existence—the understanding of which leads to the ultimate wealth.

Aside from learning about these topics, you will be given a detailed manual on exactly how to shift paradigms and experience greater prosperity immediately.

* * *

In 1962, philosophy professor Thomas Kuhn wrote a book entitled *The Structure of Scientific Revolution*, in which the concept of paradigm shifts was first introduced. Kuhn theorized that breakthroughs in science did not evolve in a step-by-step linear way, but happened through inner belief-system changes by the scientist. He observed that all breakthroughs in history occurred the exact same way—through radically oppositional thinking to the 'status quo' of what was already known. Those scientists who were willing to think in ways no one had thought before—like Einstein—made the monumental breakthroughs.

This kind of daring thinking requires a momentary

surrendering of old beliefs—which is the barrier for most individuals. Being creatures who find security in habit, people love their beliefs even if, rather than providing true security, those beliefs lead to suffering and premature death. If you see the folly in this behavior, and are willing to allow yourself to temporarily suspend certain beliefs, a higher belief can now enter in—and a magnificent change can occur. This is called a Paradigm Shift.

This curriculum will therefore focus on non-traditional thinking. Please reason through this: eighty percent of humans are more unhappy than happy, more poor than rich, more sick than healthy, and more fearful than confident. Ultimately, those are the exact results that conventional thinking and common sense will provide for you. For most of you reading this, merely thinking differently will not be enough—you must think the opposite. The man who was generally regarded as one of the most brilliant minds in history was Albert Einstein. His stunning scientific breakthroughs came from oppositional thinking, and it was about this exact topic that he said:

> *Any intelligent fool can make things bigger, more complex, and more violent. It takes a touch of genius—and a lot of courage—to move in the opposite direction.*

If you only use *common* sense, what you will get is a common life. If you want to live an extraordinary life you must use *extraordinary* sense—and you do have this capability within you.

To help you understand why seeking a paradigm shift is so important, let us outline how paradigm programs get input, and the consequences of living according to a flawed paradigm.

We are programmed first by our biological parents or caregivers. The programming continues being input by elementary, middle, high school teachers, college experiences, social friends, books, magazines, television, radio, Internet, religious leaders, scientific leaders, political leaders, etc. Each of these influences contribute beliefs that complete your paradigm by about the age of twenty-one. It is your paradigm that acts as the operating system in the computer of your mind, automatically feeding choices and decisions as thoughts into your mind. Whether the beliefs are true or false is irrelevant to our computer-like mind. Like the computer that can only run by the operating system that is installed, your mind will mechanically continue on with an outdated program *even if it has been proven to be non-functional.* Go into any computer search engine and type in 'The Flat Earth Society' and you'll get a clear idea of non-functional programming. This group is absolutely convinced the world is flat, despite all the irrefutable evidence. Not too long ago, everyone on Earth believed the world was flat, proving that just because everyone believes something doesn't mean it is true.

Prosperity Paradigm Principle

Collective human behaviors/beliefs do not qualify those behaviors/beliefs to be TRUTH.

Just because most everybody believes first in fear and negativity does not mean that you should. Many people continue to live their lives according to their programmed paradigm long after it's been proven to be non-functional—and therefore false—out of habit and fear. What proves their paradigm is false? It doesn't work! While Americans live productive lives relative to the rest of the world, most are still under-earning and unhappy with how they earn. In many cases this is because we are living by the set of rules within the flawed paradigm put there by others. Do you see the folly in living your life by a set of rules and beliefs put there by a group of people who are miserable—yet you're trying to be happy by living them?

This is because the human mind is much like the hardware of a computer. Whatever is entered into your computer as software is run by the hardware called the brain. Can the hardware choose its software? No. It can only run the programmed software that has been downloaded, and has no choice but to do so. The software is social programming (your current paradigm) and the hardware is your mind. Who are you? You are the soul in the body—the spirit in the body that has a mind, but is not the mind. The spirit—your highest Self—is the most powerful part of who you are, and the only aspect of yourself who has true authorship over your life story. By seeing your Self this way, you can stop being bullied around by your mind, recognize the defective programming for what it is, and delete it. Being stuck in one's mind is a hellish thing because much of our social programming is sick and non-functional.

Therefore, this curriculum will empower you to create results from a higher plane of potential—that which I refer to as the spiritual realm. Being spiritual and being religious are two very different things. While I am a definite proponent of the upside of religious life, it's necessary to illustrate the huge difference between religion and spirituality. Any sensible human being has respect for the upside of religion, while also recognizing its downside. It is due to the good works of a variety of differing religious groups that downtrodden people all over world have received food, clothing, medicine and shelter in dire circumstances, and this is obviously very good. The downside of religion is a dangerous distortion wrought by fundamental fanatics who use it as a political control weapon hiding behind the cloak of scripture.

Because of religious bigotry and deception, many people are turned off by the word spiritual, so I will re-define my meaning of it. When I use the word *spiritual* I refer to a choice—choosing love, faith and confidence over fear, doubt and worry. Spirituality is a *way of being* that people choose, or do not choose, every moment of their existence. It is choosing to be, and to behave, as either the God-Self or the ego-self. Studying the attributes to these two very different selves will be helpful for clarity sake.

God-Self	**ego-self**
love	fear
faith	doubt
confidence	worry
learning	blaming
serving	prideful
humble	narcissistic
asking	demanding
empowering	controlling

Thus, being spiritual is choosing love over fear when you are challenged. It is choosing to have faith instead of allowing ourselves to be filled with doubt when difficulties arise. When things don't go as planned the spiritual being focuses on learning instead of blaming, and so on with both categories of opposite qualities being virtually endless.

It is recognized that all religions are based upon the inspired revelations of an individual. Each was originally a great spiritual leader who inspired people through the radiance and presence of their own experience with Divinity. Each one spoke from direct experience with God, not scriptural authority. However, with the death of each revelator, the original principles got distorted or were used out of context. Though the intentions of all religions were initially pure, the means by which the followers continued them became convoluted. The main error is honoring scripture more than God itself. The scripture is certainly a useful road map, but any traveler knows that the map is never the terrain. From this central error sprang an 'us versus them' mentality that justifies negativity in the name of God.

To deepen the confusion, each clan points to their own differing scripture claiming that it justifies their behavior. The folly of that might be best explained using this metaphor. Imagine driving on a family trip to the Grand Canyon. You buy a map which outlines the most direct route there, including beautiful pictures of all the different canyons. So you set out, finally arriving there three days later, but instead of getting out and hiking to explore and experience the whole purpose of your journey you just sit in your car pouring adoration onto the map. Your adoration is interrupted as a car pulls in next to yours. Your license plates say New York and the car next to yours has plates from California. You notice the driver adoring his map too. You think you have something in common with him so you get out to chat about the greatness of your map. You are dismayed however, to discover he has an entirely different map even though it accurately led him to the exact same place where you currently are. Because he drove from a different starting point his map *must* be different, which of course makes perfect sense to anyone thinking clearly. But you put all your faith into your map, so you are no longer thinking clearly. Despite the fact that you both arrived at your intended destination, you decide to argue about whose map is right. And the more you try to convince each other you're right and he's wrong the angrier each one gets. So here you are in this magnificent sacred setting totally ignorant of the initial intention of the journey, trying to kill each other.

This is what many religions have become.

Out of fear, religious beliefs focus on accentuating differences, proving others wrong, moral superiority, and converting others. Each has a unique story that offers converts an edge on Truth, thus claiming all others as erroneous. This results in close-minded and fearful behavior of other philosophies outside of their own, condemning them as wrong with little or no knowledge of that which they condemn. Thus, religions have historically become an egoistic hierarchy perpetrated in the name of God.

The word religion means to 'bind back', as its original purpose was to re-legion people (meaning to form into tribal groups or *legions*). Despite this, religion has historically proven to serve as the core justification for more hateful and violent behavior than any other idea. (The Crusades, the Inquisition, Protestants vs. Catholics in the U.K., Arab/Israeli conflict in the Middle East, 9/11) Each religious 'side' has convincing rationalizations of how and why they are right, and claims the other 'side' to be satanic heathens.

Spiritual beliefs are love-based. They focus on accentuating commonalities, non-judgmentalism, and forgiveness. They are open-minded and embrace the underlying truth of all religions. The word spiritual is derived from the Latin word for *breath,* referring to the source of life itself. The origins of Christianity, Islam, and Judaism can be directly traced back to the founding father of all three religions—Abraham. His teachings focused on three essential qualities: love, faith, and forgiveness.

One can see that being spiritual may or may not have anything to do with religion, though the two words are often used interchangeably. According to the given definition given here, many so-called religious people behave anything but spiritually. Truly religious people *are* spiritual, but not all spiritual people practice a specific, or any, religion. The spiritual seeker focuses on the universal principles and values that form the basis of all religions, without the need of dogma or ecclesiastic approval. Instead of focusing on changing *others*, the spiritual person focuses on changes *themselves*. By committing to live these principles, the spiritually-oriented person gains entrance into a new field of life possibility.

The spiritual realm is the place of highest possibility, the mental realm is the middle, and the physical realm is the lowest. You spirit is the essence of that which you are. The spirit is the true author of your life story; and it is from this realm only that your soul purpose can be clearly identified. Only the true author can consciously write the software of success. Others have entered flawed software into your brain and this programming affects everything, but only the true author (the spirit –your higher self) can delete it and re-program it. The true author is the spirit, not the mind. The mind is the hardware; it has no say in the matter!

Adding to the faulty software problem most of us have, is the fact that the human mind has the virus of fear, doubt, and worry. How well would your computer work if it contracted a virus? The answer is: not at all. It would still turn on, and look like it is OK, but the minute you tried to run a program it would start to sputter, and malfunction, and possibly freeze up. Until you run an anti-viral program, it could never successfully complete an application you are trying to run.

When most people try to do a task out of their normal routine, the virus begins to short-circuit their efforts. There is no outside threat causing pain, but the inner virus is causing pain, so the person erroneously tells himself *the task* is painful. Our poor programming projects the inner fear onto the outer task, creating resistance to the task—even though it may be beneficial for all. Concerning the business realm, this limits people in areas like marketing, prospecting, effective communication, and accountability. In our personal life, it limits our effectiveness in areas pertaining to exercise, eating right, prayer, and meditation. Each of these activities is beneficial to us and to society, but is made difficult by the inner virus of fear, doubt, and worry.

The weakness and frustration that emanate from this inner virus constantly drain the person running it so they cannot advance beyond it. This results in one's doing the same thing in the same way day-in and day-out, yet expecting a different result. This is insanity, and is scientifically called paradigm blindness.

Paradigm blindness is a term used to describe what happens to people when their current paradigm prevents them from seeing new, viable options. A dominant paradigm, even though it has repeatedly been proven false, often continues to blind its owner both to its non-functionality and to other more favorable alternatives.

Here are some powerful examples of this phenomenon, from so-called experts in the areas upon which they were referring:

1. "Everything that can be invented has been invented."
   Charles Duell, commissioner, U.S. Office of Patents, 1899

2. "Who the hell wants to hear actors talk?"
   H.M.Warner, Warner Brothers, 1927

3. "I think there is a world market for maybe five computers."
   Thomas Watson, Chairman of IBM, 1944

4. "$640,000 ought to be enough for anybody"
   Bill Gates, now CEO of Microsoft, 1981

When these comments were made, each person was viewing the subject matter from an old established paradigm, and each statement probably seemed reasonably intelligent if heard by someone who lived at that time. But because you are presently viewing each topic from a 'new paradigm,' every quote seems ludicrous and short-sighted. These were not unintelligent men—they were all considered to be leaders and experts in their given field of expertise. (Janis, 2000).

We all suffer from paradigm blindness—it's part of being human. The breakthrough question is, *'am I willing to open to new unfamiliar truths for the sake of greater health, wealth, and happiness?* If you **are** open, the next question is, *'how committed am I to the discipline* *required to implement the new program?'*

If the discontent regarding your current level of prosperity is not great enough, you will most likely change nothing. If the discontent within you **is** great enough, you absolutely can do it. Discontent allows us to discover two great spiritual powers deep within – faith and will. They do not exist in the mental realm, because they are spiritual essences. It is the faith to believe in your self enough to trust that you will endure and succeed no matter what. It is then the will to tell myself the hard truth about what is working, or is not working in my life. The hard truth concludes with the realization of who is responsible, if any movement towards prosperity is to occur. This faith must then be combined with the will to admit to yourself the absolute truth about the failure of your current paradigm.

What is needed to cure paradigm blindness is a paradigm shift. A paradigm shift can only occur when the pain of running a false program has reached the point when you say—ENOUGH. The shift can begin by learning from one's discontent, remaining open to new possibilities and through a willingness to implement new truths that seem unfamiliar and therefore uncomfortable. These new truths may seem to contradict old teachings which you've heard are true, but in most people have never been personally investigated—nor experienced—as Truth. The key is to remain open-minded. If you have the courage to admit that certain areas of your life are not working, and you are open-minded to try what is being offered here, you possess all that is necessary to be far more prosperous.

Understanding the Basics

Remember—beliefs govern behavior, and behavior creates results. This curriculum has three aspects to it: *understanding* the Prosperity Paradigm, *internalizing* it, and finally *externalizing* it to create new results. By understanding it you will be educating yourself to a higher belief system, to create higher behavior and thus achieve greater results.

What is true prosperity? While most people struggle with how to have more money, many so-called wealthy people struggle with how to be happier and to find balance. Is money more important than happiness? Is wealth more important than health? What is wealth? For many, these are maddeningly difficult questions to ponder, understand, and answer. This curriculum will guide you to reconcile and resolve these important, yet confusing issues.

Whether you realize or not, one of two paradigms is currently determining all of your life results.

Prosperity Paradigm: *Beliefs that increase love/joy energy, bring inner peace, true value, and confidence to yourself and others.*
Scarcity Paradigm: *Beliefs that drain love/joy energy, destroy inner peace and confidence in yourself, in a way that undermines bringing value to others.*

You are currently running one of these two paradigm belief systems. I suffered from scarcity consciousness for the first thirty years of this life, until the discontent became great enough for the paradigm shift to be made. The difference is so astounding it is very hard to believe, which is precisely why most people do not believe it even if exposed to it! Though the scarcity paradigm always results in suffering and stress, because it has become habit, *people vehemently defend it.*

As stated before, beliefs create behavior, and behavior creates results—so if you are displeased with your results you must change beliefs. Chances are, you probably didn't put them there anyway—someone else did. Your beliefs subconsciously compel how you behave out in the world. Over time this behavior becomes habitual and so natural that it has become your style and your way of being.

I refer to the paradigm as Prosperity Consciousness because being conscious is the essence of all life. The great proof of whichever paradigm you are currently using can be easily determined through answering this question. Is prosperity something you have, or something you are? If you believe it is something to have, own, or possess—you are running the scarcity paradigm for sure. Prosperity is a *way of being* that governs one's thoughts, words, and actions. When repeated for a long enough period of time, this *way of being* becomes deeply ingrained as success habits in your conscious mind. The choices and decisions that arise from 'Prosperity Consciousness' compel you to serve others, thereby creating and offering a unique value. Creating value for others is critically important if you are to embrace this work.

Value is a feeling of ***meaningful service*** *or* ***significant worth*** *which, when provided for another, creates enhanced joy and fulfillment for* ***both*** *parties.*

There are only two ways to earn money in this world.

1. Value Creation (Prosperity)
2. Deception (Scarcity)

Some people intentionally deceive others. They don't realize that everything we do to another we are doing to our self. This is based upon the Law of One and is explained in detail in chapter eight. Thus, deceptive behavior traps the deceiver into a life of misery. The majority of people are unknowingly self-deceived. This is different than intentionally deceiving others, and is rooted in adherence to false principles. True principles work, false principles do not.

The more value you create in service to others, the more money you will earn. It's that simple. This is because in a world of seemingly continuous cause and effect, Value Creation is the Cause, Money is the Effect.

By implementing this knowledge in your life, you can never be poor or unhappy for very long. One major false belief at the essence of the scarcity paradigm is this:

HAVE—DO—BE (Scarcity)

If I **HAVE** more money—then I'll **DO** the things I really want to do—then I'll **BE** happy.

To experience True Wealth, you must believe and behave the complete OPPOSITE:

BE—DO—HAVE (Prosperity)
I choose to **BE** happy—to **DO** that which I love—then I'll **HAVE** more money

Do you know that happiness is a learned skill? Happiness is an inside job—it is nothing you can materially have, or own; it is something you choose ***to be***. Being happy leads to greater productivity, and when you're more productive you'll earn more.

In his best-selling book, The World is Flat, author Thomas Friedman writes of a first-hand experience which validates the efficacy of the Be/Do/Have paradigm shift in business terms. While booking an airline reservation with then-new airline JetBlue, he had an intriguing experience with the booking agent. A woman named Dolly was so cheerful, yet professional and efficient, he began asking her a series of questions which culminated in his interviewing the CEO of JetBlue. Friedman interviewed David Neeleman, who hired four hundred reservation agents working out of their homes, just like Dolly. His believed that without the stress of having to commute, 'dress for success' and deal with office politics his 'happier' employee might be more productive. They all worked out of their own home offices taking reservations at their personal computer in between cooking, babysitting, and exercising. Because Dolly was allowed to work from home, her energy and happiness level were heightened, which resulted in greater productivity. Neeleman said, "They were 30 per cent more productive, taking 30 per cent more bookings, by just being happier. They were (also) more loyal and there was less attrition."

Any corporation would be ecstatic to have a 30 per cent increase in productivity in a given year – as would any worker in any industry. While so many other U.S. companies were 'outsourcing' to countries like India, JetBlue invented a new model - 'homesourcing'.

Happiness is actually a pre-cursor to being prosperous, while unhappiness is the predominant emotion in the scarcity paradigm. Despite all evidence to the contrary, dare to believe that you could actually earn more money by being in a career you love. Here is the paradigm shift, first showing the scarcity paradigm most people currently operate by. Notice the dreariness and underlying feelings of desperation that emanate from this belief system;

I **have** to make money.
I **do** whatever it takes to make it.
To **be** happy is not an option – I just do what I have to do.

Now observe the very different energy pattern and thinking that comes from a total opposite shift in beliefs;

To **be** aware of a possible career I already have joy and passion for,
To **do** the study and disciplined hard work to be one of the best at it,
I'll **have** more money (and joy, fun, health, fulfillment, etc.)

The ultimate deception that hypnotizes people is to accept that the scarcity paradigm is just the way life is. Nothing could be further from the Truth.

The Power of Belief

Remember that you are the spirit in the body, who has a reasoning computer called the mind—but you are neither the body nor are you the mind. Taking it one step further, you *have* a history, but you *are not* your history. Your beliefs are part of your history—they are the past. As we look at your core beliefs, and the powerful effect they have over your life, be willing to examine them with an honest and detached awareness.

I strongly urge you to keep those beliefs that have proven to be true, loving, and healthy *beyond a shadow of a doubt*. But please be willing to surrender all others. What do you love more—yourself, or your beliefs? To really shift paradigms it is important for your Self-love to be stronger than your belief love. If you sense there is an inner destructive aspect of yourself working against you that is difficult to change, then you have come face-to-face with a major limiting belief. Remember that every belief falls into one of two categories—Prosperity Beliefs and scarcity beliefs.

As you intentionally choose to be more aware of your core beliefs, you get the opportunity to re-create them in a way that empowers you rather than limiting you. By replacing limiting beliefs with empowering beliefs, ego-negativity exerts far less power over you, while your greatness begins to emerge more and more. This emergence is recognized as a deeper belief in one's abilities to think, speak, and act with focused confidence in any given area. The belief in your own powerful ability to better your life is thus born. This occurrence is critical, for you will then begin to more deeply love and respect yourself. This love and respect isn't forced, touchy-feely or strange. It arises naturally and effortlessly as a self-evident truth that anyone who contributes to making the world a better place deserves that degree of love and respect.

The inner desire to investigate personal reality and to know who you are becomes paramount. Instead of accepting beliefs that you were force-fed by those who are clearly unhappy and unsuccessful, you begin to trust your deepest inner knowing in your own ability to create a better life. Begin to question long-held beliefs, and to enlarge your sense of who you are, and what is truly possible for you to accomplish in the world with a higher belief system.

To give an example, my family unintentionally held deep-seated limiting beliefs about money. I was raised believing that wealthy people acted as if they were better than others because of their money. I was taught to believe that if you made large sums of money the government would attack you to pay more taxes, and that you would be viciously penalized when they did so. I observed that good honest people like ministers lived in a pious poor condition which was viewed as honorable, but that many people with dubious ethics made millions. All these false ideas formed an inner belief system which caused me to unconsciously push money away. The lower self (which ran this life at that time) reasoned that if all these beliefs were true, I would never have to suffer their seeming negativity by being sure to not have money.

This all happened in the quietude of my sub-conscious mind, where deeper beliefs are typically stored. As such, they were difficult to consciously see, until the discontent became great enough. And so these scarcity-based beliefs led me to struggle financially for several years. When being broke became painful enough, I embarked upon a process of self-inquiry in which harmful limiting beliefs were seen and discarded in favor of the empowering beliefs that are now habitual. I shifted from a paradigm of scarcity consciousness to one of Prosperity Consciousness.

In the following true story, you will see the life-altering power one's beliefs have in creating and affecting life results.

Dr. Bruno Klopfer was attending to a man named Wright who suffered from lymph node cancer, which had unfortunately advanced to an untreatable stage. Every typical cancer protocol used in hospitals at that time had been tried, and yet the man was dying. Mr. Wright was strictly scientific in his beliefs, and had heard of an exciting new drug called Krebiozen that showed promise in treating cancer. Though he didn't fit the exact profile to use it, his doctor found a way to include him in a study which enabled him to be treated with the drug.

After the treatment the doctor was amazed to find Wright taking walks through the hospital hallways and seemingly normal, saying that his tumors had "melted like snowballs on a hot stove." The once-protruding tumors and chest fluid were gone. Less than two weeks after Wright's first treatment he was discharged from the hospital—as his x-rays verified him to be cancer free. He remained well for about two months, until articles began appearing that the drug probably had no real curative effects treating cancer. Almost immediately, Wright suffered a relapse and re-entered the hospital.

Having observed the oddly healing effects of his patient's beliefs, Dr. Klopfer did an experiment in which he told Wright that he had a new version of the drug which was more concentrated, while injecting the man with only water. The same healing results again occurred, the orange-sized tumors dissolved, and Wright resumed his normal activities while claiming to feel completely rejuvenated. When he had entered the hospital his breathing was so labored he needed oxygen, yet he had healed to the degree that three days later he was out flying his airplane and seemingly back to normal.

Two months later the American Medical Association published the final report on the drug's efficacy, declaring it to be totally worthless. Mr. Wright became depressed and his health deteriorated almost immediately. His cancer returned, and he died only two days later (Klopfer, 1957).

In Wright's case, he not only experienced a miraculous, yet temporary, healing from cancer, but also contributed to his own death through the powerful influence of nothing other than his beliefs.

How might your own beliefs be limiting your abilities to earn, enjoy life, and positively influence others? After reading each question below, take a moment to reflect on the truth of each answer. Please allow your commitment to self-honesty to supersede any negative judgments that may arise about the content of the answer.

- Do you love your self—and if so, is it acted on every day?
- Do you respect who you are, and if so, how do you show it?
- On a daily basis, are you living and using the potential you believe is really inside of you?
- Are you *brutally* honest with yourself, or *skillfully* honest?
- Do you berate yourself when things are bad, but rarely acknowledge yourself when you do well?
- Does your attachment to getting 'your way' cause you to worry and struggle to be in control?
- When your expectations are not met, do you get angry, frustrated and disappointed?
- Do you influence your own reality, or does fate determine results in your life?
- Is life random and accidental, or do things happen for a reason?
- Is money good or bad?

- Is who you are and what you can achieve set in stone, or are they changeable?

These questions are included to serve as a backdrop for you to observe the possibility for positive change within you by first examining recent experience. Now that you sense it may be a false belief causing this discontent, you are free to drop the old belief for a prosperity belief. Step-by-step instructions are included later in this curriculum on precisely how to do this process. As you begin to get in touch with your core beliefs about who you are, you are then freeing yourself to create who you can be. It is important to begin examining all beliefs, and determine which ones are Truth and which ones are illusions. The Infinite Intelligence will support your noble urge to know the Truth once you commit to begin the quest. All great masters urge us, "Know thyself—you will know the Truth and it will set you free."

The quest to an exceptional life thus begins by seeking to know yourself. This eventually occurs as an answer to the question, "Who Am I?" As you consistently ask this question, a matrix of specific strengths, interests, and proclivities will continuously be revealed to you. This is your soul matrix, from which you are being urged in a certain direction. The choices contained within this matrix are very clearly set for most people, while deeper self-inquiry and exploration may be required for a small minority.

You can further uncover your own unique gifts by asking the next question, "Why Am I Here?" While it may take some time of deep delving, ups and downs, and self-contemplation to ascertain the answer, it is within you and powerfully worth knowing. For this process will lead you to discover one of the greatest riches any human being can discover – your Soul Purpose.

Chapter Two

Soul Purpose

Soul Purpose is your unique series of talents, strengths, passions, interests, hobbies, attitudes, and values that form the essence of the most magnificent version of you. When these qualities are intentionally acknowledged and cultivated, they coalesce into a specific mission in service to the world. These qualities already exist within you in a basic raw form. For most people they need to be clearly discovered, then nourished, studied and refined. Soul Purpose is like gold – hidden deep within, but when painstakingly sought for and carefully mined – makes for fabulous wealth.

The common denominator of all successful and famous people throughout history is that they all lived their Soul Purpose. They all 'followed their bliss' – daring, many times against impossible odds, to be that which they believed they were destined to become. This bliss led them to do what they had an innate passion and talent for. Their cause became a life mission – a *raison d'etre*. They rarely set out to achieve fame and fortune. On the contrary, fame and fortune occurred as 'effects,' stemming from each person following their inborn 'cause.' This cause became their guiding beacon whenever fear, doubt, and worry assailed them. It guided them to have faith, and the will to persist in times of challenge.

To scarcity paradigm thinkers, money is power; to prosperity paradigm thinkers, wisdom is power. This wisdom is the recognition that you have a specific purpose here on Earth. It is this purpose that will create the most value for others, and money will follow. This wisdom is inside of you – it is something you are and it also is something that will lead you to great happiness, because it's something you already love to do.

Prosperity is not something you possess, it is a state of being. It is living the happiest, healthiest and most fulfilling life imaginable without worrying about money. It begins by opening up to the greatest human life value that exists – the discovery of your soul purpose.

You are a Soul—in a body—who has a reasoning computer called a mind. You are trapped in the mind, and as such, do not have direct access to your Soul Purpose. In fact, so many people are trapped in their mind that they don't even believe the soul *exists,* much less has a purpose. To begin awakening to your Soul Purpose, start by seeing yourself as *the spirit* in the body who has a mind, but is not the mind. To verify this as a plausible truth, let's look at what you really are with a greater awareness and clarity, perhaps more so now than ever before.

Most people consider themselves to be their body—are you the body? The body goes about its business—blood circulation, digestion, heartbeat, neuronal activity, autonomic nervous system functions—without *you* helping at all. It handles millions of physiological functions every day—fully independent of you whatsoever. Are you thinking about your heartbeat right now, commanding it to happen with each beat? Are you commanding digestion to occur after each meal? Of course not, the body does these things on its own. The more closely you observe, you will begin to see "I *have* a body, I *am not* my body." While the body is a great gift, to equate who you are as *only the body* is to critically limit your potential. Yes, you are to take care of the body as best possible, but the body functions on its own. In fact, it does many things you do not even choose—getting headaches, toothaches, stomach aches, etc.—do you control or choose any of that?

If you were the body you would have much more say over its workings—much like the owner of a company has control over what that company does. He owns it—he controls it. Since you actually have very little control over what the body does, are you the owner of it?

Looking more closely, one sees that you actually have only a modicum of control over the body, because you are much more than that. The body is the vehicle and the vessel for *who you really are*—but quite obviously not you.

Many others believe themselves to primarily be the mind, so let's investigate this idea. An analogy might be useful to illustrate this point more fully. Imagine you're watching TV. When you're bored of watching TV, you—as the owner and controller of the TV—merely choose to turn it off. Can you do that with your mind? NO! Why not? *You are not it*. Don't the inane ramblings of the mind get boring sometimes too? If you were the mind you would be able to control it and shut it off at will—which you cannot. You didn't start the mind—and you can't stop the mind. You can't shut your mind off because ***you are not it***. This understanding is a major turning point in one's soul work. Secondarily, it is important for you to recognize, 'I have a mind, but I am not my mind."

If you are not your body or mind, but instead *have* a body and a mind, then what are *you*? You are the life-force energy inside the body, or that which has long been defined as the soul or the spirit. This new belief—I am the Spirit/Soul in the body—will immediately begin freeing you from the clutches of the mental realm. As you do so, your Soul will become more powerful, because this new belief is like spiritual weightlifting. Your spirit, being the greatest part of you, begins to get stronger and stronger the more it is exercised. It only makes sense, doesn't it? Exercise the body—the body and it gets stronger. Exercise the mind—it gets stronger. Exercise the spirit, it gets more powerful, and with discipline, you eventually realize your Soul Purpose. It exists fully formed within you, but you may not see it because it is obscured under layers of fear, doubt, and disbelief.

As you gain spiritual strength you'll become aware of the unique combination of inherent talents and abilities that, combined with your life experience, point to it. By living this Soul Purpose you will offer the most phenomenal value imaginable to others, and to the world.

Discovering your Soul Purpose and living it every day is the hidden Mission of every person on Earth.

The Infinite Intelligence programs a unique purpose into the matrix of each person's soul. This unique purpose contains the solution to an existing problem on Earth. This is why you see billions of problems existing on our planet. Even problems have a purpose. They exist so each one of us can discover our own unique Soul Purpose. The unintentional consequence of not discovering Soul Purpose is that the problem your soul work can correct goes unsolved. World problems are becoming insurmountable precisely because so few people are aware of, and living, their Soul Purpose. As conscious human beings we therefore have a personal and moral responsibility to discover ours. Your soul is now awakening to the truth that you can make this kind of difference.

Notice that we are all born with a distinctive series of interests, passions, and natural talents that exist within—strongly formed in our soul matrix. As an example, Mozart wrote his first symphony at age eight. Anyone can see that this exceptional musical talent was very mature in his soul matrix at birth.

How does Soul Purpose tie into greater prosperity? It is important to recall that within a world of seemingly continuous cause and effect, value creation is the cause, and money is the effect. When value is created for another – dollars will surely follow back to you. What else could possibly offer the world the greatest value other than living that which you were specifically created for? What else would you also have the most fun doing, knowing you were doing that which you loved to do every single day? What else could you possibly do to have more fun, create more value, and earn the most money from doing than your Soul Purpose? Doesn't that resonate with you? This is the dovetail between spiritual and material wealth.

This, therefore, is a spiritual curriculum. Remember that spirituality is not the same as religion. In fact, in many cases true spiritual principles are *the opposite* of traditional religious teachings. Nevertheless, while they often oppose the *traditional* teachings, true spiritual principles are completely congruent with the *original* great teachers. Being spiritual is merely choosing Love over fear. The act of being spiritual is the moment-to-moment choice of choosing Love (God) over fear (ego). Your spirit itself is conscious loving intelligence. The spirit only wants to love, and to be loved. This curriculum centers on increasing your conscious intelligence, thereby awakening dormant powers that are within you, covered up by the layers of fear.

So the beginning belief necessary to the Prosperity Paradigm is that you are a spirit in a body who has a mind, but you are not your mind. If you remain stuck in the mind, prosperity will be quite difficult to attain. You will merely go around and around in your mind, thinking that **it** is what you are, limiting the ability to transcend the social programming put there by others. Only by understanding this can you regain the power necessary to discover your Soul Purpose.

The second new belief is that you were built and born for a very specific reason—you are here on a mission. Daring to believe the first belief will give you the courage to trust in the hope offered by this second belief. You have a Soul Purpose that the world needs desperately, and by living it you will create enormous value, and in turn will naturally receive prosperity. If you act responsibly with this prosperity you will achieve financial freedom. This is the entry point into the Prosperity Paradigm, and out of the drudgery of the scarcity paradigm.

Answering the following questions will help you get clearer about what your Soul Purpose may be. Please take the time to write out the answers. Typically, the first things that come to your awareness are right. If you get momentarily stuck, move to the next question and come back once the other questions are answered. Do not allow the 'how to do it' limiting mindset to paralyze you. Let these answers flow in a stream-of-consciousness, non-judgmental fashion.

1. What do I do that unexpectedly brings compliments?

---

2. What activities energize me and bring me the most joy?

---

3. In what areas have I enjoyed the greatest success in the past?

---

4. What is the most unique thing that I bring to the banquet table of life?

---

5. What do I know that few others' know?

---

6. What are my three greatest natural strengths?

---

7. What valuable work would I do if I were financially free?

---

8. What three principles mean the most to me?

---

9. What do I believe God is guiding me to do with my life?

---

10. What life work would I enjoy doing every single day?

---

11. What hobbies do I love doing in my spare time?

---

12. Other than my family, what would I risk my life for?

---

13. Where can I make the greatest difference in the world?

---

14. What topic could I talk about all day without being bored?

---

15. What causes are worthy of my life?

---

16. In what area(s) do I have supreme skill and effortless passion?

The answers to these questions contain many special gifts that only you possess. No one else can present them to the world in this specific combination as can you. These are clues pointing to your soul purpose. They are things you already like do, as well as talents, behaviors, strengths, attitudes, speech patterns, and many other specialties. They all inspire your passion, love and natural interest–you need exert no effort to enjoy and embrace them, for they're already written as interests in your soul. When lived as a coherent mission, they will provide tremendous benefit to society. These unique qualities are like spokes on a wheel, all leading to, and supporting, a central hub that is your essence and reason to be, or Soul Purpose.

SOUL PURPOSE WHEEL

In the above diagram, the sixteen spokes on the soul purpose wheel represent the many unique abilities you possess. Notice that the arrows simultaneously point in both directions; they represent value going both to you and to society.

The value you receive is satisfaction, recognition, money, making a difference, greater health, enhanced self-respect, and increased fulfillment. The value to society is greater service, products, processes, inventions and discoveries that uplift humanity and alleviate suffering. Understand soul purpose as something you are, not only something you do. It is not a job or a career; rather it is a way of being. This new way of being inspires new ways of thinking which inspires new ways of speaking, ultimately inspiring new activities. Once you commit to live your soul purpose, *the right job will find you.*

In the Prosperity Paradigm symposiums, these questions help people to truly discover their purpose. With the help of the instructors, their prosperity network, and mentoring, thousands of people are currently aligning with their own unique mission.

Look at the answers you wrote down, and notice that a common theme exists. This theme is most likely the area in which your soul work is meant to be done. Please write the potential theme of your Soul Purpose here:

My Soul Purpose Theme ________________________________

If you are already on your mission, but not pleased with certain results, this curriculum will help you discover the missing piece of some unique ability that you are currently unaware of. Becoming aware of this one thing may be the factor that has an enormous impact on your life results. Because this unique ability is so natural for you, you may be unaware of its value to others.

Oftentimes, our own soul purpose can be seen by others close to us, because we often do not see ourselves as clearly as do others who know us well. You probably marvel at some unique talent others possess, but they themselves may think nothing of it because it comes so naturally to them. For this reason, people often underestimate how valuable their Soul Purpose may be. Since this is your unique Soul

Purpose, you may be unintentionally devaluing yourself, while others will see its value and gladly compensate you handsomely for it.

Your Uniqueness

There is no one else on Earth who has the exact same purpose as do you, though some purposes appear to be similar. Two people may be painters, but one may paint portraits which relay a person's charm in an easily recognized likeness, while another explores the person's inner life and spiritual aura through symbolic use of line and color. Two other people may have careers in the area of finance, but one specializes in life insurance and the other is an expert in investing in the stock market. Two others might be teachers, but one teaches in a high school, and the other teaches by writing a column on nutrition for a health care magazine.

In basketball, Michael Jordan brought an athleticism combined with a competitive fire to win that had never been seen before. Magic Johnson brought a joy combined with the unique ability to bring to the moment whatever skill was needed, whether it was the right shot, rebound, block, or pass. Larry Bird brought a never-say-die will to win by raising the level of every other teammate, mixed with the talent to hit the impossible shot from any angle. Shaquille O'Neal possessed a combination of strength, power, and dominance that had never been seen on the court before. Though they are all basketball players in a sport where people thought they'd seen it all, each brought something special no one had ever seen before. And, they all became champions. They may appear to be similar but, in truth, are original and distinctive, and supply unique value to others. There is so much variety and diversity in life that anyone intent on seeking his unique niche always finds it.

If you are completely dissatisfied and unfulfilled in your current career, it is a sign you are most likely missing your Soul Purpose. This situation may show itself in different ways in a variety of different life situations. You may be doing the right thing in the wrong place (needing to change company or geography) or be within the right career path, but in the wrong job (working in a kitchen instead of opening a restaurant). One knows they are on their Soul Purpose by the level of spiritual (not just ego) fulfillment and satisfaction felt from living it.

When one discovers his Soul Purpose, a critical shift occurs. You recognize every previous life event in a way that instantly makes complete and total sense. The good times and the bad, the victories and the defeats, all are immediately seen as having been necessary and perfect. You then wisely see the necessity of every event, especially painful ones, as having molded you in all the right ways towards accomplishing your Soul Purpose.

It becomes obvious that while you are the main character in the movie of your own life, you are not the producer and director of it. You have the lead role, and a very critical role it is. One co-creates his Soul Purpose in concert with Infinite Intelligence, which acts as the producer/director of the show. Infinite Intelligence scripted specific interests, passions, and loves into your soul as guideposts for you to follow to your purpose. As you discover your Soul Purpose, the whole world is uplifted. If the ocean level were to rise one inch, wouldn't every boat on it also rise simultaneously? Because your consciousness is tied into the ocean of consciousness, all of humanity benefits from the accomplishment.

Occasionally, misunderstanding arises about Soul Purpose. It usually centers on the misperception that living Soul Purpose automatically guarantees fame and fortune. This is a fallacy perpetuated by the ego. The following understanding will erase any potential confusion.

Some people's Soul Purpose appears to be bigger and more important than others, but this is untrue. Soul purpose roles that thrust people into the spotlight are no more important than any other—they are merely more visible. It appeals to the basic human ego structure that fame and fortune indicate superior social importance, but this is not so. A mother can live her Soul Purpose merely by being an exceptionally committed parent who lovingly nurtures and cherishes her children. A traffic cop who loves what he does and performs his job with zeal, fulfillment, and precision is just as important to the world as is the president of a country.

Support team members whose Soul Purpose is supporting an onstage person in 'more visible' Soul Purpose roles are critical and necessary. These support people are sometimes more highly evolved than the famous person. Because they may be more spiritually advanced, they *prefer* the anonymity and peacefulness of their role and need no fame or fortune while relishing their simple life.

The advanced teacher may live what appears to be a simple life, but the love radiating from such a high soul uplifts all of humanity. Mother Teresa was an excellent example of this truth. Because of the enormous diversity of what is necessary on Earth for world peace, every Soul Purpose well-lived is critical and important. In this context, one can see how fame and fortune may be irrelevant.

Therefore, monetary wealth may or may not be present, or necessary, in the life purpose of many such souls. Because high public visibility is an unpleasant idea to many, it may or may not happen, and to the advanced teacher means nothing. To these souls, money is mainly used to help others, to maintain privacy, and to expand the reach of their loving message.

Soul Purpose is not only about discovering what I love to do. It is also about determining who I love to serve. This is critically important because the latter will become your market. When I clearly define what I love, and the people I love to serve, then I have a powerful combination. Taking these points and aligning them with the others principles to be covered herein will transform you into an unstoppable presence.

It is reassuring to understand that adopting the soul purpose belief system does not require you to make the ultimatum of *either/or*. It is not—***either*** I quit my job to live my Soul Purpose right now but struggle over money worries, ***or*** I stay unfulfilled for the security of a salary. <u>It is *both*</u>. You can ***both*** work your current job, *and* immediately commit to educate yourself in your unique soul work arena. This commitment will inspire you to greater happiness while temporarily working the current job, with the knowledge that you are becoming someone greater. The commitment to invest in yourself will be the greatest investment possible to increase your prosperity. This investment can be made in the following areas:

1. Identifying, and studying your Soul Purpose field.
2. Attending workshops/seminars and reading books that offer expertise in this field.
3. Networking with people at these workshops and exchanging contact information.
4. Asking them for the names of books, websites, and other possible resources that helped them to increase their skills in this field.
5. Implementing the new action steps that invariably arise from following the preceding steps. This will increase skill and expertise in your Soul Purpose field.
6. Practice these new skills as often as possible, without creating major imbalance in your family life.
7. Find which one of these skills in this given field that you excel the most at, and do that one thing almost exclusively.

This commitment to invest in yourself is the KEY—it will maximize your creating value for others via your soul purpose work while minimizing stress.

One's age, race, social status, family upbringing, educational background, and job experience offer no advantage or disadvantage to discovering Soul Purpose. The only requirement is a willingness to know it, study it, and live it in service to humanity.

Prosperity Paradigm Principle

Discovering and living one's Soul Purpose expands the greatest possibility for people to create value for others.

In conclusion: all beings truly living their Soul Purpose, regardless of other's erroneous misperception about what success is, greatly contribute to greater personal health, wealth and joy—and further world peace.

If you know your Soul Purpose, fantastic! This next component will be a deepening and a re-affirmation of how to amplify it into creating what I call your Individual Legacy.

Creating an Individual Legacy

If you know your Soul Purpose but are waiting for a more opportune time to live it, you are deceiving yourself. Every day spent not working in your Soul Purpose is a day spent moving further away from it. *Knowing* one's Soul Purpose and ***living it*** are two different things. When you live out your Soul Purpose you create an Individual Legacy.

Because the power of Soul Purpose issues forth from a higher realm, the spiritual, living it has deeply far reaching effects. A deceased person who lived their Soul Purpose continues to uplift humanity long after their death. Mozart, Mother Teresa, and Martin Luther King all created Individual Legacies that continue to uplift humanity for generations. This reveals another amazing trait of living Soul Purpose that we have yet to discuss. Your contribution will continue to serve long after your physical form is gone. This is why it is called an Individual Legacy (Coelho, 1988). Though he died three hundred years ago, Mozart's music continues to thrill and uplift people today. Mother Theresa's healing centers still successfully treat thousands on a daily basis. Dr. King's sacrifices and teachings still guide others to greater understanding and acceptance of cultural diversity. The anonymous baker who first gave an extra cookie with each dozen continues to help bakers everywhere to build a joyful relationship with their customers.

There is evidence that living your Soul Purpose is also the secret to living a longer, healthier life. Psychologist Abraham Maslow pioneered the self-actualization movement, and his life work scientifically validated this benefit of living Soul Purpose. Maslow did a life long study of human transpersonal psychology, theorizing and proving something powerful. All joyful, productive, well-functioning people have one thing in common: *chosen work* that he or she finds deeply self-fulfilling. His studies indicated that people whose career was devoted to doing that which they loved to do, also *lived longer* (Maslow, 1976). When you live Soul Purpose, it creates the highest joy factor which positively influences one's health and length of life. Because every thought affects the immune system either positively or negatively, you can see how a soulful life filled with positive thinking enhances health (Pert, 1997). It appears as if finding and living your Soul Purpose may be a secret to longevity.

The drudgery and hidden futility the average person feels as they 'run the rat race' without feeling like they make any difference in the world is in direct opposition to the feeling felt by one who lives their Soul Purpose (M. Elias, *USA Today*, 8/18/05).

You deserve to experience that feeling, but you have to believe it and completely commit to owning that belief. The power of belief cannot be understated, for your life has become the sum total of all your beliefs. If you believe this work is powerful, and you use the principles and techniques given, you will absolutely have positive results. If you believe this work is bunk, you will not do the work and it will have no effect. This curriculum is meant to expand your self-imposed boundaries so you learn to believe in yourself in the greatest way possible. If you don't believe in your Self—who will? You are here to accomplish something important and, to fulfill a sacred contract between you and the Infinite Intelligence.

Deepening your belief in yourself, and your greatness—daring to dream that you have a special purpose no one else on Earth possesses quite the way you do—is critical to moving forward. You are a part of the Infinite Intelligence itself—unaware of who you are—but you nevertheless have this magnificence within you.
Begin by simply opening up to the following possibilities right now:

- I was created by an Infinite Intelligence for a reason
- I have a Soul Purpose here—co-created specifically for me—that I came here to fulfill
- Misery and desperation are the result of the inability to discover Soul Purpose
- I will feel a deep fulfillment when I dare to believe I can discover and live my Soul Purpose
- Soul Purpose is not only about discovering what I love to do; it is

also about determining the people I love to serve who will become my market.

- Living my Soul Purpose will create maximum value for others, prosperity for me, and leave behind a permanent Individual Legacy
- Those who create an Individual Legacy live a balanced life filled with health, wealth, a greater joy, and a deep sense of satisfaction
- This Individual Legacy is timeless in its ability to continually help others

It is appropriate at this point to share a note of caution. If this knowledge is allowed to go the head (ego-self swells) instead of inspiring the heart (God-self awakens), misery can ensue. These teachings about soul purpose do not imply that you are superior over others; they mean that everyone is special. The allure of *specialness* makes the ego drunk with power, which can cause the opposite purpose of this work to ruin your life. Attribute all credit to God, parents, team mates, teachers, and to your new commitment to excellence, and your success is all but ensured. The enhanced level of prosperity, health, and happiness are all yours, and that is more than enough.

Chapter Three

The Scarcity Paradigm

The scarcity paradigm is a set of beliefs that drain love/joy energy and destroy inner peace and confidence in yourself, in a way that undermines your ability to bring value to others. How did the scarcity paradigm come to be installed in our minds?

Most of our ancestors emigrated from other countries to the United States, seeking new opportunity. They were leaving the scarcity of their birth country to try to find prosperity in America. Many, like my own grandparents leaving Italy, arrived just in time to experience the Great Depression. Food was scarce, money was scarce, and jobs and hope were also scarce. They had left the diminishing opportunity in their original country, only to find greater scarcity in America. These difficulties were compounded by cultural and language barriers. They often went hungry, and scraped by doing any job they could find, desperate to provide for their families.

Out of sheer will to survive, they developed a series of new beliefs, creating the basis of the scarcity paradigm. At that time, this survival-based 'way of being' was practical, smart, and right. Back then, if you did ***not*** live by the scarcity paradigm you would most likely die. It was not only the way they thought—it became a way of speaking, dressing, eating, saving, working—it was a *way of being* that affected every aspect of their existence.

Despite these adverse conditions, they fought through to make a better life for their children (who became our parents or grandparents). This scarcity consciousness was then handed down to our parents, who then taught it to us. Their painful experience of scarcity became deeply ingrained as a way of being in our subconscious mind. Because it is in the subconscious mind, you cannot consciously see the flawed program clearly. Much like you cannot see beneath a carpet to the sub-floor that supports it, you cannot see beneath the conscious mind to the subconscious program that supports it.

Even though American society is now stunningly abundant, most of us still operate with scarcity consciousness. *They* struggled with having enough food to eat—*we* struggle with eating too much food. Why? We're still operating from their old paradigm of scarcity! Back then you ate as much as possible if it was available because you never knew when you were going to eat again. Now, we still gorge ourselves that same way even though food is abundantly plentiful, so Americans struggle with obesity. As children, how many of you heard the following? *Clean your plate! You're not leaving this table until you finish your dinner! Children in Africa are starving!* Can you see how this way of being not only affects our health potential, but also our wealth, and ultimately our happiness too? Because it is a consciousness, meaning a *way of being*, it subtly affects all aspects of existence. It is a hidden program that dominates as the operating system in the computer-like mind. Like any program, it can be deleted and replaced by another. If you truly choose to create greater prosperity, **you must remove it and replace it.**

Scarcity consciousness affects how we eat, how we heal, how happy we are/are not, the thoughts we think, the money we make, how we feel about money, where we live, the car we drive, what we teach our kids, our level of self-respect, and millions of other factors.

Until this program is removed, no amount of earning, investing, saving, luck, time or discipline can change the inevitable negativity that results from living it. Nor can any new sales technique, process, marketing system, or tool permanently solve the problem either.

Stories abound of famous athletes and musicians who made huge fortunes, but wound up penniless because they remained in scarcity consciousness. In nature, whatever condition is at the root, will always bear the same fruit. Rapper MC Hammer made almost twenty million dollars in the music industry in the late nineteen-eighties, and two years later he was broke. The less obvious examples are people who make or inherit millions, identify who they are with their net worth and remain anxious and miserable. Scarcity consciousness has rot (fear/lack) at its root; therefore it will always bear rotten fruit (scarcity). The Prosperity Paradigm has health (love/wisdom) at its root; therefore it always bears healthy fruit (abundance).

While it is simple to outline, it is not easy to live. Though the essence of the Prosperity Paradigm already exists within you, it is covered up by habitual fears, false beliefs, and doubt. *(If it's too good to be true it probably is, or, if it's so great why isn't everyone doing it?)* Living the scarcity program is like viewing life through a movie camera that has dirt on its lens. Seen through this lens, everything is dirty and distorted. The external things which you're viewing are not really dirty, but they appear that way because your lens needs cleaning. Therefore, when Truth is shown, scarcity conscious people see it negatively because the dirt in the hidden paradigm causes them to misperceive the Truth.

The Prosperity Paradigm will help you clean the lens of your inner eye, so you can more clearly see the already existing opportunities in a new way. It will also help you to delete and re-program your individual consciousness to prosperity.

The Influence of Conscious Intelligence

The term *consciousness* refers to the fact that you exist, and you know that you exist. Consciousness is a spiritual essence, and is the irreducible substrate of human being. The term *intelligence* refers to the ability to make successful choices by studying truth, and learning from experience. Conscious intelligence is allowing the mind to be directed by the spirit, instead of by the ego (which is unconscious ignorance erroneously referred to as intellect). It is important to understand the immense power of choosing positivity over negativity, for this choice is required in virtually every moment of human existence. Conscious intelligence is choosing positivity, love, and life instead of allowing the unconscious intellect to automatically choose negativity, fear, and death. As conscious intelligence increases in a person or organization, favorable conditions occur which increase the likelihood of success. As this conscious intelligence expands, a greater power flows from this individual into their surrounding environment. Anyone or anything in this environment then receives greater value, if they are open to receive it.

Continual growth then occurs when one identifies a mission bigger than oneself, and commits to achieving this purpose in service to others. Increased consciousness equals increased power and ultimately success, and from a limited consciousness comes little growth and little success.

Why do people fail? Failure is the result of a limited consciousness—the state commonly called ignorance. Ignorance is a state that ensues when one is living false beliefs, and failure and suffering are the inevitable result. The failure takes different forms: for some it's relationship, for others it's health, and with others its money. Ignorance prevails when a person is unwilling to grow out of their comfort zone, and is often accompanied by a deep stubbornness to adapt and change.

The simple formula of this book is:

INCREASED CONSCIOUSNESS = GREATER POWER = EXPANDING VALUE = ABUNDANT PROSPERITY

Conscious intelligence is the sweet spot between science and spirituality, where they merge and exist as One Great Truth. This is the balance point where their purpose is one and the same—and that is the pursuit and expression of Truth itself. Here, the brilliant wisdom of science and the miraculous power of spirituality are not antagonistic pursuits designed to disprove each other. They are sister disciplines that confirm the existence of the source of all inspirational thought. This source is really an unseen connection—within you—to an *infinite Field* of creative genius and power that is only accessible when your motive is for the Highest Good of All. **This Field is a realm of invisible energy that pervades all of space and time and is infinitely intelligent beyond human comprehension. It opens up to, and greatly assists, those who are on a noble mission to uplift humanity—and closes to those who are selfish**. The Field is consciousness itself. It is an infinite, limitless reservoir of all knowledge and power itself, which is accessed by your own spiritual will and awareness.

If the **"Field"** is a new concept to you, bear with me and read through this chapter. As the Field concept becomes clearer to you through definitions and examples, the nature of the Field and the possibilities opened up by connecting with it will start to strike a chord with truths you may already know on a deep level or through fleeting experiences. The effect of this Field (as it will be referred to here on in) multiplies your personal power and connects you to an infinite network of people and possibilities that are unknown to most people.

The analogy of the human mind being like a computer is helpful. Imagine you are a laptop computer. You can run on battery power for a couple hours, or you can plug into a constant electrical power source and run indefinitely. ***The Field*** is the source of all power, and you are like a laptop computer running on battery power. The laptop can run on battery power for a couple of hours, but then it loses power and shuts off. However, by plugging it into the wall socket, you increase its staying power infinitely. It's plugged into a higher energy Field, right? Now realize the increase in powerful possibilities that open up when you add an internet connection. All of a sudden you have an infinitely more powerful capacity to communicate all over the world in seconds, and to access libraries of information at the touch of a few buttons. Unplugged from the Field, you are the laptop computer with very limited power and capability. The Field is all around you—

in all things—supporting all things to exist, hear, think, and see. It is literally the playing field for the game of life.

The next time you look at your refrigerator and see the magnet clinging to the door, ask yourself, "what is the source of power that holds it in place?" Is it held there by an engine or motor, is there any glue or tape? There is no man-made power source because it is the Field of Infinite Intelligence that is holding it in place. The Field of Infinite Intelligence is an unseen source of limitless power and infinite connectivity to all Knowledge. With your computer, you cannot see the electricity coursing through the wall, yet you know it is there. You do not know exactly how your internet connection ties your individual computer to the infinite network of computers, but you know it works. In much the same way, you cannot see the Field of Infinite Intelligence nor do you know exactly how it works, but it does work. When you plug into this source, you operate at an infinitely higher capacity in all areas of life.

You have already experienced this Field of infinite thinking—it is your *imagination*. Einstein constantly tapped into this Field of energy—hence his quote, "Imagination is more important than knowledge" (Einstein, 1941). He credits his monumental discovery, of the Theory of Relativity, directly to his ability to connect to this invisible energy Field. Johan Sebastian Bach was another genius who tuned into the Field to write his greatest symphonies. Almost every great musician first heard the song in his head, and then struggled to quickly get it onto paper. Thousands of other very famous people have a strikingly similar story.

But let's observe a common person, much more like us, who also received guidance from the Field. Friedrich Kekulé, the father of organic chemistry, tuned into the Field and received the breakthrough insight that broke the code of carbon/benzene chain bonding no one else could solve (Roberts, 1989). His discoveries were major contributions to modern pharmacology, without which millions would die every day. (Think of a world without penicillin, aspirin, insulin, etc.) Once he committed to his life mission of breaking the code, he began repeatedly having recurring daydreams, through which 'he received' the answer. In his own words…

> I was sitting writing on my textbook, but the work did not progress; my thoughts were elsewhere. I turned my chair to the fire and dozed. Again the atoms were gamboling before my eyes. This time the smaller groups kept modestly in the background. My mental eye, rendered more acute by the repeated visions of the kind, could now distinguish larger structures of manifold conformation; long rows sometimes more closely fitted together all twining and twisting in snake-like motion. But look! What was that? One of the snakes had seized hold of its own tail, and the form whirled mockingly before my eyes. As if by a flash of lightning I awoke; and this time also I spent the rest of the night in working out the consequences of the hypothesis.

The line in which he says, 'the snake had seized hold of its own tail', was the insight neither he (nor anyone else) had ever before realized. He applied the theory he had received from the Field to his next experiment and broke the code.

Personal study of several hundred stories with this recurring theme in the lives of the great masters guided the creation of this curriculum. Whether in daydreams, flashes of insight, dreams, contemplation, or meditation, once the higher sense of Imagination is awakened, what is imagined becomes possible. And, when each one seemed to hit a wall, at that critical moment an insight was bestowed upon them by the Field.

You can begin the paradigm shift to greater prosperity by imagining (believing it's possible) and imaging (visualizing) that a life of great prosperity and fulfillment can be yours. Is it possible? If it is so, recognize that you are already beginning to change programs, from scarcity to prosperity.

Prosperity Consciousness is a belief system that connects you to an energy field of infinitely creative thinking constantly transmitted from the Creator.

Scarcity Consciousness is a belief system based in fear that is constantly transmitted by the ego, which short-circuits your connection to the Creator.

Prosperity Consciousness connects you to the Field of infinite thinking that guides you to be a Mission-Driven Being whose value creation serves humanity and alleviates suffering. As others receive value, the person in this paradigm becomes financially abundant—because dollars follow value.

Scarcity Consciousness disconnects from the Field of infinite thinking, conditioning you to be a Fear-Driven Being who serves mainly themselves, increasing personal suffering. Others receive little value from the person running this program; money goes elsewhere, resulting in a lack of prosperity.

This is such a big concept, it must be repeated: By evolving your consciousness, you connect to Field of infinite power. **The Field is a realm of invisible energy that pervades all of space and time and is infinitely intelligent beyond human comprehension. It opens up to, and greatly assists, those who are on a noble mission to uplift humanity—and closes to those who are selfish.**

Defining the Field

Have you ever walked into a room, and felt that the 'air was so thick you could cut it with a knife?' Or you might have felt the converse positive energy by being in the presence of two young lovers whose obvious adoration was infectious. This is a description of intense energy you can sense but not see, which I refer to as the Field Effect. The Field Effect is an energy pattern that is invisible, yet is deeply felt, registered, and has measurable effects on people.

In scientific terms, the Field is called the electro-magnetic spectrum. This invisible spectrum is a combination of electric and magnetic energy waves that carry radio waves to your radio antenna, light to your eye, and thoughts through your brain. It contains many already discovered invisible frequencies and wavelengths—radio waves, television waves, microwaves, gamma rays, cosmic rays, solar rays and on and on, ad infinitum. The electro-magnetic spectrum is the size of our ever-expanding universe, cannot be drained, and pervades all of space in the universe (Capra, 1976).

Every person, thought, and substance (even at a sub-atomic level) is affected by electro-magnetism. The electro-magnetic spectrum has fascinating properties built into how it operates. Simply put, our universe appears to operate like a giant cosmic magnet. Your words are sound waves—they are mechanically magnetic. Each word, *and the authenticity with which it is spoken,* carries a specific frequency. Fear, doubt, worry—the dominant emotions found in the scarcity paradigm—carry a very low and slow frequency, and produce extremely low-level results. On the other hand, words that are sincerely spoken with love, skill, and knowledge—express fast, higher frequencies. These words can very quickly draw high-level prosperous results. Sound is a mechanical wave, and both light and thought are electro-magnetic frequencies. What you visualize, what you think, and what you say all combine to produce material substance because of the inherent properties of the Field as electro-magnetism.

The Field is like a living blank canvas of infinite possibilities, and you are like a painter who's been given a palette containing every color of paint imaginable. The different colors are your thoughts, choices, beliefs, words and actions. This invisible realm is a Field of infinite possibility which—when powered by an ethical mission that is for the Highest Good of All—can literally transform thought into matter.

If you have trouble believing that last statement, think about playing the radio in your car. You can't see the radio waves. They are invisible, yet the electro-magnetic spectrum they ride upon pervades all of space. Despite the fact you can't see them, you know they exist when you turn on your radio, and tune in to your favorite station. The conscious choice of listening to music to make your journey more pleasurable gets you to 'turn on' the radio, then 'tune in' the dial to the specific frequency. Music, in the form of radio waves, is transmitted from a radio station miles away are on an invisible frequency. Your car antenna, acting as a receiver, picks up and then sends the music signal to your speakers, and you then hear the music. Because you've grown up knowing car radios play music, despite not knowing the principles behind how it does so, you don't doubt it. We are employing the exact same principles to expand your success potential.

Can you imagine trying to explain how a radio works to someone living in the late 1800's? They'd think you were absolutely insane! When Marconi sent the first radio signal across the English Channel in 1899, people ridiculed him. This is a common theme with invention – most people mock and deny its possibility with no actual knowledge of it at all. Perhaps in much the same way, you scoffed at the concept of harnessing a previously unknown power (the Field) on your side. This is why the first prosperity principle is –'collective human behaviors/beliefs do not qualify those behaviors/beliefs to be TRUTH.' For you to create lasting prosperity you must open to new possibilities you might've previously negated only because everyone else negated it.

What familiar inventions like a car radio have in common with breakthroughs like an x-ray machine is that they are *positive* contributions to society. They all offer value creation. They fall into the category of things created for the love of oneself, one's fellow man, and society as a whole. Every invention was a physical manifestation of someone's Soul Purpose. The beauty of living this paradigm is that everyone has this kind of potential inside of them—and somehow we all know it.

In scientific terms the Field is called the electro-magnetic spectrum. In spiritual terms, the Field is individually experienced as consciousness, and more universally referred to by using the word God. I also use the term Infinite Intelligence.

The Mysterious Obvious

In 1973 an unheralded technical study changed the lives of the most well-respected physicists and astronomers of the day. Hundreds gathered in Poland that year to celebrate the 500th anniversary of the Polish astronomer, Nicolaus Copernicus. The leading scientific minds were present as the then-communist country pulled out all stops to celebrate their countryman's great contribution to science and modern day astronomy. The well-heeled audience wined and dined by night, and during the day were lectured by fellow scientists on the content of their rapidly expanding research and discoveries.

The research paper that rocked the proceedings was written by cosmologist and astrophysicist Brandon Carter from Cambridge University, who was a friend and fellow associate to the now-famous Stephen Hawking. The paper was entitled "Large Number Coincidences and the Anthropic Principle in Cosmology." The gist of the work was that Carter had theoretically proven the existence of God by using highly respected principles of physics. What made it all the more controversial was the fact that—beginning with Copernicus, then Newton and Darwin—modern science had developed the 'God is dead' theory because of the seemingly 'random universe' they *assumed* they were observing ("Is God Dead?" *Time Magazine,* 1966). But in a methodically brilliant way, Carter used the same principles many atheistic cohorts were familiar with to construct a highly technical verification that our universe was created by a "God who loves humanity." The full story is written in the book, *God—the Evidence,* by Patrick Glynn. Here is an excerpt.

> The anthropic principle says that all the seemingly arbitrary and unrelated constants in physics have one strange thing in common—these are precisely the values you need if you want to have a universe capable of producing human life. (It is) the observation that all the myriad laws of physics were fine-tuned from the *very beginning* of the universe for the creation of man—that the universe we inhabit appeared to be expressly designed for the emergence of human beings.

Applying the physics principle of Ockham's razor to his controversial theory gave it even more validity. Ockham's razor is a scientific principle that states "when two competing theories are being offered to describe the same system, *the simplest most logical explanation is probably correct.*" The theory is not perfect, but over thousands of applications it has proven to be right most of the time.

There are innumerable powers and forces in our universe that have 'constants'—the measurable values of gravity, electro-magnetism, weak force, strong force, the speed of light, etc—that never change. In a universe of constant change, these changeless constants are quite miraculous. An infinitesimal variation in any of these constants at any time would result in the end of human life in the universe. Of the two competing theories below, see for yourself which appears to be the simplest most logical one.

1. Accidental Principle: These hundreds of constants have one thing in common—but they are merely accidental, randomly never change (in a universe of otherwise continuous change), and happen to coincide in the existence of humanity. (Humanity is a random accident)

2. Anthropic Principle: These hundreds of constants have one thing in common, and are intentionally that way, and purposefully never change, because this universe is created for the purpose of the one commonality—human existence. (Humanity has a creative purpose)

As an analogy: imagine hundreds of people got food poisoning in your town last Tuesday, and they had one thing in common—they all ate at the same restaurant that day. Now apply 'the Razor' to slice open the truth…

1. These hundreds of people have one thing in common—they all ate at the same restaurant, but that is merely coincidental, and they randomly got food poisoning.

2. These hundreds of people have one thing in common, they all ate at the same restaurant, it is no accident they got food poisoning, the food there was somehow contaminated. It's the old adage, if it looks like a duck, walks like a duck, and quacks like a duck—it's probably a duck.

Being rational men of science with rapier sharp wit, the

profound Truth was hard to argue with, and the harder the atheists among them tried to disprove it—the greater the proof was found.

Another aspect of the Anthropic principle (anthropos is Latin for man), is that these values must have been perfectly set *prior to the existence of the physical universe.* The cosmos could not have formed exactly as it did if all the 'constants' weren't perfectly pre-set by an Infinite Intelligence. It's like pre-setting the oven at the proper temperature when preparing dinner. If it's too low—the food is raw and inedible, and if it's too high—the food burns. Considering the seeming fact that our universe is 13.5 billion years old and human life appears to be only about one million years old, *the Infinite Intelligence must be able to see the end result prior to its very start* (Hoyle, 1993).

The final tantalizing aspect to this theory is that there are several odd exceptions to the rules of physics that, without which, human life could not have emerged. The simplest exception to explain is: water is the only compound that is heavier in its *liquid* state than in its *solid* state. If it were not this way, the oceans would freeze from the bottom up and human life could never exist here. Ice floats, and if it didn't the Earth would be covered with ice. Water is, of course, critically essential to human life (Leslie, 1996). This is one of many exceptions in physics that must be this way for humanity to exist, and you can draw the same conclusion when viewing every other exception.

The elegant simplicity of the "Anthropic Principle," when one applies Ockham's razor, always results in a very simple scientific bottom line. It is obvious that the universe was created by an Infinite Intelligence for the existence and evolution of humanity.

The Field is everywhere, omnipotent, omniscient, and omnipresent. It is scientifically called the electro-magnetic spectrum, spiritually called God, and individually called consciousness. There is obviously some power that allows you to see, think, and hear, and makes your heart beat—electromagnetism, God, life, consciousness. They are merely different words that mean the same thing—but they are real and true. The evidence of God's Love for you is your very existence. You can show your love for God, yourself, your family and the world by seeking to make the shift to live your Soul Purpose as if it were your mission on earth—which it is!

The Mission Defines the Context

Living life as if you were on a mission is the most direct and thorough route to achieve true wealth. This is fact because **being mission-driven is the underlying context that gives all life meaning**. Thoughts, words, actions, and **all things are meaningless** unless context is clearly set. Think about it: Is money good or bad? Only by providing context do we get the answer. If money is used as a donation to find a cure for breast cancer it is good—and if it is used to fund an act of terrorism it is bad. Are drugs good or bad? Again—only by providing context do we get the answer. If drugs are used as an addictive solution to life's problems they are bad, but when they're used to anesthetize a patient for life-saving surgery they are good.

Prosperity Paradigm Principle

No truth exists in this world without context being clearly set

This Content/Context dilemma must be clearly understood for you to proceed with this curriculum. Human beings are constantly focusing their attention on something – thoughts, desires, goals, people, objects, etc. Spiritual work trains us to focus on context, whereas the world had programmed us to focus on content as the source of happiness. When we shift our awareness away from thinking some external material thing (content) will make us happy, and focus on the contextual field – happiness becomes an inner choice that can be experienced anytime. This is why great teachers say, 'happiness is an inside job.' Please carefully study the critical difference between these two concepts;

1. Content is a person, object, or idea that has erroneously been given a false value.
2. Context is the setting, circumstances, and underlying factors,

including intention, which ultimately determines meaning.

Think of the old pirate story of Black Beard whose ship, heavily laden with a treasure chest full of gold, was irreparably damaged in battle and was sinking. His greedy crew was so attached to their gold that they carried it overboard with them (focused on content), thus drowning (no awareness of context – gold is heavy).

Principles must also be used in context, or their meaning can be distorted. Any beautiful principle can, and has, been misused by erroneously thinking that *the end justifies the means.* Money is content—how it is earned and then utilized is context. Drugs are content—and therefore meaningless—how they are used is the context, which determines whether they are good or bad.

The mission-driven being is clear about the context of who he is, why he is here and what he is doing, which is always inspired by a good cause. The person on a mission to alleviate suffering for the benefit of humanity accesses the Field. My definition, then, of a Mission-Driven Being (hereafter referred to as **MDB**) is one who persists with a noble cause that is for the highest good of all concerned.

Conversely, things taken 'out of context' are in fact a perversion of the truth. Think of an unscrupulous defense attorney asking misleading yes or no questions of an innocent rape victim to imply that she is 'an immoral woman who contributed to the behavior of the rapist by dressing scantily.' Intentionally taking things out of context is a sign of a manipulative purpose with a selfish, greedy motive. This is often the way an ego-driven person manifests himself. This person can justify and rationalize any negative behavior to get his way. (The end justifies the means) He views anything outside of himself as there to fulfill his narcissistic desires.

Content is an idea or a thing—Context is the setting and situation that ultimately determines it's meaning. Let's look at how this applies to prosperity. Money is content, creating value as a MDB is a context for money. Looking at it from a business perspective, an example of erroneously focusing on content might be thinking: "I'm in this business to make the most amount of money possible." This is exactly what I have heard from hundreds of entrepreneurs, stuck in low modes of productivity. In contrast, the MDB believes, "I'm on a mission to help uplift and educate people in a way that creates great value and joy through what I do."

This is a key distinction to make because what is going on in your inner world tends to manifest in your outer world. People almost always manifest that which they hold in their mind. If we hold negative intentions they tend to manifest, and if we hold positive intentions, that is what will most likely take form (Dyer, 2004).

Like your computer ties into all computers via the World Wide Web, your individual consciousness ties into Infinite Consciousness (the Field) by being Mission-Driven. Let me definitively state this again:

> **When you commit to living your life as a MDB, you instantly create access to an inner energy Field of infinite power and brilliant ideas for serving others and uplifting the world. In the seeming world of cause and effect, this valuable service is the cause, and money is the effect.**

Anyone on a mission to help humanity 'turns on' access to the Field, which aids their success. And anyone focused on greed 'turns off' access to the Field, increasing the likelihood of failure. The nobility of your mission acts like a high-speed internet connection linking your computer to the trillions of bits of information in cyber space. Money is *content,* and therefore neutral and meaningless until *context* is clearly defined. Earning it with class and grace denote a higher meaning, and then proper utilization of the money insures one's ability to maintain the prosperous life.

Remember God—Choose Love—Create Value

The schizophrenic dilemma of being trapped in the mental realm is that you are required to make the constant choice between the ego-self (fear) and the God-Self (love).

Human life is like walking into a maze every second, requiring you to make a continuous choice to either turn one way (ego/fear) or the other (God/love). If you could see the maze from a higher perspective, you'd realize that taking the fear paths can never lead you out—they are all dead ends. This 'higher perspective' is the spiritual realm. When you are in the mental realm you are stuck at ground level, unable to clearly see that the path of love is the only way out.

Most people are programmed by scarcity consciousness to automatically turn toward their fears and ego, and this is the problem. No lasting happiness, consistent health, or wealth with any degree of certainty can exist with the fear/ego program running the show. Happiness cannot be found here even by the millionaire, because with fear as the driving force, scarcity thinking undermines his ability to feel confident and peaceful. Having more money merely means he has more to lose—therefore more to fear and worry about. He thinks everyone is after his money and feels he can trust no one. He constantly obsesses with how much he has and how much its growing (accumulation), instead of the true principle which is focusing on how the money is being used (utilization). Accumulation is content, and utilization is context. Money—like drugs, guns, and a myriad number of other things—is neutral. Its meaning is derived from how it is utilized. The millionaire running scarcity paradigm beliefs has money, but not prosperity, because he has become enslaved by the money.

You can see how the false beliefs inherent in the scarcity paradigm can make having money more of a curse than a blessing. True wealth is freedom—it results in a happy, healthy, more fulfilling life without ever worrying about money. Possessing money with scarcity consciousness is enslaving, and having money while running the prosperity paradigm is freeing.

The paradigms of the ego-self (scarcity) vs. the God-Self

(prosperity) are completely different, and in fact, opposite.

Because they are totally opposite, both cannot be correct, so we are always choosing one or the other. When you choose the God-Self, you are choosing the difference that makes all the difference. You are turning the right way and going onto the only path through which the 'way out' of the maze appears. Poet Laureate Robert Frost wrote his most famous poem about this choice—the last three lines of which are:

Two roads diverged in a wood, and I -
I took the one less traveled by,
And that has made all the difference.

Psychologist M. Scott Peck devoted his best-selling opus entitled ***The Road Less Traveled*** specifically to this same theme. This whole curriculum can be boiled down to this one fundamental Truth:

REMEMBER GOD—CHOOSE LOVE—CREATE VALUE

Falsehoods are always complex and often take a very long time to sort through and to figure out.

Truth is always simple.

This fundamental Great Truth will lead you to pursue your Soul Purpose, which leads to greater value creation, which leads to permanent wealth. If you take one thing from this curriculum, this should be it. Committing to live one single Great Truth, with discipline, can take you all the way to the greatest wealth imaginable. It only takes one scalpel to dissect the entire human body; similarly, it only takes one great Truth to unravel all others. This truth of choosing God, love and the creation of value is the only ethic that can never be taken out of context—all others can be distorted. This one great truth ensures that all other principles and beliefs are used in the highest context. Without the proper context, principles and beliefs are meaningless, and even dangerous.

This fact is historically verified when you observe how often fanatics have murdered in the name of God—whether it was the

Crusades or a Ku Klux clan lynching (both perpetrated by so-called Christians). These are unfortunate examples of taking beliefs out of context. Aren't these apparently hypocritical acts the very things that convince intelligent and caring people to explore atheism? But there is no conflict—the murderers were not acting as true believers in the first and foundational truth of Christianity—Love. This is the biggest difference between religion and spirituality. If a person talks about God without choosing love, this person is easily lost in the ego/fear maze. Every religion says that God is love. Choosing love instantly eliminates any ego-driven behavior, and enhances your ability to create value.

Prosperity Paradigm Principle

The highest context of human existence is to Remember God, Choose Love and Create Value

This one fundamental ethic will insure your connection to the Field of Infinite Intelligence that God is. In turn, the Field will guide you to make the highest integrity choices that put all of life into context. At the core of being mission-driven are ethics based on the *context* of *remember God—choose love—create value.*

So as not to fall into the content/context dilemma, these ethics must be **contextual ethics**, not unyielding principles, or they can be twisted by the ego. Many good men have fallen right here—because the ego is pride, and 'pride goes before a fall.' Only contextual ethics bring value for the highest good of all, whereas unyielding principles rigidly enforced are often used to justify hidden ego agendas.

An ancient story from India illustrates this point.

> Kauseka decided that his path to God would be realized by always telling the truth, no matter what. One day as he was sitting on the banks of the Ganges river meditating, a beautiful young maiden ran up to him saying in a fearful voice, "please sir help me! Two men are chasing me, where can I hide?" Kauseka pointed to a nearby cave hidden behind some bushes, and the girl ran

into it and hid. A minute later two rough-looking rogues burst onto the scene. With evil in their eyes they snarled at Kauseka, "a girl came by here a minute ago, where did she go!?" He pointed to the cave and they went about their evil intent.

Do you see that rigidly following his principle of 'truth no matter what' did not serve the highest good in this situation at all? He took the truth out of context in an immature, literal manner. He lived his principle, though, didn't he? Had it been a contextual ethic, he would have been able to serve the highest good—without lying. If even the great principle of **Truth** can be distorted by taking it out of context, can you see the importance of living all things in context—especially ethics?

The ethics of the Prosperity Paradigm are Natural Laws of the Universe and as such, are created by God, not men. They are provable by science and congruent with all spiritual scripture. Please be clear here: these ethics are not *optional*, only to be used when you feel like it in certain situations. Saying, as we have, that all application of ethical principles must be adjusted to the context of the situation does not mean that our central ethical values and choices are optional. These ethics are always used in every situation. The mission-driven being is guided by the Field to always use the ethic in a way that is for the highest good in every situation. The finesse with which you present your truth is precisely attuned by the Field according to the context of that which serves the highest good of all.

Here is a personal story that I experienced, showing the guidance received by the Field to tell the truth without lying or exaggerating. Notice that I was able to still serve the highest good when put 'on the spot,' unlike Kauseka.

Years ago, the girlfriend of a musician I once worked with suspected him of not being faithful. (I've given them fictitious names here.) She normally wasn't all that friendly towards me, but one night she came up to me and engaged me in much more conversation than ever before. It was really quite nice, up until she said, "Do you consider us to be friends?" A little taken aback, I said "Yes." She then said, "if you're really my friend—tell me the truth, is Bill cheating on me?" I reflected for a moment then answered, "Jane—that is a question you need to ask Bill, because it's really is none of my business—wouldn't you agree?" While unsatisfied, she nodded and walked away. Jane was a decent person who didn't really want others meddling in her relationship. My connection to the Field allowed me, without lying or exaggerating, to tell the truth for the highest good of all concerned. While I did *think* that Bill was being unfaithful, I had no proof, and the higher truth is that it was none of my business. Had I given my uneducated opinion, it would certainly have been destructive, and perhaps fatal, to the relationship. They eventually married, and as of the writing of this book are still happily married today.

Again, contextual ethics bring value for the highest good of all, whereas unyielding principles rigidly enforced are often used to justify hidden ego agendas. To alleviate any worry that may arise about how to use contextual ethics, understand that when you Remember God, Choose love, and Create Value—you are guided with amazing precision as to what to be, do and say. This guidance never fails to produce prosperity.

Because of the allure of money and the recognition it brings, ethics and values can be compromised all too often. Money and recognition are *content*—remember God, choose love, create value is the *context*. The ego-driven person is in business only for himself—and if it happens that he helps people along the way, that's fine, but as long as he's "profiting" he could care less. The mission-driven being is in business for everyone, and knows that when he helps others get what they want, he then gets what he wants, because uplifting others is the mission.

The importance of being driven by a mission is that you are inspired by a higher power to carry on, especially during difficult times when others quit. The MDB performs his duties as an agency for positive change in the world. He leads with his mission as the context for reaching out to people, opening the hearts of his clients, establishing the bridge, necessary in any budding relationship, known as—**Trust.** It has been said that 'people don't ***care*** how much you *know*, until they *know* how much you ***care***.' Trust is a heart-based, not head-based, emotion that allows people to open to new possibilities for their life. It is a well-known fact that people act, buy, and make choices for *emotional reasons* and justify the behavior with *logic*. It is only when people trust you that they then allow you to act as an agent for their highest good.

A recent example of a MDB is Lance Armstrong, seven-time Tour de France cycling champion and cancer survivor. He, along with the Nike shoe company and others, created the 'Live Strong' bracelets in May of 2004 to support the noble cause of finding a cancer cure. The simple yellow plastic bracelets emblazoned with the mantra "Live Strong" sell for one dollar with almost all proceeds going to cancer research. With little fanfare or expectation, the cause has become an unheard-of success story, selling twenty million in the first eight months without any slowdown of sales in sight. As of the writing of this book, sixty million have been sold (Murphy, 2006). People began buying first one, then ten, then twenty or even hundreds at a time! The innate goodness of the cause is instantly registered by the Field within each person, and it just feels right for people to buy many bracelets to give away. It is a mission that resonates deeply inside of people. *Because all people's lives have been touched by a cancer story, and because the Field is the energy source at the core of every atom—even inside of you—the MDB's cause compels people to participate* ***from an inner feeling that tells them to do so.***

I hope all entrepreneurs reading this point understand the implication. When you tell authentic Truths—not manipulative truisms—others receive an inner guidance to further participate in whatever you are offering. They trust you. Trust is the ensuing emotion a client feels in the presence of authentic Truth being spoken. When you add the success habit called **persistence** to your Truth, you again increase your power exponentially.

Armstrong persisted in the face of terrible adversity. He persisted in the face of a cancer so virulent that approximately ninety-five out of a hundred patients die. He persisted despite the French press accusing him of using illegal performance-enhancing drugs when traces of chemotherapy showed up in his system years later. And he persisted in winning what is arguably the most difficult athletic event of all time—the Tour de France not once, but a record seven times in a row—against tremendously high odds.

This story proves other features of 'the Field' that are noteworthy. First, one must persist in carrying out the mission—for any noble cause encounters opposition. Marconi and Einstein as well as almost every inventor were called crazy by the 'powers that be' prior to their great breakthroughs. Secondarily, the more noble and loving one's mission is, the greater the access to—and power received from—the Field. The right books and teachers appear as if by magic. Assistants appear to help you from "out of the blue" (Hill, 1960).

Clients begin to refer friends and seek you out, unsolicited, and the MDB begins to experience the phenomenon known as the *effortless effort*. Do not think of this as being on 'a roll', for in truth the MDB is on 'a role.' Being 'on a roll' always comes to an end, as any gambler knows. The MDB has discovered that being 'on a role'—meaning living your life-role and being in tune with your Soul purpose, is a way of being in the world that ultimately ensures a fulfilling, lasting career.

One theme common to every MDB is a *burning desire* to be doing what their chosen career drives them to do. It is as if the mission is inside of them like an internal compass, intuitively guiding the MDB in the right direction, like Columbus seeking the New World.

If you are not sure what your mission is—don't worry. By the end of this curriculum you will have remembered it, or certainly be much closer to realizing it. Your mission is very definitely inside of you, simply covered up by layers of fear, and this curriculum will help you remove the fear.

The beginning point to inputting the new prosperity program is to make a list of the positive things you really love and enjoy doing. These interests have always been present in your awareness from the earliest age, and you'll notice that you always had an inborn ability to do them well. By following the things that we love, we discover that we have unique talents which, when developed and nurtured, uplift humanity and create fabulous societal value. These innate talents exist in all human beings, and constitute the essence of each person's mission. As other people receive value from you living your mission, abundance follows value, and financial prosperity is the result. Einstein said, "Try not to become a man of success but rather to become a man of value."

Money appears as the **result** of the 'value creation' that others experience—but not the **cause** of it. The primary cause is the prosperity consciousness that guides your mission, the secondary effect is money.

The first obstacle that must be removed is often the misplaced focus on money. You must learn not to focus solely on money, but rather to concentrate on the mission. You do have a magnificent mission, even if you are uncertain as to what it specifically is. Your mission will create value, and money will inevitably follow. Remember this: mission first, money second.

Chapter Four

The Study

Some people work a job, others a career, and the fortunate few see their life-work as a mission. All famous and highly successful people were driven by a mission. A life-long dedication to study the greatest philosophers, economists, scientists and entrepreneurs resulted in the compilation of these mission-driven principles into a curriculum. By 1999, this curriculum had been compiled into a format that was being taught all across the U.S. to people from all walks of life via telephone mentoring sessions and quarterly seminars. Over the ensuing seven years, almost ten thousand mentoring calls were provided for financial services professionals alone. At the end of the first year a specific pattern began to emerge. As this pattern became clearer, I created a series of markers to categorize client's tendencies. They began to reveal themselves in five distinctly different categories:

1. Love-driven
2. Mission-driven
3. Pride-driven
4. Desire-driven
5. Fear-driven

A verbal questionnaire was then utilized to determine which of the five modes an entrepreneur most closely fit into when they were interviewed. I began to keep track of all of these results in a kind of informal study. I did not enter into this study looking for specific results. I was looking for the data to reveal to me if there were hidden determinants to successful entrepreneurship.

Over the years, a consistent pattern slowly revealed itself. Those people who were willing to let go of old beliefs and transcend the three lower modes (fear, desire, and pride) had enormous spikes in their business productivity and personal happiness. Those who were unwilling to do so continued to spiral into lower productivity, and suffer in their health and family life to varying degrees.

The results revealed by this study indicated very powerful and completely unexpected results.

The conversations, belief systems, thinking processes, speech patterns, productivity levels, and many other factors were amazingly similar and consistent in people favoring each specific mode. I struggled to believe what the data kept inferring, until finally it became indisputable to me. I had assumed that their life circumstances and many other external factors (education, social status, degree of nurturing by caregivers, etc.) predisposed them to success, but the opposite was shown to be true. It was their internal level of consciousness that most powerfully influenced their life results.

The quality of thoughts and choices—even their willpower to act on them—appeared to be determined by which one of the five modes people fit into. The fear-driven people spoke in almost the exact same way, had very similar beliefs about the world, and used startlingly similar excuses as to why their lives weren't better. The same tendencies, with minor exceptions, predominated for people in the other two negative modes of desire and pride.

Most illuminating was the profound shift exhibited by entrepreneurs possessing mission-driven and love-driven tendencies. They lived a highly principled and integrous life, tinged with a sense of gratitude and humility. Because they had such an evolved level of consciousness, their ability to be aware of others needs and feelings, combined with impeccable integrity, created a fertile environment for success to flourish.

For many people this is a very difficult concept, so an analogy might help. Let's equate these five differing levels of consciousness to five differing levels of electrical wattage;

1. Love-driven consciousness – 1,000,000 watts of electrical power
2. Mission-driven consciousness – 100,000 watts of electrical power
3. Pride-driven consciousness – 10,000 watts of electrical power
4. Desire-driven consciousness – 1,000 watts of electrical power
5. Fear-driven consciousness – 100 watts of electrical power

The fear-driven person carries enough power to turn on a one hundred watt light bulb, but one more thing requiring power from them will blow their circuitry. This power level can light up one room, but no more than that. It certainly cannot provide power to supply even a small home. The fear level of consciousness can barely provide the energy to sustain one life, much less a relationship, a home, a career, or a soul purpose mission.

The desire-driven person has one thousand watts of energy which is enough to power a small modest home, but not much more. Equating this power to a level of consciousness, one has much more power than in fear, but is seduced by constant craving and therefore prone to addiction. Wants and needs then get confused, often guiding this person to focus on a problem as a solution. *(Much like the alcoholic thinks that having one more drink is the solution.)*

Because pride-driven people have an even higher level of power, they can create a greater level of productivity, but can also create bigger disasters in theirs and other's lives. This is a dangerous mode because of the unique combination of power mixed with a blatant disregard for the well-being of others.

Mission-driven people carry one hundred thousand watts of power, which is enough to light up a whole town. These people make highly successful entrepreneurs, leaders, and healers because of the higher level of energy available to direct towards any task. They genuinely care about humanity, and have more 'juice' to take their mission and vision into the world. This is the first level of consciousness in which soul purpose can truly be discovered and lived.

Love-driven beings are rare. They carry a high enough level of power – one million watts in our analogy – that they can electrically light up the power needs of a major city. A being radiating the amount of power specific to this level of consciousness can easily run a large company, or even a whole social movement.

The entrepreneurs who stubbornly refused to leave the lower modes repeatedly failed and soon quit working with me in a predictable fashion, the fear-driven leaving first, followed by the desire-driven people. The pride-driven men were usually high income earners who were suffering in a different way. They were always looking to experience more balance, health, and happiness. While they had money, they were clearly not happy. Regardless of what mode any entrepreneur was in when he came to this work, anyone willing to be open-minded to adopt and implement the mission-driven prosperity beliefs experienced success.

The qualities that determined people's ability to shift higher were;

1. **Truth** – to admit they were unhappy and that they themselves were responsible, no matter how painful it was.
2. **Faith** – that they would somehow be successful no matter how bleak things appeared to be in the moment.
3. **Discipline** – to do the work even though it was very different and unfamiliar, in contrast to their dominant paradigm.
4. **Will** – to trust in the unseen grace of God, despite all inner resistance generated by the ego-self.

Each of the above qualities is a spiritual essence, and without it, the mode you are in dictates the likelihood of your success, or the lack thereof. We can elevate our conscious intelligence through the right use of will. Without utilizing your spiritual willpower, the mind drives your behavior without you even knowing it. Each mode contains social programming that dictates your way of being while you are doing or saying something. People unknowingly 'tune in to' what you're being, more than saying. This is the essence of the science called ontology, which is the study of being.

The MDB intentionally chooses to act with high awareness, knowing that this *way of being* positively influences every relationship. Plugging in to the nobility of serving others is really plugging into an inexhaustible power supply—the Infinite Intelligence of the Field—so the MDB simply cannot fail. Awareness to exercise free will and align with higher modes increases your personal power and ultimately your level of consciousness. Your *mode of being* really determines life results because from being arises thinking, and from thinking arises doing, and from doing arises achievement or the lack thereof. So the fear driven being thinks, speaks, and acts fearfully without realizing that others unknowingly feel it and want nothing to do with it.

Because of the hypnotic effect of the negative modes, many people simply cannot help being other than what they are. This is because their level of conscious being *tells them* what the world is, who they are, and what is possible in the world—in a mostly erroneous fashion.

This study indicated that people labeled thoughts 'mine', but they are more accurately 'the thoughts' that dominate at each level. From your mode of being, thoughts that are in harmony with that mode arise all by themselves without you initiating the process whatsoever. This is an aspect of consciousness itself—and the higher it evolves, the higher the quality and power of the thoughts that run through your mind. Therefore, the great achievers in history were the high consciousness beings, and the failures were low-consciousness.

All of us are simply acting out attractor patterns of conscious being as it flows through us. Being weak-willed and having low consciousness go together, and these people are easily influenced by any other negativity. Think of the lynch mob phenomenon in which a mob of angry people is storming the courthouse demanding 'vigilante justice.' A low-consciousness bystander who may know absolutely nothing about the situation gets swept up in the *field effect* of the group's energy, and a minute later is screaming for the hanging of someone he may not even know.

Take this member away from the group and sit him down in a quiet room with sensible people and ask him, "What on earth are you doing?" He visibly deflates outside of the sway of the negative attractor pattern and he answers, "well jeez, it seemed like a good idea at the time." He believes he is thinking, and doing, but this is a fallacy. He is in fear mode, and is easily mesmerized when in the presence of others in fear mode to act in mass ignorance. The being in fear mode has fearful thoughts continuously arising in his mind. The being in desire mode has continuous desires arise unbidden in his mind. He erroneously says, "I thought such and such…"—but he didn't think it really. He *observed* the thought pop into his mind all by itself, habitually claiming it to be his thought. This negative 'herd mentality' is called cognitive dissonance (Einstein, 1956).

Little moles called lemmings see other lemmings running over a cliff to their death and unquestioningly follow because of this phenomenon. History proves that people often act like lemmings, following each other to negative results just because of the mass herd mentality. They are ignorant to what effect their 'being while they're doing' has on their life success. Religious zealots do the same thing in the name of God.

The saving grace is that free will always exists as the possibility to make a higher consciousness choice. This is how one evolves to the next mode or even all the way to the highest mode if one is inspired and committed.

Life Success Paradigm Shifts

Fear Driven→ Desire Driven→ Pride Driven → Mission Driven → Love Driven

The lowest three modes—fear, desire, and pride—are predominantly negative, with certain exceptions that 'make the rule.' There *appear to be* healthy fears, but in truth healthy fear is actually based in love. Imagine a mother seeing her three year old riding a tricycle too closely to the road. Out of love for the child's safety, healthy fear propels her to shout "stop!", and run to guide the child away from the street. The exception in desire mode is what we already referred to as burning desire, which is noble in contrast to selfish desire, which is the negative mode outlined below. The exception as it pertains to pride mode is 'pride of ownership,' in which a person is compelled to habitual respectful maintenance of a possession like a dress, a car or a house. This is really not pride, but actually a commitment to excellent stewardship.

The same specific situation—one's reaction to being 'cut off' in traffic—is given in each of the following explanations for comparative analysis. This is done to help you further understand how a person in each specific mode is driven to handle the same situation differently. In this way you can learn the profound shift in possibility that occurs towards greater joy and wealth when one chooses higher ways of being. The two highest modes—mission and love—are what this book is attempting to help you attain, for these are the modes of people living the Prosperity Paradigm.

The Five Modes of Being

Fear Driven: This mode is all about survival. Most everything and every one are scary, threatening, and a potential source of danger which lurks around every corner. In this mode—love, tolerance, and ethics are seen as weaknesses to be exploited. One's own feelings of resentment and hostility are viewed as powerful and justified. On the back end of this person's every thought is fear, doubt, and worry. The constant fear is fed by inner feelings of futility in seeing the unsolvable negativity of the world, which serves to continually drain him of the energy needed to complete things start to finish. He is constantly starting activities that rarely get completed, making the 'appearance of being active', but somehow never 'productive.'

This person is struggling with surviving and therefore incapable of thriving. He is often focused on just trying to pay the mortgage or rent, keep food on the table, and/or not get the credit cards or gas and electric turned off. This mode is all about getting, not giving. The person cannot think about giving to others because he believes if he gives, he will only have less for himself. The act of giving implies a feeling of depletion. He is primarily focused on 'getting' as the means of advancement in life.

The dark, complex negativity of a fear-based life gets suppressed into his subconscious mind, where it festers just waiting for one event that explodes the emotional dynamite. This person gets cut off in traffic and sees it as the perfect opportunity to release all their repressed negativity through violence. This is why a person trapped in fear mode often experiences 'road rage' which makes them fantasize about killing another driver who may've cut them off unintentionally. The unfortunate truth is that many people in this mode not only get into physical altercations, but also do kill each other, as the recent spate of LA freeway shootings confirms. (Marquez, *ABC News,* 2005).

From a business perspective he feels paralyzed to assert himself outside of his comfort zone out of fear of rejection, being misperceived, and misunderstood. This person may talk forcibly on the outside—but it is a mask—for on the inside he is unsure and scared, and therefore emanating negative energy. The dichotomy between the outer façade and what's really happening inside results in his secretly feeling shame and guilt. This compounds the fear, and he punishes himself inside for "not being ______ enough." (smart, industrious, eloquent, handsome, tall, muscular, witty, courageous, persistent, etc.) Self esteem and self-respect are therefore seemingly insurmountable inner issues.

The thought of reaching out to people is frightening, until the discontent becomes great enough to break out of his shell. Though it is negative energy driving him, for a short time it can force him out into the world, to eventually have a positive result, whether in business or in life. If he can persist long enough to do so, the resulting success hopefully empowers this individual out of 'fear mode' into the next mode. If not, this person quits the job, the team, or the relationship. If this pattern is allowed to repeat itself, this being becomes a candidate for criminal activity.

Sees the world as a battlefield

The fear-driven being views the world as a dog-eat-dog society based on survival of the fittest. It is a kill-or-be-killed world where charity is for fools, and the only way people get ahead in life is by climbing over the bodies of others. In this mode, the idea is to beat people to the punch, because they're out to get you if you let them. Or, fear-driven beings see the world as a cold, harsh, hateful environment in which terrible things happen to good people. Playing small and self-isolating behavior are seen as intelligent options, because you'll only get crushed if you dream big. To a person trapped in this mode, the earth is a battlefield.

Desire Driven: This mode is a huge breakthrough from fear mode, because one is now inspired by what is possible. It is in this mode that one discovers the power of 'giving' versus always, and only, 'getting.' Instead of feeling *depleted* from giving, as in the previous mode, this person feels *completed* from the act of giving.

The problem is that at this level of consciousness there is not enough positive energy available to keep one's intent pure. Ultimately, desire is a state of wanting. With desire as the central driving force, we're continually subjected to the feeling of *wanting* more. This is because desire—**as a way of being in the world**—almost always turns into *selfish desire*. What begins as 'I want money because I want to help more people'—which is dignified and decent—becomes an endless circle of 'I wants,' unintentionally becoming the barrier to greater success.

The *noble* intent can quickly turn into *selfish* intent—in which forever higher goals are set in an endless search for the happiness that they supposedly will bring. As 'desire consciousness' kicks in—"I want the latest greatest luxury car, I want a new home, I want to own the building "- one's lifestyle rises to meet income, and what was once *wanted* is now ***needed*** (Parkinson, 1957).

This is an insidious mode of being, because in many cases the current dominating business paradigm supports this mode as good and right. This 'desire consciousness' drains the joy out of any success, because constant victories are expected and mandatory, and therefore cannot be celebrated. 'Desire mode' fast becomes addiction-to-money mode. When one desire is satisfied, the next 'want' kicks in automatically, along with the resultant pressure—"I want more money, I want more referrals, I want more quality clients, I want more sex, drink, food, drugs," etc.

If this person gets 'cut off' in traffic, he might recklessly chase the other car even breaking laws to 'right the wrong'. Like a moth is drawn to the flame, he is unable to resist the desire to catch the other driver at the next light to throw them the finger or roll down the window and argue with them.

The desire-mode person often has a secret inner fantasy life that he is often consciously unaware of. There he thinks dark thoughts in the privacy of his brain, which often drain him without his full awareness. These thoughts often center on desire fulfillment to compensate for what is not being accomplished externally.

The positive desire that once compelled him has now turned into a negative energy that drains him. This mode is insidious because the desire-driven person may often function as seemingly normal, but often feels a hidden internal self-loathing. In the business world, he has unknowingly formed major attachments to things going 'his way', and his desperation can be subconsciously felt by clients who intuitively sense "commission breath." The client often senses that this being is more interested in the money he makes from the sale than in helping the client to solve a problem.

A high number of seemingly successful career salespeople get stuck here, enslaved to this level of production while constantly wondering why they can't actualize their latent potential.

Sees the world as a trap

The person stuck in this mode believes there is a hidden catch to everything, no matter how good it may seem. They are ignorant to the fact that human beings are creative manifestors—in that we powerfully influence our own reality. This results in their inability to see that they destroy their own happiness with negative beliefs. They believe idioms like "if it's too good to be true, it probably is." This belief has the unplanned effect of making them believe that only bad things can be true. Therefore they live life constantly waiting for *the other shoe to drop*, and it's always a negative 'shoe'. Everything and everyone is seen as having a hidden agenda to disrupt their life plans. This results in viewing Earth as a trap.

Pride Driven: In contrast to the lower modes, a man feels positive as he reaches this level. Many big earners see this as the pinnacle of success and get stuck right here. With the increased financial success, his self-image rises, serving to heal all the discomfort he felt in the previous modes. We see pride readily accepted in our society—even encouraged. The glitter of the pretense of success still fools the masses who have been led to believe that fame and money always lead to happiness. Crowds still pay good money to see pampered, spoiled athletes who may cheat by using performance enhancing drugs, or sneer at making *only* seven million dollars a year. We see the power of pride corrupt politicians, as the allure of prestige and kickbacks erodes a good man's judgment. These same politicians still hold sway over large demographics of people, and often get re-elected.

If one does not have an enlightened teacher present to 'temper' this rapid rise in self-esteem, the ego begins to inflate and can spin out of control. The person now believes they deserve more than others, can play by a different set of rules, and a sense of entitlement develops. He gets blinded by pride, like the rich CEO manipulating to secretly steal from his employee's pension fund. Though he believes it is wrong for others to break the law, he rationalizes that it is acceptable for him because pride has distorted his judgment. This is precisely why it is written in every holy book in the world, "pride goes before a fall."

If this person gives, it is for the tax deduction and for the 'rush of pride' ***he** receives*, more than for the actual good the charitable contribution will do in the world (Giblin, 1968).

Pride wears a mask that appears calm and collected on the outside—but this person's happiness is delicately dependent on the external conditions he sets that must continually be met. This is precarious—because when the external conditions aren't met, *the individual invariably reverts back to the lower modes.* The inflated ego of pride is a house of cards, quickly susceptible to collapse, and is easily sucked backwards into fear and desire.

When cut off in traffic the pride mode person probably won't chase the other driver as in the previous two modes. He feels a quick flash of anger, and then the superiority complex of pride mode often directs him to derisively condemn the other driver as an inferior deemed unworthy of any response. He speeds past the other car at the first opportunity and stares at the other driver suppressing the urge to do more harm. He is experiencing the 'fight or flight' stress response indicative of one still caught in the lower modes (Selye, 1978).

Many entrepreneurs have the trappings of success, but because they're in pride mode they're not consistently happy. It is typical for the person caught in pride mode to add guilt to the negative cycle through thinking "I am more successful than most people in the world, and I'm still not happy?!"

The outer success in these people therefore is a front, easily 'seen through' by any aware observer. As long as things are going this person's way, he carries himself with a false confidence tinged with arrogance based on the 'my way or the highway' mindset that typifies pride mode. As a result, most people stuck in pride mode are secretly considered by others to be control freaks. Of course, this unnatural need to control is masking inner feelings of being *out of control,* causing greater attachment to getting their own way.

The attachment to being in control, evidenced in the constant need to be right, often leads to addictive behavior as one seeks relief from the inner unhappiness. This person cannot see that the block is the ego, *which they have been viewing as an ally.* Often times it is the occurrence of a life-shattering event that creates enough discontent to propel one to move beyond pride. It takes a special person or situation to break through this mode, which can only be transcended via **conscious humility**.

Sees the world as their chessboard

These people are capable of dangerous things because they are usually incredibly bright, yet seriously self-deceived. Derision and mockery of large demographics of people, professions, and entire countries is common. Someone trapped in pride mode views the world as their personal pleasure device. Because of their high intellect or talent, but low emotional awareness, they are coldly desensitized to the feelings of others. People are viewed as objects, not living beings with a personal story. Understanding each person's story would explain each person's behavior, but pride-mode people do not care to. People exist only in terms of either helping this being get what pleases him, or not. If others assist their goal achievement they are tolerated, and if they do not, they are often vilified and even hated. Winning, being right, controlling people, and manipulating outcomes are of paramount importance. Consequently, Earth and her inhabitants are viewed as mere pawns on their chessboard.

Mission Driven: The experience of discontent has a humbling effect on people, which leads to deep reflection and self-assessment to find a way to heal their pain. One becomes acutely aware of real suffering in the world as a result of having experienced one's own, and the need to serve others becomes a driving power. The MDB has finally become aware of a higher purpose of life on Earth—and, with it, the stunning realization that if all would only serve others, humanity could positively transform immediately. This person now wants to truly serve more than just earn. He is no longer interested in only making a living or achieving recognition; he is now out to make a *difference.*

This mode is a huge breakthrough because one has now tapped the infinite Field of limitless power and possibility. The three previous modes are based on 'force,' while this mode is based on 'Power.' Forcing anyone or anything is fear-based, while empowering people is love-based.

Force is an energy field that is initiated from the idea of manipulating others for the good of the few. Force, because it is manipulative and based in greed and selfish ends, always creates counter-force, and is therefore in constant need of re-supply. Power is an infinite Field of energy based on an idea that is for the Highest Good of All. Power has no agenda other than serving and helping those who allow us to help them. Force pushes people—whereas power pulls and magnetizes people, uplifting them via a dignified and noble Mission. Power needs no re-supply because its goodness is multiplied exponentially by the Field (Gandhi, 1962).

A better understanding of power vs. force might come by imagining that someone who is unable to swim is floundering in deep water. Using our metaphor—by pushing the person (force), they'd go further underwater, causing them to drown. But by pulling (power), you are taking them away from danger, uplifting them to safety. Using the financial services industry as an example, in today's society people are drowning in money problems and need financial guidance more than ever. The MDB leaves force behind for the infinitude of the power received from the Field. Clients feel pulled to safety with power, and pushed uncomfortably by force.

When the MDB is cut off in traffic he shifts the context of what is happening (recontextualization), and, instead of taking it as a personal attack, sees it as a harmless slight. He has experienced the lower modes, so he is glad he can graciously provide the little happiness boost the driver in front of him may feel from the mini-victory of being in front. He intentionally chooses to see his brother's innocence instead of automatically assuming his guilt, and he then experiences an empowerment from the event instead of feeling weakened.

The MDB constantly remembers he has something so phenomenal to share with others, that the thought of serving and helping other people far outweighs the fear of rejection or being misunderstood. This positive energy Field is carried with them into every interaction, and helps establish a heart-based (instead of head-based) connection that is received and felt by others as 'Trust.' Trust is simply the emotion one feels in the presence of Truth.

People feel so inspired through not only the value they receive from the process, but also by the means with which the MDB has conducted himself. In business, being uplifted by a person, a process, and a product is such a unique experience, the client ***wants*** to go out of their way to give referrals. In this way, the Field magnanimously attracts more and more clients to the MDB because of the overall uniqueness of the value he provides.

Sees the world as a school

Mission-driven beings recognize that every person and event is there for a reason, and not by random accident. They know that all things in their awareness are purposeful, existing to teach a very powerful lesson. Through life experience they have connected the dots enough to see a direct correlation between their own behavior and what manifests as a result of it. Love attracts heavenly people and experiences, and hate attracts the opposite. They have experimented with the lessons to the point that they recognize one almost instantly. They have experienced discontent to the degree at which they can easily practice the gratitude attitude when a negative event occurs. They put their hand on their heart and say, *"Thank you God—this is a gift—show me the lesson."* They are advanced enough to recognize that Earth is a school. (Chapter Nine has a section specifically devoted to further explain this idea.)

Love Driven: A major transformation takes place in this mode. One has discovered and experienced that happiness is an inner condition that can be chosen at all times simply by choosing to *remember God, serve all, and love all.* Their joy is no longer contingent upon external conditions, and an aura of peace and confidence flows from them that silently nurtures others. The being in Love mode sees 'the whole movie' instead of one disjointed snapshot—therefore acting from a more complete understanding of the dynamics of each relationship. It is as if he has been given an inner secret about everyone that makes others open to his teachings. No one can really give or take away from this person because his source of power is inside, therefore requiring very little outside.

Unlike the last mode in which the externals still matter—

attaining goals, measuring linear progress, keeping score—in this mode one has entered the non-linear domain in which happiness and success are internally created and therefore independent from any external cause or condition.

Goals are replaced by preferences, as attachment to external gain is totally replaced by the infinite fulfillment of love as Prosperity Consciousness. All is given freely from this level as the Give vs. Get mindset allows one to continually give from an infinite supply that is inexhaustible. Because of the purity of intent at this mode of being, the more one gives, what is given is replaced ten-fold.

Love is not passive, gullible, or weak—as it is erroneously interpreted by those blinded by the ego in the negative modes. Love is the ultimate power which guides this being to concentrate on others' beauty and best efforts—deconstructing evil by recontextualizing it, rather than attacking it. If a being in 'love mode' is cut off by another driver in traffic, the anger felt in the lower modes is replaced by the understanding to give the transgressor the benefit of the doubt without feelings of hostility or frustration. Instead of condemning the other driver, the loving one thinks 'bless you,' sending a silent prayer to the other driver who he recognizes as himself, and the whole scenario is transformed. The other driver may even feel a strange sense of peace without knowing why.

Love becomes a way of being in the world, not because people have earned it or deserve it. The love-mode person loves others as the inevitable emanation of who they themselves have become, for at this level there is only one relationship, and all in one's presence are subject to it. Love has become *who they are,* and lovingness is the style through which one expresses it. The degree to which clients are drawn to someone immersed in this Field of Love is astounding, as the 'field effect' effortlessly replaces—and far exceeds—any traditional marketing efforts.

Sees the world as perfect

The Love-driven being recognizes that people are always doing the very best they can given their life history, level of conscious intelligence, and intensity of aspiration to evolve. This understanding allows them to recognize the purpose of earthly life from a macro-cosmic perspective instead of the limited micro-cosmic view others in the lower modes see. It is the difference that makes all the difference. If one can see that Earth offers the perfect opportunity to evolve and learn everything, from the horrible to the divine, then one could understand the necessity of such a wide range of available choices. Divinity is not earnable without criminality as a choice; prosperity is not earnable without scarcity as a choice, and so on. The Love driven being sees all from a higher vantage point. Like flying over your town in an airplane gives you a new perspective of how all the streets and buildings fit together, so too does love explain how all creation fits perfectly together. If this universe exists for the express purpose of human evolution towards Godliness, Earth is perfect—*exactly as it is.*

* * *

The valuable truth revealed by this research is that whether you realize it or not, people are simply doing the best they can, with who they are and what they have, given the conditions of their life. The realization of this truth heals the impatience and intolerance most entrepreneurs feel on a daily basis, replacing it with compassion and forgiveness. Most importantly, this realization helps you re-capture the 'lost opportunity energy' one inevitably wastes when stuck in the lower modes of fear, desire, and pride. Instead of wasting energy complaining about what he is upset about and is opposed to, the MDB is focused totally on what is working well and what he is a proponent of. He is not *against* war, he is *for* peace. In the presidential election he doesn't vote for 'the lesser of two evils,' he realizes he is voting 'for the greater of two good men.' He has no time to hate, because all his energy is focused on love.

Through awareness, choice, and discipline one commits to being a MDB, receiving an enormous boost in energy from the recaptured energy you once frivolously wasted. This new energy makes all the difference in the world for it helps you actualize your once-hidden latent potential to further accomplish your mission and experience greater prosperity.

The Results

The informal study that I conducted included the following financial services careers: mutual fund owners and managers, insurance agents, financial planners, mortgage brokers, attorneys, realtors, money managers, several life coaches, and accountants.

The results shown below indicate what mode these people were in when they came to this curriculum. More importantly, they give the general public a useful barometer of the probable intentions of people in business today. This is precisely why referring people to a MDB in every area of business and life is so critical.

1. **Love-driven—.02%** (very high consciousness and understanding—a true teacher/healer)
2. **Mission-driven—33.8%** (high consciousness, high integrity and commitment to excellence, a balance of higher productivity, family joy, personal health and awareness)
3. **Pride-driven—7.4%** (passive/aggressive conflicted consciousness, high producer, happiness tied to money, controlling, always thinks he's right, high intellect, low emotional intelligence, variable integrity)
4. **Desire-driven—15.8%** (medium consciousness, average production and happiness levels, aware they can do better, no idea what he's doing wrong, self-sabotaging)
5. **Fear-driven 42.9%** (low-consciousness, low production, low happiness, stubborn refusal to change, mostly blames others, addictive personality, inability to look within)

(Other than in example #1, the fractions were rounded off to the nearest tenth)

These are the results within my sample, and indicate easily observable tendencies. The study indicates that calling a professional out of the phone book would most likely bring you a high integrity person only one-third of the time (mission and love-driven). A very small percentage, only one person out of five thousand, would be motivated by love.

The mission-driven person knows that he will serve his own greatest self-interest by first focusing on the client's needs and beliefs. He then carefully shapes his presentation to fit the client's understanding without compromising truth or self-respect. He is always authentic in what he can, and cannot, do. Another common trait is that he is continuously educating himself to increase conscious intelligence.

The other two-thirds of the time you'll get someone more interested in their good than your own. The pride-driven person is often very good at what he does, but attributes his accomplishments solely to himself instead of to his family, teachers, and God, as well as to his own will. He unintentionally makes everything all about himself. This often takes the form of belittling other companies or products to make his look bigger and better (7.4% of the time).

The desire-driven person is so focused on making a sale, and it may be so obvious that it becomes ludicrous or comical. It is obvious to the customer but not to the salesperson (14.7% of the time).

The fear-driven person's approach is so convoluted that it can evoke a gamut of feelings in the customer—ranging from pity (because of ineptitude), to outright anger (because of deliberate disrespect), at the salesperson's fear-driven mediocrity (42.9% of the time).

The results of my study were compiled between 1999 and the end of 2004, and tested in 2005 at a year-long series of quarterly workshops with a major life insurance company in Baltimore, MD. Out of one hundred fifty total employees, the company had one hundred eight that attended my initial workshop entitled The Mission-Driven Agent Process. The course consisted of a total series of four modules to be taught one module every three months beginning in January, 2005. The owner paid for the first one, and then each attendee would have to make the decision to pay to attend the three following modules.

After the first workshop, which they attended for free, forty-four agents chose to attend module two. Thirty-eight out of the original one hundred eight completed all four modules. The productivity of those thirty-eight agents (the study group) rose **81.7%** in 2005, as compared to their collective productivity over the exact same time period in 2004. The collective productivity of the rest of the agency (the control group) rose **3%** applying the same parameters over the same time period (S. D'Annunzio, Q.Crawford, J.Ransone, 2004). The only known differing factor between the two groups was that the study group used this curriculum and the control group did not.

Could this startling rise in productivity be attributed to the application of this curriculum alone? No. (Clearly, willingness to invest time and money in the curriculum was another difference, perhaps reflecting a higher level of awareness coming in.) Did this curriculum help to create *favorable conditions* for greater prosperity to occur? Absolutely, yes. This proves the amazing efficacy of the mission-driven principles, and has nothing to do with this author as a workshop presenter.

The test also proved the five-year study to be useful and accurate. Thirty-eight participating attendees out of the original one hundred eight equal 35.1%...this percentage is interestingly parallel to the 33.8% found to be mission-driven in the five-year study. It is interesting to theorize why the non-participating agents chose not to attend the other modules. They probably found no relevance in attending a workshop centering on being mission-driven when they were predominantly fear, pride, and desire-driven. This result is most likely due to paradigm blindness. They were only in business to make money, so they were therefore blinded as to how the context of being mission-driven had any relevance whatsoever to adding to their bottom line.

The test and the original study both allude to the same truth. Mission-driven agents are living their Soul Purpose, serve their clients better, are more educated to true principles, have higher integrity, and earn more. They do the right thing when no one is looking, and always treat each client as if he is their friend.

This is why referring and recommending a MDB is such an

important habit. It allows those you love to receive better services and products, and also results in putting the unethical businessmen out of business. Both are valuable, because the ensuing discontent the disenfranchised agent feels will hopefully compel him to change, grow, and be more ethical. Referring Mission-driven Beings is so critical because you are voting with every dollar you spend. If we continue to send money to unethical businessmen, we are voting for mediocrity to grow in the marketplace. Evidence from the test also pointed to the importance of referring ethically. It revealed that the study group received more quantity, and a higher quality, of referrals than did the control group.

All that was required for anyone in the study or test group to shift paradigms was a willingness to admit the truth. (Example—*I'm in fear mode—what do I do?* Or, *I'm clearly being pride-driven, how do I correct it?*) Some even made public admissions, and experienced faster paradigm shifts through this public declaration than did the others.

It is through this act of conscious humility that the doorway of infinite prosperity is thrown wide open. By owning up to our negative 'shadow self' does the light of the sun (God) make the shadow self (ego) disappear.

Chapter Five

Enlightened Capitalism

As you shift your core beliefs from negative to positive ones and apply them out in the world, you will begin to receive an immediate verification of whether they are true or not. The verification will be a realization of the goal. When you live your soul purpose mission in the world, profit is far more likely, because the Field acknowledges Truth with success, and falsehood with failure. This is because the Field is a Truth barometer, and its measuring stick is functionality.

It is important to acknowledge when something functions, and when it does not. Failure in any endeavor is a sign from the Field that changes are necessary. Repeated failure causes major pain and discontent, doesn't it? The Field lets each individual know if they are on the right track, or not, simply by one's level of discontent. When people are content, they tend to take life for granted. It is an odd truth that not until one suffers do they decide to search for a way out. Discontent doesn't mean you're a bad person, but it is a clear signal you are operating from a non-functional paradigm. Continuously experiencing discontent is the way the Field, programmed by an Infinite Intelligence to do so, gets one's attention and says "WAKE UP!"

The fact that much of humanity live their lives by the cultural paradigm they were raised with, yet so many are experiencing major discontent, is a signal to the wise that a paradigm shift is necessary. This is the powerful purpose of discontent—it is a sure sign that one is going the wrong way. Discontent is the way that one finds out how **not to** succeed at something, because of adherence to false principles. The Field gets your attention that you are headed down the wrong path when that path repeatedly does not work—it is *non-functional*. Einstein said, "Truth is what stands the test of experience. "

The power of being mission-driven resides in the fact that it accesses a greater possibility for life success than ever before known or available. (That is, the Field as a source of infinite power—willing to support and inspire any noble cause, person, or country.) The United States of America sprang forth as proof that a Mission-Driven society offers greater hope for peace and prosperity. The abundance experienced in the U.S. verifies the existence of the Field, and the Prosperity Paradigm as an entrance point into it.

Let's test this idea by observing world history. Democracy in the United States has proven to be a Truth because it functions in its founding mission to support a relatively peaceful, happy, and prosperous population. Theocracies in Iran and Syria do not function in providing a balanced infrastructure for a happy populace. Communist dictatorships in Russia and Cuba have proven not to work in sustaining those same qualities for its people—they are non-functional. Their falsity is revealed by the simple fact that they don't work.

Other dictatorships have also proven to provide the same fate for the populace of each country—they are non-functional, and therefore collapse under the weight of the dictator's greed. The people suffer as a result of the non-functionality of these systems of government. Because dictatorships are not for the highest good of all people, but based upon what is good for the few, the Field of infinite intelligence makes it obvious that, as systems to govern others, they are based on falsehood. Notice this innate knowledge already exists within you—it exists in your conscious awareness in an obvious way.

You don't have to be convinced of it—you just *see* it and instantly *know* it. The dictatorship currently governing North Korea proves this point.

Looking again through the lens of world history, observe systems of commerce using this same idea as a measuring rod. Historically, capitalism functions well in creating prosperity, while socialism and communism do not. The self-correcting nature of capitalistic society in the United States has proven that it offers a unique opportunity for the Prosperity Paradigm to be experienced like never before.

It is self-correcting because Americans have freedom *from* religion, and freedom *for* religion. They have freedom *to* elect leaders, and freedom *from* electing leaders. They have freedom *for* creativity (entrepreneurship) and freedom *from* creativity (blame others). This unique set of freedoms (and many more too numerous to mention) exist in the U.S. like nowhere else on Earth, making it the perfect field for prosperity. The competitive business model offered by capitalism allows the most effective value creators to rise to greater success. Capitalism is free markets, allowing inventive people to see what society needs, and by filling that need, their product or service returns money back to the entrepreneur.

While the operational engines that serve as the foundation for American culture are not perfect, their obvious functionality proves they are based upon Truth, and therefore wisdom. One of the seeming flaws of capitalism is that it can crack under the greed of pride-driven people who lose sight of its original intent. These people blindly seek profit at the decimation of the environment or towards the very citizens it was created to serve. The answer may be found in the mission-driven model offered by this book, which I call Enlightened Capitalism.

In living soul purpose, the enlightened capitalist has a heightened level of consciousness guiding his behavior. Because soul purpose can only be accessed by transcending pride, the enlightened entrepreneur is inbred with a social responsibility to tithe money back to society. The enlightened capitalist does not feel forced to do this; he or she feels honored to be able to change the lives of others through these gifts. Living soul purpose is such a blessing; it is no longer necessary to focus on making one's own life better. They have hit the earthly life-lottery; thus, the next measure of success then becomes, "how many other's lives can we help be happier?"

Knowing your Soul Purpose is the first great breakthrough, but by itself is not enough to create lasting prosperity. Soul Purpose is like a coin that has two facets; the first is doing what I love, and the second is *serving people I love*. Many people get the first facet right but totally miss the second which is equally, if not more, important. This is the critical missing component for many who are exposed to the concept, but never succeed in bringing it to the marketplace. The marketplace is the specific group of people who are suffering in some way that your soul purpose alleviates. By identifying people you love who can be served through your product or service, you have created a market. A magnificent Mozart concerto is worthless without the ears to hear it. Those who love rock and roll are not the right market, are they? A cure for cancer has no value if it stays in the laboratory—it must get to those who have cancer. By identifying the people you love who need what you offer, you again create favorable conditions for prosperity to blossom. The free markets of the U.S. provide the fertile ground to plant the seedling of your Soul Purpose.

The Perfect Prosperity Field: the U.S.

Put simply, a Democratic republic based in enlightened capitalism offers a free and balanced self-correcting society in which anyone trying to better themselves, with the right driving motives can greatly prosper. The United States functions precisely because it operates in harmony with the already existing natural laws of the Field of consciousness. That is, the freedom to recognize that which makes people's lives better and happier, and to make it readily available to them in an affordable way. This freedom allows people the choice to pursue that which they love, creating value for society by doing so, which eventually becomes their mission.

These freedoms were brilliantly orchestrated and protected by

America's forefathers in two of the greatest documents ever written—the U.S. Constitution including the Bill of Rights, and the Declaration of Independence. These documents operate at such a high level because they contain a series of contextual ethics that can be wisely interpreted to generally function for the highest good.

You can see how these principles set the U.S. on the optimal track for prosperity. The oldest historical documents in existence bear out the exact same point.

Thousands of years ago the ancient sages of the Far East also connected to this powerful Field of potential. In ancient India, the Yoga Sutras were treatises written by Patanjali (Pa-tán-jah-lee)—detailing how he had personally accessed the Field for attaining his goal of unity consciousness, the mystical enlightened state. The word yoga means unity of body, mind, and spirit—because the Field affects the physical, mental, and spiritual realms. Patanjali was recognized in his time as being a leader among the enlightened masters. The following quote is an excerpt from the Yoga Sutras.

When you are inspired by some great purpose,
Some extraordinary project,
all your thoughts break their bonds;
Your mind transcends limitations,
your consciousness expands in every direction,
and you find yourself in a new, great
and wonderful world
Dormant forces, faculties and talents become alive,
and you discover yourself
to be a greater person by far
than you ever dreamed yourself to be

—Patanjali, 1st to 3rd century B.C.
(Shearer translation, 1982)

Thousands of years ago Patanjali talked about this "consciousness expanding in all directions" (connection to the Field) when empowered by a "great purpose" (your mission). At the core of you is the simple fact that you exist, you have consciousness—You Are. The essence of existence from one's own standpoint is called—I

Am. The 'I Am' essence—consciousness itself—has a very definite programmed intention.

This intention is written beautifully by America's forefathers in the Declaration of Independence: *...that they are endowed by their Creator with certain unalienable Rights, that among these are Life, Liberty, and the pursuit of Happiness.* The Declaration wisely acknowledges that these rights are God-given, and therefore innate to all citizens who, by their very existence, are deserving of them. This triune quality of consciousness can be understood as follows.

1. Human beings seek Life.

The properties of consciousness itself seek to live, and to continue Life. You exist, and within you is a continuous drive to further exist. The important point from a MDB perspective is that anything that is life-building, life-enhancing, and life-affirming *accesses and expands the power of the Field*. This principle is at the core of value creation.

2. Human beings seek Liberty.

One of the greatest programmed aspects of humanity is to be free. Conversely, one of the greatest tyrannies is enslaving people. In the American Civil War, the confederacy could never have won the war with slavery as an underlying principle. It is simply a self-defeating, life-destroying cause that could never prevail in the long run. Because its intention was selfish, immoral, and for the good of the few—not the whole—it cut off access to the Field, ultimately resulting in defeat. In contrast, the Union forces' freeing of the slaves was in accord with the innate quality of consciousness that is deeply ingrained within each human being as the desire to be free. Even though the freed slaves could have run away from the battle, most joined in to fight for their brothers' freedom, even willing to give their own life for the nobility of the cause.

Freedom is that which brings greater ease to life, and the opposite of freedom brings dis-ease. The entrepreneur who operates in concert with this principle will prosper repeatedly. Because the U.S offers its citizenry the most freedom of any other country on Earth, prosperity is more easily achieved in the U.S than anywhere else.

3. Human beings pursue Happiness.

Everything you do has the pursuit of happiness, and ultimately love, at its core. There is an old game called—*Why do you do that?*—that bears out this point.

You say, "I go to work."

Playing the game I ask, *Why do you do that?*

"For fulfillment and to make money." '

Why do you do that?

"For personal satisfaction and to take care of my family."

Why do you do that?

"Because it's the responsible, right thing to do."

Why do you do that?

"Because it makes me happy."

The MDB builds upon this directive tenfold by making a living out of expanding other's happiness. When you perform a job well-done that you know really helps others, the sense of inner satisfaction is extraordinary. The MDB fulfills this inner directive of consciousness because he experiences great joy in making a positive, loving contribution that far outweighs money or recognition. Inevitably, money and recognition flow in greater abundance as a by-product of being a MDB.

Many times the MDB is so lost in their cause they appear oblivious to the money and recognition. Looking at it from a cause and effect standpoint, the mission is the Cause, and money is the Effect. Again, this driving power turns on and amplifies the help received from the Field to enhance the efforts of the MDB.

The Field is accessed by ideas and people who are life-building and simply cannot respond to that which is against Life. The Field is accessed and expanded by ideas and people that add to people's freedoms, yet cannot respond to those things that enslave others. All enslavers meet a bad end—Mussolini, Hitler, Hussein. The Field effortlessly empowers those who make a living centered on making others happy. This is evidenced by the relative 'Golden Age' the United States of America has long been experiencing with the principles of life, liberty, and the pursuit of happiness as the central theme of government.

Crucial Scientific Breakthroughs

Mission-driven principles transform reality via a specific scientific process that is truly remarkable. This process was clearly identified when computer technology and micro-processing opened new avenues of study to scientists. Powerful new computers could now make millions of calculations per second. As research boundaries expanded, reams of information were entered into these computers that no human mind, or even research teams collectively, could make any sense out of. The information was called incoherent data, because the data had no common thread—it was seemingly chaotic and meaningless. The computers determined something astonishing.

Underlying everything that exists is a fundamental coherence that acts as the causative organizing principle. The coherence was given a name—***attractor patterns.*** There are two kinds of attractor patterns—weak-force, and strong-force.

Every thing in our universe—every person, idea, company, book, food, song or movie—possesses one attractor pattern or the other. The people or things that possessed a strong-force attractor pattern exhibited consistent results—growth, joy, and greater health and wealth. Those people and things that contained weak-force attractors consistently resulted in atrophy, decay, and failure. This was the birth of the radical new science called Chaos Theory, which has proven that from chaos, patterns emerge (Lorenz, 1993). The astonishing aspect was proof that these attractor patterns are the underlying influence that determines results in our lives.

As research continued, it was discovered that human beings continually align with attractor patterns throughout their day. Approximately eighty percent of humanity aligns with low energy, weak-force attractor patterns, unknowingly maximizing failure

(Hawkins, 2003). The remaining twenty percent of people align with high energy, strong force attractor patterns, consequently maximizing success. This is why success breeds success—it is no accident!

Prior to the development of chaos theory, a new branch of scientific study had been unfolding. Einstein founded quantum physics and mechanics, which morphed into advanced theoretical physics, as other great minds 'followed the breadcrumb trail' of mathematics and atomic experimentation. New discoveries that shattered centuries-old beliefs were happening so quickly that the outside world is only now finding out about it. Advanced theoretical physics morphed into a new branch of knowledge termed non-linear dynamics. It may sound hard to understand, but it's really simple to explain.

Linear objects are things like cars, people, houses—they possess tangible, apparent form. Non-linear things are intangible and formless—emotions, thoughts, intentions. Non-linear dynamics was proving the same thing as chaos theory. That motive, emotion, and intention formed the unseen attractor Field that immensely influenced the outcome of virtually every human effort. Now, please recall the programmed intentions of consciousness itself—life, liberty, happiness—and realize they spring from a *primary causative essence* that is the prime attractor pattern of them all…

LOVE.

These aspects are all non-linear. Love is formless and intangible, as are freedom and happiness. Despite the fact that you can't see or prove their existence, everything you do is compelled by them!

Non-linear dynamics was proving that the unseen power of love, as a motive and intention, created the ultimate strong-force attractor pattern that influenced all life. Conversely, the seeming opposite to love was determined to be fear (Jeffers, 1987). Fear is coming to be recognized as the ultimate low energy weak-force attractor pattern.

One of the greatest success edicts is to **give up aligning with weak force attractor patterns and consistently focus on aligning with**

strong force attractors.

We have included the following chart for you to become familiar with what these patterns might look like:

Strong Force	**Weak Force**
Emotions	
Love	Fear
Happiness	Sadness
Acceptance	Rejection
Peace	Anger
Confidence	Worry
Movies	
Field of Dreams	Friday the 13th
Forrest Gump	Psycho
Pay it Forward	Natural Born Killers
The Color Purple	Nightmare on Elm St.
It's a Wonderful Life	Apocalypse Now
Music	
Classic R&B and Rock	Gangster Rap
Gospel/Spiritual	Death Metal
Smooth Jazz	Grunge
Classical	Punk Rock
Activities	
Self-Help or Spiritual Reading	Violent Video Games
Work / Study	Bar Hopping
Prayer/Meditation	Pornography
Exercise	Gambling
Creating Value	Habitual TV Watching

It is often helpful for people to see that the attractor patterns they unknowingly align with have very predictable consequences.

As an example, any police officer can tell you it is a fact that domestic violence cases almost always involve the abuse of alcohol and/or drugs (Coleman, Strauss, 1983). Gambling almost always ends in money problems and/or marital problems (Rosecrance, 1986). These are the predictable consequences of aligning with weak force attractors.

In contrast, extra study in one's career, exercise, prayer/meditation, and reading personal development books, all have profoundly positive effects in one's life.

In business, every product or service has an underlying attractor pattern, as does the company marketing it, as does the individual who delivers it to the public. If it is love driven and mission based, its purity of intent is felt by the client. If, however, the salesperson's intention is really primarily focused on personal gain and ego-gratification, the client feels 'in his gut" that something is amiss. It doesn't *feel* right.

The logical reasons to buy make sense, but the non-linear dynamic of fear as greed causes him to feel a weak force attractor and back off. Those who align with an industry or career that is based upon alleviating human suffering, and that clearly is beneficial to society, maximize their prosperity potential.

As will be scientifically/spiritually verified herein, there is absolute genius in doing so. The following table clearly outlines the enormous difference in the powerful attractor pattern of the Prosperity Paradigm in contrast to the weakness inherent to the Scarcity Paradigm.

Prosperity Paradigm	**Scarcity Paradigm**
Love	Fear
Abundance	Scarcity
Now	Someday
Giver	Taker
Confidence	Worry
Responsible	Blaming
Value	Price
Learning	Complaining

Utilization (Context)	Accumulation (Content)
Producer	Consumer
Certainty	Luck
Expansion	Contraction
Infinite	Finite
Interdependent	Independent
Creates a Prosperity Network	Does it all himself
People are the Asset	Money is the Asset
Wisdom is Power	Money is Power
Disciplined	Procrastinating
Open-minded	Closed-minded
Decisive	Hesitant
Creation	Reaction
Money works hard for me	I work hard for money
Love people/use money	Love money/use people
God-Self	ego-self

Each of these seeming opposites is repetitively examined and explained throughout this curriculum. The scarcity paradigm activates finite thinking in which fear convinces you to believe that there is a universal conspiracy for you to fail. It makes people paranoid, habitually suspicious, and they then believe that behaving with resentment and hostility is wise. One unknowingly disconnects from the higher power emanating from the Field, and by so doing, increases and magnifies the likelihood of failure. This program comes installed in most versions of homo-sapiens. All the negative qualities it contains automatically fire in most people's brains when opportunity arises. It typically paralyzes the person with feeling *fear of loss*, both if they act, and if they do not act. It is a Lose/Lose.

The Prosperity Paradigm empowers you to remember you live in a Field of infinitely abundant possibilities that, when chosen, activate a universal conspiracy for you to succeed. In this program, the success you are seeking is also seeking you, and is only one choice away. This choice is to be a Value Creator instead of a fear reactor.

Creation: An infinite process of eternal expansion of possibilities.
Reaction: A finite process of eternal contraction of possibilities.

Reactions are typically fear-driven behaviors done habitually that repeatedly manifest as limited results. Creations are typically love-based behaviors done habitually that repeatedly manifest with powerful results.

Here is a simple example. Out of love for each other, a husband and wife choose to bring a child into this world—they choose creation. In a co-creative decision they make love. At the peak of this act is an experience called orgasm in which the miracle of creation is conceived. It is a physical representation and experience of actual connection to the Field. People often describe the experience of this exact moment in the following manner: "we felt as if we were One…we felt infinitely powerful…the feelings of love/ecstasy were indescribable by words…it felt as if time stood still…" This is another internal verification that the Field not only exists, but can be universally accessed by choosing creation. It also verifies the qualities contained within the Field that one experiences through connection to it—Oneness, Infinite Power, Loving Bliss, and Eternality.

At a lesser level you are creating and birthing a new possibility for yourself as a Mission-Driven Being who is magnificent at creating value for others by living your Soul Purpose.

History of a Mission-Driven Industry

We've outlined the success and opportunities offered by living in a mission-driven nation, now observe an industry that is mission-driven. Because this curriculum deals with money as a by-product of living the paradigm, I chose the life insurance industry as a useful example because it was founded upon a noble mission.

England, under the oppressive rule of George I in the late 1600's, had become a country where freedom and the pursuit of happiness were only available to the small minority called the upper class. All others died fairly young (average age 25), felt trapped and enslaved by the rich, and were governed by a royalty that mainly made all decisions based upon the highest good of the few—themselves.

Courageous people and their ministers began leaving England to seek freedom of religious expression in the New World of the Americas. One minister died prematurely leaving a young widow and children destitute and alone in the new, harsh, foreign country. There was no welfare or Social Security of any kind for them to turn to. A group of Presbyterian ministers, seeing the plight of their deceased brethren's family, decided to create a fund that each would donate money to. They called it the Fund for Pious Uses. They gave their friend's widow and her children a portion, literally saving their lives. Sensing the power of the idea, they collectively decided to continue putting small amounts of money into the fund every month. They created a mutual agreement that if any contributor died prematurely, a portion (plus a small amount of interest—later called a dividend) would go to his survivors. They further agreed that if any contributor lived a full life to maturity, they would get to take the money out at an agreed upon age. The widow's fund eventually became the first life insurance company, incorporating as the Presbyterian Ministers Fund in Philadelphia in the year 1717 (Brackenridge and Boyd, 1988).

It was a noble cause whose intention was for the highest good of the whole. As with many great high-minded causes, its original mission became diluted, misunderstood and weakened by greedy people over the ensuing three hundred years. This created a negative perception in the mind of the general public. The industry that began with such great intentions currently labors under the thinking that life insurance is a necessary evil. But remembering that no truth exists without a context, life insurance can be either good or bad. In the hands of the MDB, permanent life insurance is at the center of a prosperity plan that has tremendous power (Castiglione, 2005).

Focusing on the positive aspects of this mission-driven industry is where the true power lies. Ultimately, buying life insurance is an act of Love. Loving people buy life insurance because they love their spouse and/or children so much that when they die, they want the sorrow of their death to be tempered by financial security. They also recognize that whole life insurance contracts can act as a 'bank of money' that can be used like banks use the public's money (Huebner, 1929). Whole life insurance, when used in the context of the Prosperity Paradigm, has phenomenally abundant possibilities. When people reject buying it, it is because one of two things has occurred. The first occurrence is that they are operating from the scarcity paradigm and are seeing a MDB through a dirty lens. Some financial planner with pure intentions has entered this person's life, but is erroneously seen with suspicion. The client may be a good man, but his faulty paradigm is feeding him bad information based on someone else's experience.

Second, they may be accurately tuning in to the weak attractor pattern that the ego-driven agent (or company) has unknowingly emitted. This weak-force attractor phenomenon is well-known by success coaches who call it 'commission breath.' It is the feeling a client gets when she senses that the salesperson is more interested in the money he'd get from making the sale, than in helping her solve a real problem. As a teacher in this industry, my motto has always been, "Remember the Mission, forget the commission." Mission-driven financial advisors are really teachers of the Prosperity Paradigm.

All that has given this industry a negative perception in the eyes of the general public is due to those who are running faulty programming. Scarcity consciousness has the selfish desires of one's own ego as its primary motivation. Here is an example of how this negativity manifested in this industry.

One insurance company that had been experiencing a down year was referred to work with me by a prominent client. The owner of this company eventually hired me to do a productivity training seminar for his firm. He had recently fired his sales manager and was attempting to personally lead his team to achieve greater results.

I began the seminar by stating my mission in being there for the attendees, and then asked them to write out their intention in choosing to attend. I then asked if anyone was willing to share what their purpose was in choosing the insurance industry as a career. The room went silent for a moment, and then the owner raised his hand to get the ball rolling. His answer was "To make lots of money and recognition, and for my ego." In others words, it was all about him, and nothing about helping others. This is the person responsible for training forty people in his company, and unfortunately the underlying message had set a negative example to all employees. Here was an illustration of an ego-driven person whose greed had polluted the results of a whole team of people. Consequently, most of this man's employees were more focused on what *they themselves* got out of each client interaction, than what *the client* was getting. The whole sales staff was laboring under a greed-based way of thinking that had caused the office to slide into poor production and major discontent.

You can imagine the tremendous good that can occur from living as a MDB, but you must also recognize the damage that can result from working as ego-driven beings. In their inner consciousness they were focused on the commission and could care less about the mission. There is no power available here because the source of all power—the Field—is inaccessible to these people.

What the leader of this office was holding in his mind was manifesting for almost everyone, because people tend to actualize that which is held in mind. Leadership is much less *what you do,* and is much more *who you are,* and the example you set. Who we are determines what we do. Everything that exists in your life has only one thing in common—that one commonality is YOU. You are experiencing—<u>and creating</u>—all things outside of yourself, from inside of yourself.

So it only makes sense that if you seek to experience meaningful changes in your outer world (more money, enhanced relationship, better health, etc.) the most efficient way to do so is by changing your inner world. What is this 'you' on the inside? It is your conscious awareness itself—the fact that you exist, and know that you exist. This consciousness is your connection to the source of all true power. As this inner 'you' grows and expands, so will your outer results. As the inner consciousness becomes more prosperous, the outer results will reflect it. When you change and evolve your inner world, only then will you see lasting and meaningful changes in your outer world.

How do I proceed with changing my inner world? Look at the strong-force attractor emotions—love, happiness, acceptance, peace, confidence—and now realize they can, and must, be *internally* chosen. You really can choose to be that way instead of allowing the old paradigm to dictate how you *have to react*. Next, look at the activities that are shown in the strong-force attractor list. The strong-force attractor emotions are more consistently felt when you focus on immersing yourself in the strong-force attractor activities.

1. Study that which you love.
2. Commit to increasing your personal knowledge in the areas in which you want to experience greater success.
3. Go out of your way to reflect on how to always make your contribution exceed your expected compensation.
4. Read self-help and spiritual material that resonates with the highest version of who you really choose to be.
5. Study the great success stories in your chosen field of endeavor.
6. Choose to spend time around those people who are committed to act on, not only talk about, being successful.

Remember that prosperity is never accidental—it is first imagined on the inside, then chosen and created on the outside.

Prosperity Economics: Increasing the *Velocity of Value*

All human interaction that has the purpose of making life more meaningful is generally referred to by using the term ***Business***. At the heart of business are transactions between people. There are two kinds of business people in our world—those who love what they do, and those who do their work begrudgingly. We have all experienced the former, who we almost envied because it was so obvious that they were overjoyed with living their mission. All of us also know this second kind of person. It may have been a cashier at a local store who, as they cashed you out behaved miserably, conveying the feeling that they were doing you a favor by taking your money. This depicts the huge difference between living, and not living Soul Purpose. Not working in our Soul Purpose increases resentment, detracts from human interactions and undermines society. It leads to sloppy workmanship, poor performance, and ultimately opens the door to economic uncertainty.

The first principle is educating ourselves, and then our children, to the Prosperity Paradigm. We are then driven to discover that which we were born to do, by asking ourselves the right questions and developing the right prosperity habits.

The beauty of each person doing their Soul Purpose within the context of business is this: you know and do something that I cannot do. Because it is easy for you, you aren't clear about how valuable it may be to me and others. Because it is your Soul Purpose and not mine, that thing is harder for me to do than it is for you; therefore I perceive it as being more valuable. So we co-create a transaction in which an exchange of products or services for money occurs, and we both believe we have gained. The wonderful truth is that *we have both gained,* because value has been multiplied. But more has occurred than just that.

When you are doing business with someone who is on their Soul Purpose, can you see how the energy around the exchange is one of gratitude, utmost integrity, and delightful service? It is the opposite feeling of the disgruntled employee that is described above. Rather than being an upsetting experience, *it is an uplifting, exhilarating experience for both of you*. They're doing what they love, and getting paid for it. You are not only receiving tangible value from the product or service they provide, but you are also receiving the intangible value of human warmth, kindness and connection. This makes you want to go out of your way to reciprocate to them by recommending anyone you know to use their service or product. The value for both of you, *and others*—both tangible and intangible—has been exponentially multiplied. This multiplication can be called the ***velocity of value***. Observe how the increase in value takes place in transactions with a MDB:

1. The level of joy one feels when doing what they love to do is so contagious, it creates favorable conditions for greater joy to be experienced by their clients.
2. Their product or service is of the utmost integrity and worth because Soul Purpose is God-given and therefore spiritually inspired.
3. They are better at their soul work than I ever could be, and I'm grateful for them in my life. Because it's what they would be doing even if they never got paid for it—their expertise is obviously superior.
4. The world is uplifted because each person's Soul Purpose uniquely solves a world problem.
5. Soul Purpose interactions are so exceptional, clients are inspired to refer others to work with the MDB so their friends can value from this person's unique talents.
6. The whole business world is bettered. As we refer business only to Mission-Driven Beings, the ego-driven beings will have less business, and eventually go out of business. This is the beauty of competitive commerce in the U.S.—it weeds out those who have no business doing what they are **not** meant to do. The discontent they then experience will potentially guide them to seek their own true Soul Purpose.

From a macro-cosmic perspective, observe how all parties have exponentially gained in ways that are too numerous to track.

The value of every business interaction this author currently enjoys can be directly sourced to my very first spiritual student. This underscores the exponential power of the velocity of value that led to the creation of a multi-million dollar company.

Money, through the Lens of Prosperity Economics

I have heard money referred to by spiritual teachers as being *energy* and I have also heard money referred to by economists as being a *commodity*. Both are relative truisms depending on context. By using Prosperity Paradigm principles, money can be understood in a more absolute sense within a broader context. While scarcity economics are often complex, confusing, and contradictory, prosperity economics are simple, direct and obvious.

Money is a tool of exchange that serves as a conduit of value. Money is called *currency* because it carries an energy current similar to electrical current. Like copper wire is a conduit of electricity, money is a conduit of value. The copper wire is conducting the electricity, but **it** is not the power—*it merely carries the power*. It is the electricity that is the powerful thing, right? When you need to plug in a lamp, you don't look for copper wire do you? You look for an electrical outlet because that's where the power is.

Similarly, money is not the power; it is merely the conduit for the real power—which is ***value***. Checks, dollars, francs, lire, all revenue and income are attracted to you—relative to the exact amount of value you are producing in the world. Every time you receive money, you must stop and recognize it as an effect. It appears as an end result from something you did prior to receiving the money. This something was the cause.

Recognize that there are only two ways to make money in this world:

1. Creating Value for others—this is maximized and expedited by discovering Soul Purpose and externalizing it via the Prosperity Paradigm (God-Self)
2. Deception over others—this is the result of living in a state of self-deception and/or aligning with an organization that is deceiving others. (ego-self)

If you are working for an hourly wage, look at your paycheck at the end of the week and notice that you went to an employer's place of business, somehow offered value to his customers, and afterwards received compensation. If you are in sales, you first offered a product or service to a potential client, and only when they received value did your compensation then follow. Though it has been previously stated, repetition is appropriate to help you memorize…

<u>Prosperity Principle</u>

In a world of seemingly continuous cause and effect—the *creation of value* is the cause, and *money* is the effect.

The grandiose error made by people who want more money, is that they focus on the wrong end of the equation. If you seek more money, do not think about money. Focus instead on what *you can **be**—then do*—to offer the maximum value to the world. Look at things like: 'besides money, what do **I** need to be happier," and ask yourself, "does the world share in that need? What does society need? Where are people suffering? What niche can I fill that hasn't quite been filled to the degree my vision may offer? What do I love to be, and create, that might be a valuable service or product out in the world?"

At this stage of inner 'thought travel' you must suspend 'how to do it.' Dream about what your Soul Purpose may be, contemplate it, and above all remember the 'how to' is not important at this stage. The *how to do it* is not important because you are educating yourself—and that is enough for now.

There are so many unrealized opportunities out there to create greater value in the world, it is amazing. This is true because what people view as valuable is completely subjective. To some, an old baseball with ink scribbling on it is valuable, to others used postage stamps are valuable, and to another the old shoes of a movie star are valuable. Like all of life, value is subjective, and what is valuable varies according to each person's specific likes and preferences. Whether you are exchanging money for a product or service—or vice versa—all money transactions are based on exchanging value. Remember that value is a quality of **meaningful service** or **significant worth** which, when provided for another, creates enhanced joy and fulfillment for **<u>both</u>** parties. By creating value first, money will appear second.

So money is currency, which carries the energy of value. Remember that all income is attracted to you in direct proportion to the exact amount of value you are producing in the world. In prosperity economics, we **produce** more value than we *consume.*

Mission-driven beings are producers. ***Producers*** intentionally create value by consistently under-promising while over-producing. Scarcity conscious people **consume** more value than they *produce*—they might be called consumers. They consume time, value, food, joy, peace of mind, and every other valuable commodity—to a far greater degree than they produce these things. Consumers take much more than give and have a habit of over-promising and under-producing. They become energy vampires who drain your energy every time you are around them.

Focus on under-promising and over-producing, always making sure your contribution exceeds any expected compensation. This is the commitment to excellence that is the hallmark of any MDB.

This habit multiplies the amount of value created in any given transaction. Clients receive so much value from a producer that they go out of their way to glowingly refer others to them. This causes the amount of people he can help to effortlessly grow. Not only has the quantity of clients increased, but the quality of clients also increases. As the volume increases, the amount of money returning back to the value creator also exponentially multiplies. Only by increasing the frequency of value can we possibly increase the velocity of money earned. Once this principle is correctly aligned, working with a mission-driven being whose Soul Purpose is financial planning will insure greater financial certainty.

Operating according to the scarcity paradigm makes your bank wealthy—operating according to prosperity consciousness will make *you* wealthy. In scarcity thinking accumulation is the goal, while in prosperity thinking utilization is the goal. Utilization theory is important because it puts money into the highest context. Money is content—how it's used is context—and remember, no truth exists without context.

Let's use the electricity analogy again to aid in making this point clearer. Remember the analogy; *money is a conduit of value like copper wire is a conduit of electricity.* Now imagine you just added a new addition onto your house, prompting the need for more electrical power. Will stockpiling copper wire do the job? Of course not. A garage full of copper wire spools will do nothing to solve your need for more electricity. If accumulation theory were correct, stockpiling copper wire would solve the problem. Now apply utilization theory. The right amount of wire intelligently connected and strategically utilized transforms your house from one hundred to two hundred amps. Can you see that accumulating chunks of money will do nothing to guarantee prosperity if it is not intelligently utilized?

In the scarcity paradigm fear is the dominant energy. Fear-driven people with little money believe if they had lots of money all their problems would end. Wrong. Fear-driven people with money merely worry more because they have more to lose. But if the right amount of money is intelligently connected and utilized, you can transform your life.

As an example, traditional scarcity thinking tells you to get out of debt as quickly as possible and save as much as possible in a bank account. So you pre-pay your mortgage with your hard-earned cash and donate it to the bank prematurely and what happens? You lose the interest you could have made on that money and the bank reinvests it, making more for the bank by *using* your *money*! They focused on convincing you to *accumulate*—but they *utilize* your money to their benefit. You also lose the yearly tax deduction you would have kept had you not pre-paid it.

As a rule, banks never pre-pay their own loans—just ask any banker. Consumers have been taught to hoard their money out of fear, taking it out of circulation, reducing the potentiality of its creating value by being used in other transactions. It is the fear-based belief of potential scarcity that compels them to do so. If you put it under the mattress, no value can occur to you or anyone else—unless you like a lumpy mattress. If everyone did this, there'd be no transactional business and the economy would collapse. The scarcity paradigm guides us to *stick money in the bank and save for a rainy day*—right? Why would you do that when you can use an umbrella called insurance when it rains, and use your own money on investing in YOU and your own soul purpose, instead of donating it to the bank?

Even though ninety-five percent of people still erroneously do this, do you know why the economy hasn't collapsed? ***Because the other five percent are the wealthy people and they're behaving according to Prosperity Paradigm principles—which is precisely why they are wealthy and getting richer.*** By familiarizing yourself with these principles, you can use this technology to shift the way you spend, save, earn and invest. The principles de-mystify wealth creation so that that any disciplined person committed to learn and apply them in context will better themselves financially.

Having money is a responsibility that requires wise stewardship. Using it wisely is so important because *you are voting with every dollar you spend*. When you put your hard earned dollars into mediocre, weak-force attractor products and ideas, you are voting for those things to grow. When you stop doing so, mediocre products, services, and things disappear. They will then be replaced by more valuable products, services, and things. You can stop rewarding mediocrity right now by referring the right business to the right mission-driven professional. These are the entrepreneurs who understand and apply macro-economic utilization principles of prosperity.

When you intelligently invest money back into the playing field of life (especially in support of your Soul Purpose)—and utilize the efficiency—you then increase the velocity of *money*. This is how you can use the same dollar multiple times to increase your return on that dollar, without any additional risk to your money.

Increasing the frequency of value will make you more money in a joyous fashion. Increasing the velocity of money will help you exchange the same dollar several times, maximizing the protection, savings and growth of your assets through optimal utilization. By doing so, you can truly achieve a lifetime of economic confidence with certainty, not luck.

Chapter Six

The Financial Freedom Blueprint

True wealth is not accidental, magical or mystical. It is the result of the pragmatic implementation of the following concepts, which are intentionally presented in a specific order. Like anything you build on Earth, you must start with a firm foundation and build from the bottom up.

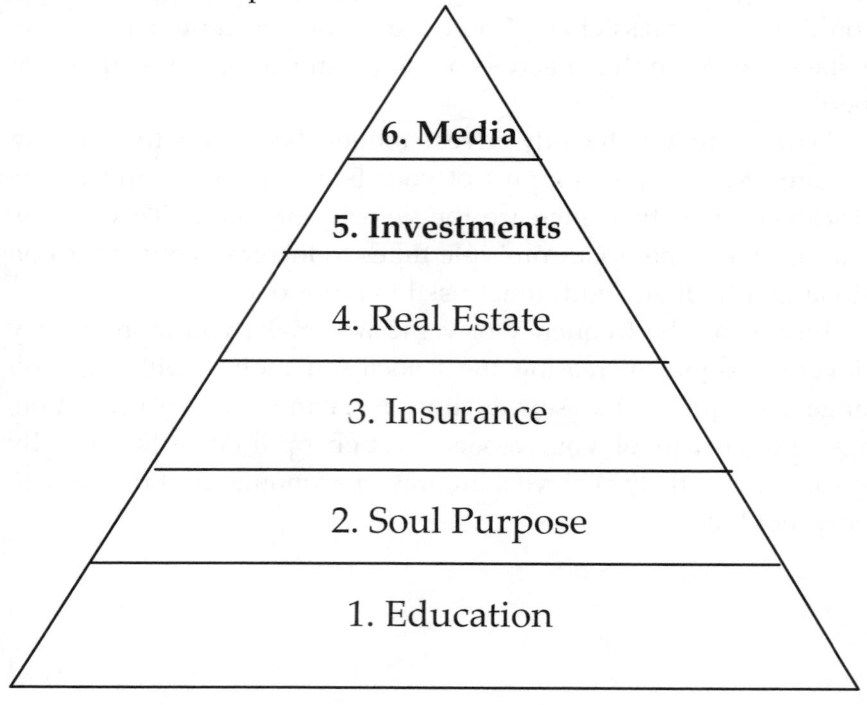

1. Education – Educating yourself to learn and apply prosperity principles is critical to wealth creation and preservation. The prosperity paradigm teaches timeless principles that result in success regardless of what the desired outcome is. When applied to finance, they create favorable conditions for an economic certainty that is irrevocable by governments and immune to market fluctuations.

When automobile pioneer Henry Ford lost his fortune in the stock market crash of 1929, friends asked if he contemplated suicide as a solution to his problems. Ford was rumored to have said, "Are you crazy? I was a millionaire once and I'll be one again - I may've lost my money, but I still remember how I did it." Three years later, he again joined the short list of millionaires at that time in the U.S. He had the wisdom, and had no doubt he could again achieve prosperity. Though he had lost all his money he retained the true source of wealth which was the wisdom to do it again. Despite market collapse and governmental failure, Ford was able to rebuild his fortune. With this wisdom you can create wealth that is timeless and permanent.

Real wealth exists as wisdom in the minds of people. People are the only real and true asset in this world. It is people who invent, build, heal, construct, and improve society. Productive people are producers – they uplift and evolve society. Destructive people are consumers – they destroy and undermine society. Remember that there are two ways to make money on Earth – value creation (producers) and deception (consumers). Consumers are not to be vilified, they are to be educated, but only if they allow you to help. Any consumer can become a producer, and self-reliant through education, by studying the principles of success and applying them in context.

Because wisdom is power, (and not money), it resides within people and once found and applied it can never fail. Erroneously believing that money is power destines people to live in fear, which is the trademark of the scarcity paradigm. When money becomes more important than people, negativity is the inevitable result. This is evident when watching the average person make a buying or investment decision. Because of the predominance of scarcity thinking, the bottom line for most people is price. Therefore, as manufacturers lower prices to stay competitive, eventually they have to lower quality to stay in business. Look at the end result. Mediocrity is rewarded by scarcity thinking, while quality goods and services suffer.

This was the thinking that guided the construction specifications behind the building of the levees that protected the city of New Orleans. Weather experts knew a thirty foot storm surge was inevitable someday, but nevertheless decided that building safer, higher levees would be too expensive. They were instead built high enough to only withstand a twenty-five foot storm surge and saved several millions of dollars. In the richest country in the world, the decision came down to price. For many years the levees held, until the inevitable storm hit in the form of Hurricane Katrina. Consider the precious loss of human life, the suffering and the billions of dollars of destroyed property that didn't have to happen–all the result of scarcity thinking.

Hence, the primary factor in any buying decision should be learning the precise value proposition of any exchange or business deal. Money can never be the primary reason to do, or not do, anything. If it is, you are absolutely stuck in the scarcity paradigm. Money should always be regarded as the secondary consideration. Again, when making a buying decision, identify and learn to understand the value proposition first, and then factor in the price second. This can bring the vicious cycle of the true causes of scarcity to an end, this cause being limited fearful beliefs erroneously held in the minds of people.

Productive people are the true asset and it was these people who invented the idea of money. This invention is significant because it is far more useful than the barter system which it replaced. Money increases the world-wide ability for people to exchange goods and services. Without money we could never barter for all the goods and services we use on a daily basis. To see the purpose money serves, for a moment think about a world in which you had to barter for everything. Can you imagine a carpenter having to barter his carpentry skills with the phone company, for gas & electric, with insurance companies, doctors, gas stations, toll booth operators, grocery stores, clothing stores, theaters, restaurants, and all the hundreds of other items we use on a daily basis? It would literally be impossible. Money definitely increases the utility of societal exchange.

Prosperity Paradigm Principle

Money is a useful tool of exchange, but people and wisdom are the true assets.

Our society collectively agrees to honor the exchange of paper money and coins for valuable goods and services. Money is a conductor of value called currency, and is therefore a very useful social agreement. The problem is that because of the scarcity paradigm, money has been elevated in relevance to be viewed as more important than the people it was created to serve.

Because money is a social agreement created by man, it is finite and changeable. Take one U.S. dollar to Jamaica and exchange it – their banks will give you thirty-eight Jamaican dollars. Why? There is a different social agreement there. Go to Europe and the same U.S. dollar is worth much less. Again, in Europe there is a different society which abides by a different social agreement as to how much value U.S. money can buy. Value exists only in the minds of people, and constantly changes according to context.

As you can see, money is a useful tool created as a social agreement among men, but it is finite and changeable. Value creation is an aspect of God and is therefore infinite and unchangeable. The wisdom to create value has, and always will result in wealth with certainty, because it is an infinite success principle. Value creation is the reality (originating from God) – and money is a useful tool of exchange (invented by man). It is the by-product that appears secondary to value creation. Through the lens of the prosperity paradigm, money is the secondary consideration, and understanding the value proposition of a potential buying decision is primary. This is why money can never be the primary reason to do, or not do, anything.

Prosperity Paradigm Principle

When making a buying decision, the primary factor is understanding the value proposition, and the secondary factor should be money.

A limiting belief projected through scarcity thinking is that it takes money to make money (money is power, money is the asset). It does not take money to make money – the true requirement is the education to use true principles in context to produce value for others. In the late 1980's real estate mogul Donald Trump hit hard times, reportedly owing investors close to a billion dollars. Things were so dire that, upon seeing a homeless man on the streets he commented to his wife, "Honey, that man is a billion dollars richer than we are."

What the homeless man did not know, which Trump did, was the secret to create wealth with certainty, not luck. What Trump had was his good word and reputation, plus his knowledge of how to create value in his industry. He called every investor and bank, telling them the hard truth of his situation, but with a game plan of how and when they could expect re-payment. Inspired by his debtors' faith in him, he repaid each one earlier than expected, while rebuilding phenomenal wealth in the process.

Learning to be productive and creating value for others inevitably results in drawing abundance (whether monetary or otherwise) to you. Remember - wisdom is power and people are assets.

2. Soul Purpose – Once you have the proper education, it takes approximately five to ten years of life searching for soul purpose to fully reveal itself. It cannot be forced or sought after; it reveals itself when the obstacles that the ego presents us with are removed. This occurs through a combination of grace, karmic merit, and spiritual discipline.

Living your soul purpose does not mean you have to own your own business or be famous. It means that you are doing what you are naturally passionate about doing every day, whether working for yourself or as an employee. Many people know their soul purpose but refuse to acknowledge it because doing so may require uncomfortable decisions. The real pain and suffering from human existence comes from ***not*** making these decisions.

The width and breadth of your soul purpose may be large or small, it may result in fame and fortune, or it may not. Regardless of its scope, discovering and living your soul purpose is the greatest gift a person can give themselves. Offering this gift of service to humanity is the greatest gift you can give to the world.

3. Insurance (Life, Disability, Liability, Health) – Being properly insured keeps you in the prosperity paradigm, and being under insured or uninsured is an indicator of the scarcity paradigm.

Insure everything you can (especially your life) for full market value. Why? Being uninsured results in living life fearfully and destining you to live the scarcity mentality inherent in the scarcity paradigm. Secondarily, being uninsured shows poor stewardship over one's family, car, home, and self.

Imagine owning a late model Mercedes, but you decide the insurance is too expensive to put on the car. (This is obviously an imaginary scenario, but so many people think with scarcity that if state law allowed it, it would occur.) Without insurance, would you be driving this very expensive car fearfully or fearlessly? Fearfully, right? If you had a home worth one million dollars, what would you insure it for? One million dollars, right? For roughly two thousand dollars you can insure it for full market value. That's a good deal isn't it? Almost all people know this, until it comes to buying life insurance. Isn't insuring your full human life value far more important than having full market value on your car or your house?

I've found that highly rated long-standing life insurance companies are really very wise. Whatever they will offer to insure me for – I purchase and put in force. Why? It's their soul purpose, and they would never offer me more than my true human life value. With all their amazing actuarial formulas and expertise, they are truly more qualified to determine my real economic human life value than I am.

Who is more qualified to tell you about the workings of your heart – you or the cardiologist? Much like a cardiologist expertly knows the heart, so too does the insurer better know how to determine people's economic human life value. So if they think I'm worth that much, why shouldn't I? The answer most people give me is because the premiums are high, especially when it comes to the most valuable life insurance which is whole life, or permanent life insurance. They tell me to buy term and invest the difference. Term insurance is cheaper over a short period of time, but if held over a lifetime is far more expensive. The only reason to get term insurance is because of price, *and* because of an incomplete understanding of the value whole life insurance offers. This is a violation of prosperity principles because money should never be the primary reason to do or not do anything. Getting the right amount of death benefit is therefore the key, with the predominance of it being whole life insurance, which offers the greatest value. If money truly prevents one from doing so, term insurance, or a term/whole life blend, with the intention of converting it later to 100% whole life is also a wise choice (Renier, 2004). The most important thing is the certainty that your family is safe and secure under any circumstances.

Seeing this useful tool through the eyes of prosperity reveals another utility of insurance. With permanent or whole life insurance, the accrued cash value eventually exceeds the amount paid in as premium payments. (This is true when using a reputable insurance firm, and, after approximately twelve years of making monthly premium payments.) This makes whole life insurance a good investment, considering that you can often buy ten dollars of protection for one dollar out of pocket. It grows at approximately 7 – 8% (the dividend) while you are alive, and 1000% (the death benefit) to your heirs. Also the dividend, and in some cases the death benefit, can be leveraged while you are alive for many different investment uses. The dividend the company pays you can actually serve as your own private bank. By meeting with an advisor who is experienced in prosperity economics, you can often buy life insurance with no additional out-of-pocket expense, much like real estate. Life insurance is actually prosperity paradigm insurance because it empowers you to live life fully and fearlessly with the certainty that your wisdom and financial legacy continues long after your physical death.

Implementing a will and trust further guarantees that your preferences are fully realized no matter what. Using these financial tools along with disability, liability, and health insurance policies indicates the wisdom of having educated oneself to true principles. It also proves excellent stewardship towards taking care of one's family.

4. Real Estate

Hundreds of years ago in Europe, as in much of the rest of the world, the general populace worked on land owned by a wealthy lord and were considered indentured servants or serfs. Because property was virtually unattainable by most families, around the year 1640 English author John Locke coined the phrase *life, liberty, and the pursuit of property*. It became the standard and the goal of most men at that time. The idea was that an individual's freedom is greatly expanded when a man owns his own land. Thomas Jefferson thought enough of this idea to borrow a portion of it for the Declaration of Independence. (Jefferson modified it to life, liberty and the pursuit of *happiness*) Real estate is more than a modern way to potentially make money; it is an innate drive that aids in the enhancement of one's self-respect and sense of autonomy. Any young adult experiences this feeling when he moves out of a parent's home or apartment into his own property and excitedly walks his own land for the first time. The humanistic principle behind this is; individual freedom is expanded through ownership of private property.

Today, the owning of real estate can create steady portfolio income through the leveraging of several key ideas. First, notice the term *portfolio income* instead of calling it *passive income,* which can imply that no value was actively created to earn the income. Second, if the business of real estate is not your soul purpose, wisdom dictates creating a strategic partnership with someone who loves it with passion and integrity. You can leverage your own credit, energy, or dollars in a partnership which allows you to be a partial owner with someone living their soul purpose in this industry. This person can receive value through using your credit, cash, or wisdom on a variety of topics to justify your place in the partnership. People whose soul purpose is real estate successfully create value by finding:

1. Discounted properties
2. Distressed properties
3. Conversion opportunities
4. New construction – (housing developments or commercial property like buildings or strip malls, etc.)

Because this curriculum focuses specifically on the macro-cosmic and macro-economic view of prosperity, the precise action steps to acquire and sell real estate are not included herein. There are many excellent books that outline precisely how to do so successfully, one being The One Minute Millionaire by Robert G. Allen and Mark Victor Hansen.

If you are clear that the real estate business is not your soul purpose, you can still use real estate to create portfolio income through a strategic partnership with someone whose purpose it is.

5. Investments – Soul purpose must always be realized as your primary source of income, and then all other investments as secondary or multiple streams of income. Unless your soul purpose involves offering a uniquely valuable yet unknown idea into the investment world, investments are best utilized *after* you discover and successfully live your soul purpose. This is a very controversial viewpoint about investing, but one that has been diligently studied for over twenty years by this author. Unless it was in pursuit of one's soul purpose, virtually no one ever became financially free *only* by investing in the stock market.

Investments can be very efficient as a secondary income stream, but when viewed as a 'get rich quick scheme,' can be disastrous. People become wealthy when living their soul purpose. This is the surest means to financial freedom. They then create a series of multiple income streams by investing a portion generated from their primary source of income with a trusted advisor who is living his own soul purpose. To find such an advisor is simple once you get on track with your soul purpose.

Recognize that all human beings travel in soul groups. Artists hang out with other artists, athletes hang with other athletes, and those who are living their soul purpose also congregate with other like-minded beings. Once you discover yours, you'll be amazed at how effortlessly you will attract the right doctors, lawyers, home builders, and financial planners. The investment world, like any other career path, is populated by people who are in one of the five main modes of life – fear, desire, pride, mission, or love mode. If you are in the lower modes, you will attract advisors with the exact same energy that you are emanating. If it is the scarcity paradigm, it matters not what the investment is – with the energy of scarcity driving any investment, the outcome will most assuredly result in failure. Because of this truth, it is always the behavior of the *investor* and never the behavior of the *investment* that is the key. The following story will help you to understand this point more fully.

In 1999 one of my very good friends went to work for a new real estate company. He agreed to a smaller salary because of the promise of a large potential payout of company stock linked to his performance. Despite his best efforts the company fired him after only a year, but because he had created an excellent relationship with the CEO, he was allowed to keep the stock. He closely monitored the price per share, and when the stock peaked he sold his shares at close to a half-million dollar profit. At that time the stock market was at an all-time high and because of the advent of on-line trading, but with very limited knowledge, he decided to invest in stocks and commodities. In three months he had lost every single cent! Why? First, his soul purpose field was not in the stock market nor in the commodities market – the only reason he had invested the money there was to make more money. (Remember - money should never be the primary reason to do or not do anything. If it is, you are absolutely stuck in the scarcity paradigm, and investing with a scarcity mindset can only reap scarcity results – always.) Second, he had no clue of the value proposition of any of these commodities; therefore his 'investment' was really legalized gambling. One thing any gambler knows is that the only sure winner is 'the house.' There was no *investment* that could have ever been successful because his behavior as the *investor* violated true principles.

Once you discover and begin creating value for others with your soul purpose, you will attract the right financial advisors. They will be mission-driven financial planners with an impeccable level of integrity. Because they are immersed in and love their career, they will have done their homework. They know precisely how and where to confidently invest your money to create the utmost in favorable conditions for investment success. Therefore it is critical to first focus on soul purpose, and then the education to contextualize true principles. Then and only then, begin to build multiple income streams with certainty through insurance, real estate, and then investments.

6. Media – The power of using the media is that you can use one performance to reach thousands of people. Any medium that allows you to write or speak once, but have that performance repeatedly go out to large numbers of people, will be a key means of increasing your personal prosperity. I believe that everyone's soul purpose is so unique and interesting that it deserves to be written in a book. Yet that is only one way to utilize media.

It may mean writing a pamphlet, brochure, or book, constructing a commercial website, doing radio and television interviews, or writing articles for newspapers or magazines. Seminars are another effective way to expand the reach of your message. Leveraging the powerful tool that media offers, will multiply and magnify the reach and efficacy of your message.

The internet now reaches billions of human beings. Imagine if you had a website that concisely offered one dollar of value to two billion people. If you had a shopping cart with a Pay Pal account on the site, and you effectively communicated that idea to two billion people who clearly saw one dollar's worth of value and half of them bought – you'd be a billionaire! With the power provided by today's media opportunities, this scenario is now possible.

The Importance of Wise Stewardship

Stewardship is the habit of respectful maintenance over the gifts you have been given or earned in life. *Wise stewardship* is correctly **prioritizing** these gifts in a way that creates favorable conditions for continuous prosperity.

A common theme in today's society is for people to have prioritized money over family, only to suffer very hurtful consequences. This is the moral behind the parable of King Midas. By erroneously loving gold so much, he wished for, and was granted, the ability to turn all he touched into gold. After turning every family member, pet, and friend to lifeless matter, the loneliness of living without loved ones drove him crazy. Though this is a fable, it clearly depicts the importance of wise stewardship.

Here is the prioritized order of how I recommend honoring these gifts, including suggestions to nurture and further develop each one.

1. **Spirit** – Chapter 12 is dedicated entirely to this subject.
2. **Body** – Proper diet, sleep, hydration, and exercise
3. **Mind** – Proper study of, and alignment with, all strong-force attractor people and things. (Books, time in nature, puzzles, movies, games, music, etc.)
4. **Family** – This category pertains to the soul group of people most important to you beginning with nuclear, then extended family, friends, neighbors, employers, employees, co-workers and clients. Living by the knowledge contained within this manual will enhance your family life, while being certain to balance spending as much time as possible with nuclear and extended family.
5. **Career** – Discovering and living your soul purpose.
6. **Money/Finance** –
   a. Adhere to the financial freedom blueprint in this curriculum.

b. Create a workable budget and use it with discipline.
c. Hire a financial advisor who is living his soul purpose and practices macroeconomics and true principles.
d. Live beneath your means.
e. Tithe to wherever you are spiritually fed.
f. Be certain to draw up a will so that all your financial wishes are realized no matter what.
g. Find a cause or charity you are passionate about and donate money to it.

7. **Earth** – Wise stewardship of our planetary resources is probably at an all-time low now more than ever. That is why it is critical for all conscious beings to show greater awareness and respect by doing the following simple things;
   a. When in nature, don't litter, and pick up others' trash if we spot it while in nature – practice leaving each natural setting in better condition than you found it in.
   b. Learn to utilize planetary resources wisely. Don't over-hunt, over-fish, over-farm, or over-strip any resource regardless of what it is. (whether plants, animals, or minerals) By learning to 'tap' the earth gently, whatever you need from her will be given to you at the right time.
   c. Most terrorist organizations are funded by westerners' dollars for eastern oil. Consider supporting and putting your dollars into green technology (Ethanol or electric cars, etc.) This does two powerful things. First, we clean up our atmosphere and prevent ozone depletion, greenhouse gases, and further glacier melting and erosion. Second, we end the western world's unintentional funding of terrorist activity.
8. **Other Material Possessions** – in order of personal preference like; Home, Clothes, Car, etc.

Wise stewardship is the prioritized application of these following success qualities; excellence, discipline, responsibility, commitment, accountability, focus, and persistence.

When we practice wise stewardship, we earn the right to

receive more. Because earth is much like a school, by learning the lesson of wise stewardship, we are given more to be steward over.

An example of this is the Bill and Melinda Gates Foundation. They personally funded this foundation with thirty billion dollars (yes, $30,000,000,000) earned as owners of Microsoft. Two thirds of this money goes to solving infectious diseases, lack of housing, and starvation problems world-wide. The other third is used to reform and restructure the American education system. They have single-handedly done more for people in Africa to cure typhoid, malaria, diarrhea, starvation and AIDS – and many other diseases – than all other countries and companies combined. Because of this spectacular philanthropy, the foundation recently received another stunning donation of wealth from business tycoon Warren Buffet (Loomis, 2006). Buffet gave thirty-seven billion dollars in stock, which may end up being fifty billion dollars by the time it's converted to cash for usage. When he was asked why he chose to give his money where he did, Buffet answered, *"If you think about it – if your goal is to return the money to society by attacking truly major problems that don't have a commensurate funding base - what could you find that's better than turning to a couple of people who are young, who are ungodly bright, whose ideas have been proven, who already have shown an ability to scale it up and do it right?"* Because of their wise stewardship, the Gates Foundation received the largest philanthropic donation in modern history.

<u>Prosperity Paradigm Principle</u>

Wise stewardship increases personal power, thereby increasing one's ability to receive more abundance in return.

Finally, we reach an interesting question – when is enough prosperity, enough?

Gates never set out to make sixty billion dollars – he merely focused on living his life fully. By doing so, he discovered a means (the PC) of connecting the whole world, which served such a valuable need; he became the wealthiest man in the world (Money followed value). More so, he helped launch the soul purpose careers of millions of software designers, technicians, micro-processors, and hundreds of other new careers. Similarly, there are millions of careers that are just waiting to be developed through the discovery of this generation's life purposes. Looking at the Gates family's phenomenal example of stewardship verifies the power of earning that amount of money. While others might have criticized them for earning so much, the way they use the money makes any responsible citizen glad they earned it!

The flawed thinking behind the concept of 'enough' is this; to think of prosperity as only money is a serious misperception. True prosperity is being in a flow with all of life, in which the perfect thing shows up in a way that serves the need of the greatest good. It may be the right book appearing at the right time, being stranded in the wilderness and food appearing 'out of the blue' to save you, or a workshop invitation that shows up in your mailbox which, after attending, perfectly transforms your life.

When wise stewardship is applied, the word 'enough' is therefore meaningless.

PROSPERITY PARADIGM PRINCIPLES

1. Collective human behavior/beliefs do not qualify those behavior/beliefs to be TRUTH.

2. No truth exists in this world without context being clearly set. (Material things are meaningless unless they are used to uplift people - how a thing is earned and used gives it meaning.)

3. The highest context of human existence is to Remember God, Choose Love, and Create Value

4. Discovering and living one's Soul Purpose expands the greatest possibility for people to create value for others.

5. In a world of seeming cause and effect, value creation is the cause, money is the effect.

6. Money is a useful tool of exchange, but people and wisdom are the true assets.

7. When making a buying decision, the primary factor is to understand the value proposition, and the secondary factor should be money.

8. Wise stewardship increases personal power, thereby increasing one's ability to receive more abundance in return.

Chapter Seven

Making the Shift

It is advantageous to recognize where you are stuck, by observing the common themes every paradigm contains. Each paradigm contains rules and beliefs which assist you in achieving a certain level of success; then you reach the limits of the paradigm and they no longer function.

As has been previously stated, the pattern for change begins with repeatedly experiencing discontent. One must then tell the truth and admit what is not working. If you are seriously ready to change, you will experiment with new paradigm possibilities, and then learn from the conditions these new experiments reap. This trial and error process is commonly called the 'scientific method,' and is the basis of all current scientific experimentation.

Though they often go by unnoticed, these are the phases that every individual goes through on the journey to success. All people get stuck in one phase or another at certain times—it is a natural part of being human. Becoming aware of these 'phases' can be of great help to becoming financially free, as you recognize what is needed to move on to the next paradigm.

Phase One: Discontent, frustration, and disappointment because of inability to reach one's goal.
Phase Two: Willingness to admit the current paradigm is non-functional.
Phase Three: Openness to seek and implement new, unfamiliar strong-force attractor possibilities that are Mission Driven.
Phase Four: Applying the new pattern to attain the goal using a 'trial and error' approach, finding what doesn't work and discarding it, and discovering what does work and running with it.
Phase Five: Persist, Learn, Course Correct; Persist, Learn, Course Correct; Persist, Learn, Course Correct; Persist, Learn, Course Correct; Persist, Learn, Course Correct
Phase Six: SUCCESS!

Highlight which phase you are currently in, so you can determine the next appropriate phase necessary to move one step closer to success. Right now, the goal is far less important than being truthful about where you are.

This paradigm shift has been studied and contains many precedents. When strong-force attractor paradigms are studied and used, profoundly beneficial changes occur *worldwide*. To explain how this happens, scientist Rupert Sheldrake uses a theory called the Morphogenetic Field (M-field). Simply put, morphogenic fields are precedents for change; people see other brave souls do what was once deemed impossible, and they then believe they too can do it. Sheldrake theorized that an idea gathers momentum until it reached a tipping point at which point an invisible shift occurred—throughout the whole of the Field. Sheldrake's theory explains the dramatic breakthroughs that occur when one makes a paradigm shift. His research discovered that every great invention was preceded by the discontent caused by paradigm blindness. Then, when the paradigm shift occurred, a new M-field of energy literally raised the consciousness of the inventor. Due to the inventor's raised consciousness, he had a breakthrough, which created the model for others to have the same breakthrough by observation of the new precedent of possibility. Electric light, the telephone, and the computer are all examples of this scientific process. Each of these inventions were initially ridiculed by the doubting populace, then generally accepted, used, and praised.

Examples of M-fields are fascinating. In Olympic running it was a well-known belief that running a sub-four minute mile would cause a human being to die. When Sir Roger Bannister broke the four minute mile barrier, he created a new M-field. People saw that it was possible, and the precedent caused a paradigm shift worldwide. The *next day* the mark fell again, and has been broken hundreds of times since (Sheldrake, 1995).

We see another example in the following aviation story. Though man had dreamed of flying for thousands of years, paradigm blindness caused this quote to be generally agreed upon.

> "When we left at the end of 1901, we doubted that we would ever resume our experiments. Although we had broken the record for distance in gliding, and although our results were better than had ever before been attained, when we looked at the time and money which we had expended, and considered the progress made and the distance yet to go, we considered our experiments a failure. At this time I made the prediction that men would sometime fly, but that it would not be within our lifetime."

Can you sense the discontent? Now think of whatever discontent is occurring in your own life—and be encouraged. The quote above was uttered by Wilbur Wright in 1901. Yet in 1903, he created a new M-field by flying eight hundred feet in the world's first power-driven, heavier-than-air machine. Along with his brother Orville, they further developed the airplane, taught men to fly, and opened the era of aviation. By 1928 the first passenger commercial flights were available, and in 1932 a half-million passengers flew commercially.

Despite being an expert pioneer aviator in 1901, Wright was yet to shift paradigms, doubtful he would ever see it in his lifetime. With the paradigm shift a mere two years later, the M-field he created attracted thousands of others whose own personal contributions exploded the industry into what it now is. The M-field establishes the precedent of 'miraculous possibility' as the strong-force attractor pattern of a new paradigm propels the success momentum of the MDB.

Observe these principles in action and see how they work. The following model represents paradigm shifts with which you'll be familiar. Each arrow between paradigms represents the discontent that compels people to seek greater productivity. This seeking causes an inner shift in consciousness itself—and a commitment to learn and persist—as the MDB is guided by the Infinite Intelligence to a higher and greater possibility.

Below we see the evolution of paradigm shifts in travel.

Travel Paradigm Shifts

Walking →	**Horseback →**	**Wagon →**	**Train →**	**Automobile →**	**Airplane →**	**Jet**
1,000,000 BC	4000 BC	3000 BC	1804	1885	1903	1930

Early man traveled by walking, and the discontent caused by the limitations of a hunter on foot were many. Being outrun by game, being devoured by bigger and faster animals, plus distance limits were all solved by taming and riding horses. But imagine being the first person to jump on the back of a horse, only to get violently thrown to the ground. Picture how crazy it must've looked to others who, out of fear of such a huge powerful animal, ridiculed that first person's brave efforts. Then imagine him trying and trying, learning from what did and didn't work, until finally success!

Ah, but a horse carries only one, maybe two riders...what about my family? This discontent contributes to the invention of the wheel (3500 BC), then the cart, then the wagon. Roads of rails called wagon ways were being used in Germany as early as 1550. Drawn by oxen or horse, the wagon carried settlers across Europe and then the wilds of America by the late 1700's. Alas, horses need hay and rest, and have troubles over mountains, and are killable by bandits. This discontent led to the invention of the first steam engine locomotive in

1804. The resulting M-field that was created expanded the minds of hundreds of other inventors, and by 1830 the first sleeper cars were being used by the public.

But, again, railroads can only go where there is track—a discontent that led to the invention of the automobile in the late 1800's. But the drawback in automobile transportation is that cars need roads, and are limited to land travel. What if we could fly? Hence, we see the invention of the airplane in the early 20th century—jet travel in the mid-twentieth century, and space travel today. Soon, commercial space travel will be available first to the wealthy, and in the not-so-distant future, to many other social stratas as well. Though it may sound far-fetched, the next frontier to be explored is time travel. Physicist Stephen Hawking has a theoretical time travel equation that is being worked on right now. Did you sense any inner resistance arise inside of you as you read that last sentence? If so, you may have just experienced the edge of your current paradigm.

Another notable quality is the quickening of time that occurs as higher consciousness paradigms gather momentum, resulting in new discoveries at an ever-increasing rate. Almost one million years passed between foot travel and the invention of the wagon, but a mere one hundred and sixty-five years passed between the first train and Neil Armstrong walking on the moon! A metaphor might help clarify the power of this point further—as it relates to you.

Imagine trying to push a car that has stalled, and you are on level ground. You push with all your might and it barely moves, but as it rocks back from the small degree you initially moved it, you push again. The car begins rocking back and forth, and you can feel you are about to reach the 'tipping point' at which the car will roll forward. Inspired by impending success, you're empowered to push the hardest yet, and the Law of Momentum carries the car forward. The faster you go, the more momentum the car gets, and you can keep it rolling with far less effort.

This describes the unique evolutionary point in history that we now find ourselves. There have been greater breakthroughs in science, medicine, technology, and industry in the last one hundred and fifty years than in the previous million years combined. This quickening of the Law of Momentum means the time is now for you to shift your paradigm to one of prosperity, by casting off the pre-programmed shackles of fear.

Yet in the beginning, while one is in Phase One of the awakening to the Field (discontent) it is very difficult. The mind plays clever tricks with us. It projects that the problem is 'out there,' when in truth, the real culprit is the virus *inside* our mind-computer called fear. The exact same Prosperity Paradigm beliefs that countless business, scientific, and spiritual leaders (all mission-driven beings) have used throughout history are herein detailed for you to follow. But expect there to be inner resistance, and expect the inner demon called the ego to do its best to derail your efforts. We'll tell you why in ensuing chapters. You must persist, persist, persist—on through to the inevitable success that is waiting for you, and in actuality, is your birthright! *It is a fact that the same level of success you are seeking is also seeking you* (Proctor, 1996).

An excellent example of this process can be found in the life work of Thomas Edison. He is referred to as the greatest inventor in history, and still holds the world record for the most patents held by an individual with a total of one-thousand ninety-three. In the course of inventing the electric light bulb, he tried and failed approximately ten thousand times. Can you imagine that level of persistence? Here are Edison's thoughts taken from his journal;

> Restlessness and discontent are the first necessities of progress. I never perfected an invention that I did not think about in terms of the service it might give others. I find out what the world needs. Then I go ahead and try to invent it. I didn't fail ten thousand times. I successfully eliminated, ten thousand times, materials and combinations which wouldn't work.

If you reflect back on the explanation of Phases One through Five a few pages back, you'll notice that each sentence of Edison's quote aligns phase by phase, as a verification of each step in the process. Phase Six is success. Besides the light bulb (1878), the phonograph (1877), the central power station (1881), the motion-picture studio (1892) the system for making and showing motion pictures (1893), and alkaline storage batteries (1901), he also enhanced original versions of the stock ticker, the telegraph, and Alexander Graham Bell's telephone. Edison succeeded in inventing or refining devices that profoundly influenced people lives, and still do today.

What Failure Really Means

There is an *enormous* difference between failing repeatedly—as many of you may believe about yourself—and 'successfully eliminating combinations that don't work,' as Edison says.

This came to the fore with a client who, as a life insurance agent, had recently experienced a terrible business year. I asked him what he had learned from the past year. He looked at me like I was crazy and said, "What could I possibly learn from such a painful experience? " I asked him if he was open to my help, and he agreed. I began by asking a couple simple questions.

I asked if he had a time management system that he used faithfully. He said, "I have one and use it occasionally, but that isn't going to make me more money. " I made a note, and as I did so, I noticed him squirm a little. I then asked, "Did you make an hour worth of prospecting calls every business day?" He said, "No, but nobody in my business really does that either." I wrote that down. I said, "Did you focus more on serving people, or selling life insurance, when you were face-to-face with clients? He defensively said, "Now wait a minute, what are you implying?" I shrugged and again wrote down some notes and said, "I'm sorry Bill, I'm really doing this to help, but I can see it's frustrating you—should I stop?" He instantly softened and said, "No, go on." I asked one more question which was, "Did you 'plant referral seeds' in every meeting to maximize the possibility of receiving personal introductions to other new potential clients?" He replied, "No, I try to remember to do that but I somehow rarely get them." I nodded in understanding, and then told him the good news. "Bill, you have successfully eliminated several behaviors that result in **not** selling life insurance!" I showed him my notes, and the paradigm shift I was suggesting, which looked like this;

Old paradigm habit: Poor or no time management.
<u>New success habit</u>: taking 10 minutes every night to create tomorrow's plan including planning for an hour of phone work.

Old paradigm habit: No consistent prospecting, not enough prospects.
<u>New success habit</u>: Make a minimum of an hour of prospecting calls every work day, with the goal of creating one new appointment each day.

Old paradigm habit: Focused on money/selling life insurance.
<u>New success habit</u>: Focused on the mission/serving people.

Old paradigm habit: Not asking for, and not getting, enough referrals.
<u>New success habit</u>: Planting referral seeds in every client meeting.

This is a success plan that has proven to be tried and true in the life insurance industry, and in any sales practice. When one persists in implementing a proven 'track to run on'- and is willing to persist, learn, and course correct—amazing successes often occur. This event is so prevalent among researchers and inventors that a phrase has been coined—Creative Failure Methodology—to describe it. Richard Feynman, Nobel Laureate Physicist, stated: "To develop working ideas efficiently, I try to fail as fast as I can." This story has been intentionally included for you to see problems as *seeds of opportunity,* to be germinated via persistence and creative determination.

One of Edison's students was a man named William Mason. He was inspired to create his own contribution to society by seeing the good works Edison created in his capacity as a MDB. Mason began looking for his own niche, having observed all of his teacher's great inventions that had been born out of 'creative failure' and persistence.

He eventually noticed that all lumber yards produced tons of wasted wood bits from the board trimming process. He repeatedly failed in different ways to make something creative from the problem—but still persisted. During one experiment, he accidentally left a pile of fibers in a steam press that had a leaky valve. He forgot about it, and upon returning after an extended period of time, found that the prolonged heat and pressure had formed a durable, firm board. If you were to enter any construction site in the U.S. today, you'd see his success literally hanging wall-to-wall—and he named it after himself—Masonite.

This story explains one of the most important benefits of making the prosperity paradigm shift to the higher mode of serving. The MDB experiences an increase in the inspiring, healing energy that helps you persist that I call *burning desire*. Mason caught 'the bug' from Edison. He left his teacher's tutelage with a *burning desire* to make his own individual contribution, first to society, and then to himself. He was uplifted by witnessing Edison's example first-hand, and then applied the MDB mindset to achieve the potential of that which he was really capable of. Burning desire is noble—and the opposite of selfish desire, which is crass.

The MDB, having made the commitment to uplift humanity, has serendipitously discovered hundreds of inventions that were not the original intent. The value of the new product or service almost always exceeded the inventor's original intent. This occurred as an accidental by-product of their creative perseverance and dedication. This wouldn't be noteworthy if it hadn't happened so often, a book was written to document this phenomenon, entitled <u>Serendipity: Accidental Discoveries in Science</u> by Royston M. Roberts. My assertion is that these discoveries were/are not accidental. They are gifts granted by the Infinite Intelligence as a consequence of connecting to The Field.

The Attractor Pattern of True Abundance

Being a MDB guides you to align with the highest strong-force attractors available in any given moment. In simple terms, this means choosing Love, which is the penultimate strong force, over fear. It is then critically important to transfer that Love energy into action. This action plan is clearly outlined later, but for now; focus on understanding the importance of choosing Love (aligning with strong-force attractors) over fear (aligning with weak-force attractors). It has been generally agreed upon by all students of Truth, (whether secular or non-secular), that the desire to love and to be loved compels all human activity. Interestingly, love cannot be scientifically proven to exist, can it? Love has never been seen, proven, or clinically verified. Despite this, it is the reason you exist, why you work, feed your family, and even brush your teeth and exercise.

Every true spiritual path in the world contains the basic precept that God is Love. Though all enlightened beings agree on this point, neither **God** nor **Love** can be scientifically verified. Since every reader of this text has experienced love, according to the greatest teachers in history, in those exquisite moments you have also experienced God.

If Love compels all human behavior, and God is Love, the first priority of the Prosperity Paradigm is a relationship with the God of your understanding. Let me define what I mean when I use the term God. I mean a Higher Power based in Love, which represents a greater possibility for your life. From that place of greater possibility, your connection to the Field is firmly established, and several qualities emerge in our consciousness. These qualities may be called the Priorities of Life Success on Earth, and look like this:

1. Relationship with the God of your understanding

↓

2. Inner Peace, Confidence, and Power

↓

3. Emotional and Physical Wellness

↓

4. Family Unity and Growth

↓

5. Life Work based in Value & Service to Others

↓

6. Financial Freedom

↓

7. Time/Space Freedom.

It may still seem odd to equate prosperity to a relationship with God until you observe that people prosper only when they have created some product or service that offers value to others. Even the triviality of the business adage, 'build a better mousetrap and the world will beat a path to your door', shows that unique value creation in a free society results in prosperity. Any process of ***creation*** includes ***inspiration*** to birth an original idea, and ***enthusiasm*** to execute its getting to the marketplace. Creation, Inspiration (in Spirit), Enthusiasm (derived from the Latin words *en theos* meaning In God) all initiate a Higher Power. In Truth, this Higher Power is the origin of all creation, and the source and substrate of all prosperity.

Money flows into one's life as an *effect.* The *cause* is creation of value in service to others. When this cause is forgotten, it often results in a life without meaning, even though the person may still be financially well off. I have personally known, and coached, several miserable millionaires. They were miserable because they loved money, and used people. In the name of money/career lust, they mis-prioritized their family, then their health and inner peace, all to maintain egoistic control of what they erroneously thought of as wealth. By erroneously making priority number six (money) their number one priority, they lost all. Some died lonely miserable deaths with full bank accounts. Their priorities were out of balance. What good is having all the money in the world if you're mentally or physically sick, or you lose your family along the way? Having a relationship with God teaches us to <u>love people and use money</u>. This builds lasting happiness, health and wealth in a balanced way, by first connecting to the true source and substrate of that which makes all things possible.

When you align with this Higher Power, an important series of discoveries follow shortly. You discover: 1. Who you are, 2. Why you are here, 3. Where you are, and 4. What is the true goal of human life on Earth. Understanding these points alleviates almost all suffering and fear attributed to being human. Can you imagine how much greater your life can be when you eliminate fear?

The life story of John Templeton is an excellent representation of one who lived these priorities, experiencing fantastic financial wealth as a result of doing so. He is widely known for having pioneered the global birth of the mutual fund in 1954 eventually selling his various Templeton Funds to Franklin in 1992 for four hundred forty million dollars. That is the story the public knows. The essence of his success is credited to his relationship to God, which he claims has always guided his life. This relationship positively influenced every aspect of his life. He looked at his business career as his spiritual mission, in which ethics and service to others were the guiding behavioral beacons. Mr. Templeton said:

> "For one thing, it (business) enriches the poor more than any other system humanity ever has had. Competitive business has reduced costs, has increased variety, and has improved quality." And if a business is not ethical, he added, "it will fail, perhaps not right away, but eventually. I focus on spiritual wealth now, and I'm busier, more enthusiastic, and more joyful than I have ever been. The question is not 'is there a God, but (rather) is there anything else except God?' God is everyone and each of us is a little bit. If we become increasingly humble about how little we know, we may be more eager to search."

In 2004, the Templeton Foundation donated forty million dollars to philanthropic causes that support the relief of suffering in the world. Over the years, many of these donations have funded the scientific study of spiritual realities and how they affect humanity. Observe how the number one priority of the Prosperity Paradigm (relationship with God) tremendously affects your level of inner peace, health, and family unity and growth (which are priorities two, three, and four in the paradigm as shown above).

Figure 1

Clinical Effects of Spirituality on Human Behavior

Condition	Number of Studies	Number of Studies in which spiritual work had positive effects	Total percentage in which positive results occurred
Alcohol	18	16	89%
Nicotine Addiction	6	6	100%
Drug Abuse	12	12	100%
Stress (Coping & Adjusting)	15	14	93%
Depression	17	12	71%

It is obvious that, for those tested in the extensive studies (a total of sixty-eight) shown in Figure 1, a relationship with God had profoundly measurable effects. Their inner peace increased, verified by the reduced stress and depression markers. Their need for chemical dependence also decreased to an enormous degree.

In Figure 2, notice the significant effects that spiritual work has on the emotional and physical wellness of the test subjects.

Figure 2

The Influence of Spiritual Work on Health

Condition	Number of Studies	Number of Studies in which spiritual work had positive effects	Total percentage in which positive results occurred
Anger/Hostility	4	4	100%
Anxiety	11	8	73%
Fear of Death	15	10	67%
Overall Health Improved	5	4	80%
Reduce Blood Pressure	5	4	80%
Increased Longevity	9	8	89%
Improved Quality of Life In Cancer Patients	8	7	88%
Improved Quality of Life In Heart Disease Patients	6	4	67%

Lastly, observe the effects which occurred that favorably increased family unity and growth. Of particular interest were the studies done by the Templeton Foundation that measured marital happiness as influenced by spiritual work. In all three studies, one hundred percent of the subject couples tested said their marital lives improved.

Figure 3

Influence of Spirituality on Human Psychology

Psychological Factor	# of Studies	# of Studies in which spiritual work had positive effects	Total percentage in which positive results occurred
Greater Life Satisfaction	13	12	92%
Improved Marital Life	3	3	100%
Increased Sense Of Well-being	16	15	94%
Increased Caring for the Well-being of Others	5	3	60%
Enhanced Self-Esteem	4	2	50%

Data Source: *The Faith Factor: An Annotated Bibliography of Clinical Research on Spiritual Subjects, Vol. 1,* D.A. Matthews, D.B. Larsen, C.P. Barry, (John Templeton Foundation, 1994).

The potential that is unleashed when you unite with the Infinite Power in the Universe has a cascading effect in your life. It affects all areas in ways that are virtually impossible to track and comprehend. Combining intention with the God-force energy of continuous creation causes the latent potential within each person to flow from the unmanifest into actualization in the manifest world. This is what spiritual work does, in a way that no other power or energy can. Again, the scientific evidence that the Prosperity Paradigm reveals is that the attractor pattern of true wealth flows thusly:

GOD→ Power→ Health→ FAMILY→ Career→ Money→ Free Time

The paradigm also contains the explanation as to why all people have uniquely specific talents, proclivities, and strengths they are born with. It has been said that the greatest way for a man to find meaning in life is to find a way to do that which he loves doing. Why does one person love architecture, the other business, the next computers, another one cars, someone else loves art or music, and so on? Everybody loves doing what they love to do in their own unique way, in their own portions and timing which are perfect and distinctive to each. As we follow what we love, an interesting question arises, "how do the things that I love come to be so? " The Infinite Intelligence is guiding us into doing that which we are divinely meant to pursue, by placing the love of this thing in our consciousness. When we follow that which we love, we are actually following the guidance of God. So we can, in fact, directly trace money via value creativity to a relationship with God. This is precisely how we discover our Soul Purpose, which is the unique means through which we are meant to serve others.

This discovery causes the individual to feel 'at peace' and satisfied with their life in ways that must be experienced to be understood. It is from that new peace that a greater power flows, releasing chemical informational messengers which alter brain chemistry. This increases immune system functioning, resulting in a greater level of emotional and physical wellness.

As this trickle-down creativity continues, all relationships are positively enhanced. Your business career begins to shift in powerful and positive ways.

1. Your ability to communicate and concisely articulate value-based statements is enhanced.
2. Your capacity to accurately assess potential dangers and foresee problems increases.
3. Your ability to act on these situations with confidence and clarity is expanded.
4. You learn to hear criticism or 'bad news,' without being weakened by it because you are no longer taking it personally.
5. Your ability to delay gratification until tasks are completed becomes stronger.
6. Your power to anticipate consequences by learning from experience grows enormously. This magnifies your success-ability multifold, resulting in greater value-creativity, strategic alliances, and overall productivity.

As personal revenue increases, one must be careful to have a money management system in place, as well as a process that increases the velocity of your money. Those who fail to do so often squander huge fortunes. Meeting with a financial planner who is working in harmony with the principles of the prosperity paradigm is therefore critical.

Finally, as you achieve greater financial prosperity as a result of living the paradigm, having the time to enjoy it can be challenging. This is why having a time management system is critical for all entrepreneurs. The basic adage is that if you fail to plan, you are planning to fail. Further personal results will be directly proportionate to your willingness to act on the guidance contained herein.

The Obstacles to Shifting Paradigms

Now that you see the significance of your determinant paradigm, it is vital to understand the nature of why it is difficult to shift from a lesser to higher paradigm. The life stories of all exceptional people detail their struggle with doing so because, without doubt, being human is difficult. The inherent dilemma can be transcended by first being exposed to, then contemplating and understanding, a series of somewhat startling Truths. They're startling because so few people are aware of them. I now ask you to open your heart and higher mind, and, as best possible, to suspend any negative judgment.

As a result of a study done over the past thirty years, (compiled through well over ten thousand private mentoring sessions with clients), the following realizations became stunningly obvious. Uncertain of exactly what my analysis of this data meant, I then saw that my conclusions were corroborated via the work of the greatest ancient philosophers: Socrates, Lao-Tzu, and Patanjali; modern social scientists Carl Jung, Abraham Maslow, and David Hawkins; and ultimately confirmed by the great savior/avatars Jesus Christ, Buddha, and Krishna. I became aware there had to be reasons why people refused to shift paradigms though they were suffering miserably. All these indicators point to the same conclusion. That humanity has struggled for eons to learn how to be more consistently happy, peaceful, and successful because of the following reasons:

1.) Ignorance of the fact that the reasoning computer we use to navigate our way through life (the mind) is flawed, and that it contains a hidden virus (the ego). Imagine journeying across the ocean with an onboard navigational computer system that is state-of-the art, and quite impressive looking with all the latest bells and whistles. The catch is that unbeknownst to you, it has a serious computer virus in it. You program your destination, get out to sea with nothing but water around you, and it malfunctions. You keep sailing around in circles, wondering why you can't get to the destination. Until you run an anti-viral program to cleanse the computer, and download the correct program, the same thing must occur over and over. This is analogous to the human experience of setting a goal, knowing it is possible, but for some unknown reason continually going off course.

2.) Because of this critical unknown flaw, people are easily programmed to negativity and, without guidance, cannot tell truth from falsehood.

The mind is like the hardware of a computer, and one's paradigm is like the downloaded software that has the virus. The hardware can only run the software program that is loaded into it, right? For example, if someone broke into your home and loaded a pornographic screen saver software program into your machine, when you turned it on what would run? The hardware has no choice—it is innately innocent—it doesn't know what it is doing or *even that anything is wrong.* It simply runs what has been input. The hardware of the mind doesn't have a way to verify whether its software is false or true. The brain is the hardware—cultural and social programming is the software.

In Sierra Leone, murderous older tribal leaders always recruit young impressionable boys to do their killing for them. To them, killing others isn't wrong at all! The innocence of the young mind's hardware is so easily programmable, they happily kill without guilt. This psychotic behavior prevails to varying degrees in gangs, in the boardroom, in politics and religion, and in every area of human behavior.

3.) The distortions of the ego result in the inherent inability to solve the content/context dilemma. The distortions result in people continuously taking things out of context, accepting mediocrity, fear, and failure as normal. Without proper context, no Truth can be consistently experienced, making life success (for most people) appear to be hopeless or a stroke of luck.

4.) These factors confuse us as to our True Identity; consequently we do not know who we really are. (Notice the gnawing ancient inner question, *"Who am I?"*)

Imagine someone getting knocked unconscious, and waking up with amnesia. Where and how does he proceed to go about finding out who he is? In a phone book? He'd have to know his name first, so what good would that do him? Even if he knew his name, without remembrance of the experiences associated with that life, would it be real? This is precisely how many people currently feel today.

They know their names, but that is all they know as to *who* they are. Many refer to their occupation as 'who they are' (e.g. I'm a plumber, teacher, lawyer etc.). But if they retire or change jobs, they have not ceased to exist, so that label cannot be correct either. Even their name was given to them, it is not something they themselves chose, therefore not really who they are. A woman marries and changes her name, but has the essence of who she is changed? Of course not. This obstacle can only be resolved by seeking Soul Purpose through spiritual work. Not knowing 'who I am' leads to the despairing human feeling that "I know I'm here to do something meaningful, but I haven't a clue as to what it is."

5.) Wandering around somewhat lost, we then unhappily discover we don't know *why* we exist, reinforcing the feeling that <u>life is meaningless</u>. (This inner longing arises as the question, *"Why am I here- what's the purpose of it all?"*)

As in the commentary above, so many of the clients who were interviewed expressed the innate feeling that they were put here to do something of importance, but they hadn't the foggiest idea of where to begin looking. The societal need for money drives most people to find and settle for jobs that provide income, but not life purpose. In most cases the income is extremely limited as well, because they are operating from scarcity consciousness.

6.) We do not know where we are, or where we are going. (One eventually becomes aware of this realization as the emergence of the questions *"Where am I, and what happens after death?"*) The apparent answer to where we are is *here*—or, *on Earth*. This is true in a relative sense, but not **Truth** in an absolute sense, for *what* is Earth and *where is here*? Isn't the place that you call 'here', *wherever your consciousness is* at any given time? 'Here' is not a location (at the office, at home, at the store) ***it is a state of being present and awake***. This is true of an astronaut in space too—so one can see that 'on Earth' is also limited in truly answering this question accurately. Where you are depends on how present and awake you are. Your confidence and inner power will expand tremendously as you understand this.

Questions about the afterlife really have to do with the evolution of the soul. 'What happens after death' is irrelevant—the relevant and more valuable question one might ask is 'what happens <u>before</u> death?'—because that is where you are right now! It is by focusing your energy on this more relevant choice of a question, that the safe and certain evolution of your soul is guaranteed.

7.) People constantly projecting their version of the world onto others, believing others could/should be doing better. All people are doing the very best they can, with what they have, given the conditions of their life. If people could be doing better, they would be doing better. But how much time and energy is wasted condemning others for not doing better? What do you feel when you see someone standing at an expressway entrance with a 'homeless' sign? Disgust? Now think about it...you're not suffering their paradigm one millionth as much as they are suffering it! That is simply their best. You believe they *could* be doing better—because YOU can do better—but they cannot. If they could, <u>they would</u>. This is far-reaching and true in all areas of life. (With your employer, employees, clients, parents, children, co-workers, etc.) Again, the relevance is the amount of energy that is wasted through these erroneous projections.

8.) The final problem is people's ignorance of the universal Natural Laws and the importance of living life in harmony with them, instead of continuously violating them. It is an obvious reality that without national law a society decays rather quickly into anarchy. (Remember the horrors that took place after Hurricane Katrina struck New Orleans in 2005) It is also a reality that without an understanding of and adherence to Natural Law, people's lives similarly decay into misery. People consistently have worthy ideas fail, due mainly to their ignorance of the Natural Laws. Conversely, other entrepreneurs have succeeded precisely by working in harmony with them. Could the Wright brothers possibly have succeeded in creating manned flight without operating in harmony with the natural laws of Gravity? National law (man-created) varies from country to country, whereas Natural Law (God-created) is infinitely powerful, and universal. Both understanding, then operating in harmony with, the Natural Laws of universal success are critical aspects to living the Prosperity Paradigm.

These issues constitute the core of what might be called The Universal Human Dilemma. Happily, the way to resolve the dilemmas listed above is detailed throughout the rest of the book.

Chapter Eight

The Natural Laws

The principles of the Prosperity Paradigm function because they operate in harmony with a very precise set of observable natural laws. The ancient Greeks realized the power of these principles and in 600 BC named the study of these laws *physis,* meaning "natural philosophy." They were aware that there was an underlying natural order to all of life that was put there by an Infinite Intelligence. This is the root of the word *physics,* which is the scientific study of the truth of the natural essence of life *as it is*. Regardless of their given area of expertise, all successful people know of—and work in harmony with—these natural laws.

They do so because they have verified that operating in harmony with these principles expands success immeasurably. Violating them is a sure path to failure and pain. As you explore these natural laws, especially if they are new to you, a key point to understand is that *the natural laws affect your life even when you are oblivious to their existence.*

To prove this, let's refer to a natural law that everyone is familiar with called gravity. Three hundred years ago Sir Isaac Newton was sitting under an apple tree contemplating the universe, when an apple fell on his head. At that moment, he discovered gravity. The relevant question to ask is, did the Law of Gravity exist before the apple fell? Of course it did! The force of gravity keeps things on the planet, and without it, life on Earth could not have evolved. It is one of the constants mentioned earlier, without which human life could never have developed. You are now ready for the next series of these 'constants' to be revealed—and used—as evidenced by the fact that you are reading this right now. A metaphorical story may help you to see the importance of understanding and using these laws to further your life success.

When I was a young man vacationing in the Florida Keys many years ago, my friends and I found what looked like a small stream that intersected this particular key (which means island). The island itself was about a mile across, with the Gulf of Mexico on one side and the Atlantic Ocean on the other. This fairly innocent looking stream was only ten to twelve feet across, yet oceanic power pulled a deceptively swift current through it. We saw it was running fast, but we were young and foolish, so we jumped in—bound and determined to swim against the current. In seconds we were swept far downstream and, grabbing any panicky handhold we could find, scrambled onto the banks of the stream while our other friends laughed hysterically. Did you ever try to swim against a really strong current or tide? For a short time you may succeed, but in the long run the current is too powerful, isn't it?

That is what one experiences when trying to actualize a new idea while swimming against the tide of Natural Law. When you violate Natural Law, success is impossible to maintain. All of creation automatically operates according to a set of very precise natural laws. They are so exact, science can launch a rocket destined to land on the moon three days later, and, at launch, accurately predict within seconds its exact time of arrival. About this subject, Einstein said:

> His [the scientist's] religious feeling takes the form of a rapturous amazement at the harmony of Natural Law, which reveals an intelligence of such superiority that, compared with it, all the systematic thinking of human beings is an utterly insignificant reflection.

The specific laws that are being taught here are the ones naturally found in our world—and universe—which *also* appear in every main sacred text of the world's great spiritual traditions. When a principle is proven to be factual scientifically and spiritually, the wise accept it as a Universal Truth.

It is of critical importance that, when aligning with a new paradigm, one chooses a proven path of Truth. Careful explanation has been given supporting the reality of the science behind the hidden power of being a MDB. The teachings of Einstein, Maslow, and Hawkins confirm what Jesus Christ, Buddha, and Krishna taught over the last five thousand years. When we are presented with the brilliant teachings of some of the greatest scientists in history, and those teachings are essentially the same as those of the most enlightened spiritual figures in history, it is worthy of our attention. The power of these Truths is undeniable, regardless of whether one's preferred path is atheist, agnostic, or spiritual.

The central text of the teachings of Jesus Christ is the New Testament (the Bible is composed of the Old and New Testaments—the latter consisting of twenty-seven books detailing Jesus life and teachings), the central text of Buddha's teachings is the Tripitaka (a voluminous compilation of Buddha's life and philosophy) and the central text of Krishna's teachings is the Bhagavad Gita (meaning The Song of God, taken from the ancient great book of India—the Mahabharata).

I acknowledge that there are many other valuable paths to God that I regard with great respect. I have chosen these three great beings as authentication from the spiritual viewpoint of 'the laws,' because of my own familiarity with their timeless Teachings. I also chose them because of the legacy of peace and joy that endures in the true followers of these teachings.

These three beings are regarded by some spiritual scholars to be the highest consciousness beings to ever walk the Earth (Hawkins, 1995). It is important for Western people to understand that Krishna and Buddha are as beloved and revered in the Orient as Jesus Christ is in our hemisphere (Yogananda, 1974). Many Christians go into fear when words like Buddha and Krishna are used. This fear is the result of seeing these advanced teachers through the distortion of the scarcity paradigm of either/or, when it is a both. Jesus Christ is an unparalleled Presence in world history—no one else like him has ever existed, nor will likely ever again exist, in human form. His clear purpose was Salvation. Buddha and Krishna serve a very different purpose; they are teachers of Enlightenment. If you are Christian and can view Christ as Savior, and Buddha and Krishna as valuable Enlightenment Teachers, you will explode into prosperity far more quickly.

Being a student of comparative religion, these teachings have been studied for the better part of the last thirty years. While there are definite differences, the greater portion of the three great master's teachings are thematically identical. Among students of Truth, the Oneness of this path is commonly called the "Perennial Philosophy" (Huxley, 1944).

The first principle is called the Law of Vibration and Attraction, which for our purposes will be defined from a very humanistic standpoint.

Law of Vibration and Attraction: Human beings constantly emanate energy via thoughts, words, and actions. Whatever energy I 'vibrate,' I instantly 'attract' people and events in harmony with that dominant vibration.

Here is what the three great masters say about this law, and what they called it…

Law of Sowing and Reaping—*Do not be deceived, God is not deceived: Whatsoever a man sows, that he shall also reap. He who sows things of the flesh, from the flesh shall reap corruption, he who sows things of the spirit, from the spirit shall reap life everlasting.*
Jesus (Gal 6:7)

Law of Causal Condition—*For every event that occurs, there will follow another event whose existence was caused by the first, and this second event will be pleasant or unpleasant according to whether its cause was skillful or unskillful.*
Buddha (Dhammapada—314)

Law of Karma—*From the mode of truth and goodness comes success, from the mode of selfish desire comes grief, and from the mode of ignorance comes madness and failure.*
Krishna (Bhagavad Gita 14:17)

From science and physics:

Law of Sympathetic Resonance—All objects vibrate at specific frequencies, and when brought near another object with similar frequency, cause the second object to vibrate as well. This is because like attracts like.

These laws allude to the exact same point. Human beings are continuous manifestation machines. We manifest into physical reality whatever we think, speak, and act. This is because the universe behaves much like a giant cosmic magnet. ***Everything in our universe is energy,*** in a constant state of vibration. Even the chair, the lamp, your car, everything, at a sub-atomic level, is particles and waves in an energetic state of constant movement. The universe is a frequency spectrum of infinite vibration. Physical matter possesses a great variety of vibration speeds and frequencies. For example H_2O molecules vibrating very slowly are seen as ice, when sped up are seen as water, and speeded up even faster become steam or vapor.

Thought waves are also pure energy that vibrates at a much higher frequency (Briggs & Peat, 1984). Whatever frequency we externally send out or 'vibrate'—as thoughts, choices, words, and actions—automatically 'attracts' people and events to us that match whatever energy we originally sent. When I think negatively, I draw negative people and events into my life. When I speak with hatred, I draw hateful people and events into my life. When I act violently, I attract violent people and events into my life.

If one lives by the sword one dies by the sword—and if one helps others, one is helped when they need it most. This is the connection that the ignorant fail to make, which proves that the thief is stealing from his own pocket. How? Our universe is one thing, completely interconnected. If you are mean to someone, the meanness you sent out will come back from somewhere else. The beauty is that the same thing happens with kindness.

The old adage, 'birds of a feather flock together,' is another way of expressing this ancient truth. This 'flocking together' refers to groups of people that gather together into *Soul Groups*. Gamblers hang out with other gamblers, athletes hang with athletes, successful people choose to associate with other successful people, and so on—they flock together because they are drawn by the unseen Law of Vibration and Attraction.

You continuously tune in to and emanate these vibrations, and you've encountered people who are negative and perhaps referred to them as having 'bad vibes.' Conversely you've met others with positive vibrational energy and refer to them as having 'good vibes.' Most people have already experienced the proof of this law without knowing it. Have you ever thought about someone you hadn't spoken to in days, weeks, months or even years, and all of a sudden you run into them somewhere or the phone rings and it's them? Or maybe you were the caller and they answered saying, "I can't believe it's you—I was just thinking of you!" Almost everyone has had this experience, and it verifies this Law.

From a science standpoint, an experiment that proves this Law involves taking a tuning fork calibrated to any specific musical note—for this example we'll choose "middle C". Imagine tapping it on your knee, and then running it over the strings of a harp, very close to the strings but not touching them. Nothing occurs until you get to the string that is also middle C. When the tuning fork nears this string, the string turns on as if by magic and sings as if it were struck—though nothing touched it. The invisible sound wave coming from the vibrating tuning fork excites the dormant harp string and attracts it into making sound because *like attracts like* (Beaulieu, 1987).

Here's how it applies to you. Science tells us that the average human being thinks 5,000 thoughts a day (many say the average number is closer to 15,000, but assuming people think 5 thoughts every minute in a sixteen hour day = 4800. Therefore 5000 thoughts a day is a workable, conservative estimate). In many people up to 90% of them are negative, fear-based thinking (Jampolsky, 1993). Invariably some of the internal thought negativity becomes externalized as words. Then, when you choose to speak predominantly negative, it eventually turns into acting negatively, and now this pattern becomes a habit that is very difficult to break. Now apply the law of Vibration and Attraction. This means that the average person is vibrating approximately 4,500 *negative* energy signals daily, and therefore attracting many, many *negative* people and events to themselves—simply as a fulfillment of their own thought processes!

This is exactly how thought-seeds begin the process of creating form. When you are thinking something over and over, whether intentionally or not, your thought vibrations instantly begin forming into reality at some level. Thought begins to coalesce energy together into material form, forming something out of nothing. So the rich get richer predominantly because they emanate 'wealth thoughts'—or prosperity consciousness—and therefore attract more of what they send out. Negative thinkers send out consistent negativity which acts as a continual self-defeating pattern. Most poor people emanate 'scarcity consciousness' attracting more of the condition that supports poorness. People and events—either positive or negative—are attracted to you by the quality of your thoughts, choices, words, and actions. You can now see why so many people are suffering, without realizing that they themselves are short-circuiting their own happiness and ultimately, life success.

An important quality to know is that all three great masters teach that the attracted result occurs *not as a punishment,* but rather as a gift. Perfectly created by the Infinite Intelligence, this law takes care of all behavior in an impersonal and ultra-personal way simultaneously. It is impersonal in that God is not punishing anyone, for it is our own free will choices—whether good or bad—that automatically determine what befalls us. The hateful being condemns himself to a living hell through his acts of hatred, while the MDB creates his own heaven through consistent acts of service.

It is ultra-personal in the stunning perfection with which the energy that was sent is received back. Carefully notice every detail of the following story to see the amazing perfection of this law and how what is sent, when done with awareness, is returned with mind-boggling precision.

In the late nineties I did a workshop at a hospital in New Hampshire that paid me my standard honorarium, plus a bonus of fifty percent of attendance income minus their expenses. You'll see why I include this detail later on. The attendance was good, but not great, therefore there was no bonus. I received my honorarium and went home.

A few months later, I was driving in a new vehicle on the first warm spring day with the windows down and a favorite song on the radio. I was much more focused on enjoying the new car in the great weather (I live in upstate New York) listening to great music, than on what the speed limit was. A minute later a policeman on motorcycle was pulling me over, and as he approached my car I noticed something unusual. My heart began pounding and I was clearly vibrating negative fear-based energy. This is precisely what I had been teaching others not to do in these kinds of situations, and here I was doing it. Because I did not want to attract negativity, I acted on the Natural Law, putting my hand on my heart while saying out loud, "Thank you God for this gift, show me the lesson."

The officer was an absolute sweetheart, and opened the conversation by saying 'Do you know why I pulled you over, sir?"

Steve: "Yes, officer, I was speeding." (His jaw drops that someone actually told the truth.)

Officer: "Was there a reason, are you late for work, or is there some other emergency?"

Steve: *Thinking to myself, 'What a nice guy—he's giving me the benefit of the doubt'*, "No, sir. I just got this new car, and because of the nice weather and this great song, I just wasn't being at all mindful of my speed."

Officer: "Yeah, I've done that too…Do you have any idea how fast you were going?"

Steve: "No sir."

Officer: "I clocked you going fifty-three in a thirty-five."

Steve: "Wow…I didn't realize I was going that fast."

The officer took my license and other info and came back in a couple minutes saying, "Because of your honesty, I'm giving you a reduced ticket for two points on your license, for failure to obey a traffic device instead of six points for a speeding ticket." I thanked him profusely and left. I pled guilty to the infraction, and sent the ticket in to the town court.

A few months later I received the response in my mailbox with only one other piece of mail. I opened the letter from the town court, informing me to pay a sixty-five dollar fine. I was grateful, knowing the six point violation at that time would've cost much more, and I thought 'thanks, God—I learned my lesson—be more mindful of my speed.' Oh, but I hadn't seen the whole lesson yet. I then looked at the other piece of mail, and by the return address I saw it was from the hospital in New Hampshire where I'd done the workshop months before. With no clue as to what the correspondence could be, I opened it.

Dear Rev. D'Annunzio,

I'm the comptroller at ________ Hospital, where you did a workshop several months ago. We had a contractual agreement to pay you an honorarium of $______plus a bonus of fifty percent of attendance income minus the expenses of hosting the workshop. At

> the time, there appeared to be no bonus, but we were in error. It's not much, but to fulfill our contract with you we have enclosed a check. Thank you again for a fine workshop.

The check was exactly sixty-five dollars and thirty-two cents. Now look at the amount of the fine, and know that at the time, stamps were—you guessed it—thirty-two cents.

I believe—no, *I know*—that my new choice at the critical moment created a completely new result. At the moment I was about to 'vibrate' negativity, I instead made three positive choices that totally altered the end result.

First, the awareness to interrupt the old pattern of fear—second, thanking God with gratitude despite being in an unfavorable situation—and third, being totally honest with the officer. Hundreds of seemingly chance events instantly began aligning so that the Field responded first to **my awareness**, by having the comptroller at the hospital *become aware* of their oversight. Second, **my honesty** made them want to *be honest* by sending me money that I never knew was even owed to me. Third, **my sending gratitude** by saying the prayer, "Thank you God for this gift, show me the lesson" attracted a 'gift' out of thin air to be *grateful* for—money appearing out of the blue to pay the ticket, down to the exact price of the stamp!

This is a pivotal prosperity principle. The abundance of the Universe paid the fine because I acted in harmony with God's Natural Laws. Money is not always necessary to fulfill your needs when you are operating in harmony with natural law. Problems get solved that money could never have solved. A stranger pulls over in the middle of the night to help fix your flat on the lonely desolate country road. The right book containing the perfect message appears at the precise moment of greatest need. A friend recommends meeting just the right person in the nick of time to prevent some life crisis that could have been disastrous.

This is one of literally hundreds of similar events I have experienced that prove how perfectly the Law of Vibration and

Attraction operates. Again, I do not *believe* this knowledge to be true—I **know** it is **T**ruth by repeatedly experiencing it throughout a multitude of life situations over the years. *Belief* is based upon another's explanation of something that may resonate within you as being possible, but in truth their explanation does not make it so. *Knowingness* is based upon one's *own deep inner experience* which is incontrovertible—you know it through personal experience. Belief can lead to *knowing* only through subjective experience, which then becomes ***wisdom*** when you habitually apply it. Wisdom is the state that the MDB continuously duplicates on a daily basis; people feel it and are deeply drawn to it. Remember, money is not power—wisdom is power.

In this part of the work I am outlining the existence of the Field and the Truths it contains merely as an introduction, knowing that in many readers it may be your first exposure. For now, please focus only on absorbing them as new possibilities for your life. I must confess that upon my initial exposure to this work in 1976, I did not like much of it because it contradicted so much of what I had been previously taught. Over time my commitment to happiness and success became so important that I was willing to do whatever it took, as long as it was honorable, to accomplish my goals. When I found the true reason for my resistance to this work was the pain of giving up my old beliefs and habits, I discovered that the MDB path was the *ultimate honor—with the ultimate payoff.*

The Law of Creation

With the previous law, I have referred to both scientific and spiritual examples from the scriptural texts of the teachings of Jesus, Buddha, and Krishna. For simplicity sake, I am choosing from here on out to reveal the essence of each of the following laws, without citing the specific scriptural references. Please remember that all of the following laws are also specifically referred to by the masters in the same way that I treated the Law of Vibration and Attraction.

Law of Creation—I create favorable conditions for reality to actualize. Reality is created through my choices, words, and actions.

The Rorschach inkblot test conveys the power of the Law of Creation (Rorschach 1921). People were shown pictures of his inkblots and asked, "What do you see?" The responses were as varied as the number of people who took the test, but proved one thing. Reality is like an inkblot upon which people project their inner ideas, fantasies, and beliefs. This book speaks about fives levels of consciousness that people belong to: (from lowest to highest) fear, desire, pride, mission, love. A fear-driven being might look at the first inkblot of the Rorschach test and see the devil looking at them with intense evil. A desire-driven being might see a sexual act being performed from looking at the same inkblot. A pride-based being might look at it and say "it looks like a woman exposing herself to me." A mission-driven person might say, "it looks like two people doing yoga", and a love-based person often sees a spiritual master in meditation.

We all project our inner world onto the outer world; therefore we are constantly creating our own reality (Talbot, 1991). As previously stated, **we rarely see the world the way *it is*—we see the world the way *we are*.** We can create favorable conditions for any desired reality within the framework of our Soul Purpose—which contains the most loving reality we can imagine living.

The power is in Choice, not Thought

The Law of Creation operates via the trinity of **choice**, then **word**, then **action**. Let us first observe and explain choice.

It is important to recognize that thought is not a choice. Every human being has a constant dialogue of thoughts that happen all by themselves. Consciousness is most easily understood as the awareness of the constant dialogue going on in your head. Thoughts arise all by themselves. You don't ask them to; they occur in an almost constant progression of their own. Consciousness itself is the thinker, and you are the observer of the thoughts (Hawkins, 2003). We all have negative thoughts, but the key to applying this law is to STOP GIVING YOUR

PRECIOUS ENERGY to negative thoughts. This is **the** choice you must make.

When you give thoughts energy, they become a created thing, *but the thought itself has no intrinsic creative reality—until* ***you*** *give it energy.* When you give any thought your energy, it then becomes a choice. Now it is a created thing—regardless of whether it is good or bad. Free will has been given for you to learn to very carefully select which thoughts deserve to be given energy. Once you have done so, the movement of this law begins a creative flow with a certain momentum. If the thought you give energy to is positive, the momentum you feel is empowerment. When you give energy to a negative thought, the momentum you feel is weakness. *Your thoughts don't mean anything*—until you give energy to them—only then do they begin to have meaning (Schucman, 1976). This is the important difference between thought and choice. *Unconscious* thought arises from the animal self and mostly results in negative consequences. Choice is *conscious* thought, which arises from the higher self and always creates favorable consequences.

Words—the second quality of the trinity of the Law of Creation—begin to further increase the manifestation of whatever choice you have made. Notice that when you have made any choice, you use words to discuss it with your spouse, business partners, friends, and so on. Words are sound waves, which is an unseen frequency that magnetizes your choice to you. Words are so amazingly powerful, that I have seen someone destroy a thirty year relationship in thirty seconds with poorly chosen, intensely hurtful words. As words flow, at one level a plan is being developed, while at another hidden level the desired reality is beginning to take material form. The form is yet incomplete, and requires the last of the trinity of this law to operate—and that is action.

Action is simply applying the choices and words out in the world, seeing which ones work and which do not. The key to the 'action phase' is to have a plan—which should be created prior to taking action. Your plan will require constant tweaking as you learn what does, and does not, work. Every great invention happened this way. It began as a high-frequency valuable idea chosen to focus on (choice); was discussed and turned into magnetic sound wave energy (word); and then experimented with (action). And when choice, words, and actions are used with persistence, the probability for success is maximized.

Staying positive when you are learning *what does not work* is critical to maintain persistence with any success idea. Remember Edison saying he 'successfully eliminated ten thousand combinations that didn't work'—for this is a crucial component to the MDB mindset. This is precisely where many people flounder. When you are applying your plan and it appears to be unsuccessful, negative thoughts invariably flow through your mind. Here is the crucial paradigm shift the MDB has learned to make to positively engage the Law of Creation: ***to observe negative thinking without giving it your precious life energy.*** To the best of your ability for now commit to very disciplined awareness of your inner thoughts—speaking and acting on the positive ones only, while observing the negative thoughts without giving them any energy (D'Annunzio, 2004).

Most people do not believe this law at all, which is so unfortunate. They have been taught to believe that life just happens to them through fate or by chance, and that they have almost no creative control over life whatsoever. So they live life in opposition to this law, believing that 'other people or fate creates my reality,' and end up living their whole life as a *play thing to outside forces*. You are a creator, whether you like it or not. You are creating either negative or positive results constantly, and only limited awareness prevents you from realizing this. You must recognize that you are always creating—*always*. To believe oneself to be weak and a failure, actually creates it being so. Think about scarcity paradigm mottos like, 'You can't fight city hall,' or 'life is a bitch and then you die,' or 'the only thing that's inevitable is death and taxes,' or Murphy's Law—'if anything can go wrong—it will at the worst possible time.' If you have lived your life believing these error thoughts, you now see how you may be unintentionally undermining your own life success.

The powerful truth of the Prosperity Paradigm is that God

always says YES. The Infinite Intelligence of our universe is an 'on' mechanism, meaning it always says "YES"! Gravity is always on, isn't it? So is electro-magnetism, and all the natural powers that govern weather patterns, the earth's rotation, and the sun and stars and so on. If the universe were a light switch, recognize that it is in a continuous *on* position. The problem is, if it is saying "YES", and we are being negative, the result is discontent. Failure is simply the universe saying 'yes' to your negativity.

If you were to go to a restaurant and place an order, you'd expect the meal to arrive minutes later exactly as you ordered it, right? Look at the universe like a big cosmic restaurant in which you are always placing an order. If you place negative orders, they will absolutely show up a little bit later. Because most of us are so internally confused, or negative, the Infinite Intelligence is saying Yes to your negative beliefs about yourself, your world, and what is possible within it. If you say 'no I can't do it,' then the Infinite Intelligence via these natural laws says "Yes, you're right—you can't do it." If you say to yourself "I'll never be successful" the universe goes, "Yes, you'll never succeed." It's only when I begin consistently saying yes to myself that I will see the *yes* confirmed by the universe.

Each one of us is in a constant process of creating our own reality. You are currently creating your reality from one of the following three levels of Awareness:

A.) **From Social Programming** within, you are allowing the rules of your culture to create your reality.

Example: *A woman meets a wonderful, single man, they date and over time fall in love. They are attracted to each other, get along well, have good jobs, and are responsible people. Eventually he asks her to marry him—and she wants to—but he is African-American and she is Caucasian. Her family, particularly her father, is angry and vehemently opposed to the marriage. She tells her beloved no.*

In this case, the woman allowed her cultural upbringing to destroy her own ability to create a happy life for herself. Suffering from the paradigm blindness of her cultural programming, she was unable to determine truth from falsehood. She couldn't see that if those who said they loved her (her father) really did, they would've accepted her choice simply because it made her happy. While the father truly cared about his daughter, his racist beliefs made him more focused on how others would perceive him if his daughter married a black man, and/or had a child of mixed race. Consequently, selfishness overrode his love for his child, and his daughter paid the price.

B.) **From the Ego-Thinking Mind** within, you allow your uncontrolled negative thoughts to create your reality.

Example: *A man is the regional director of a financial services company with about one hundred employees under him. He has successfully played the stock market for many years, but his ego has led him to believe he needs help from no one and consequently makes critical errors. Eventually, market changes beyond his control cause him to lose the majority of his fortune. Seeing the mistake of pride too late, he begins to internally berate himself continually repeating the thought, "I'm so stupid—there must be something wrong with me," over and over. The same market changes also affect his salespeople's results and he agonizes over letting some of them go, which his superiors demand. Every day he walks into the office feeling stressed out saying to his secretary, "I feel like I have a pit in my stomach." His uncontrolled thoughts torture him as they keep repeating over and over, and he keeps feeding them his energy. He hesitates laying off the sales people because the stress has confused his decision-making ability, and his superior fires him after 27 years of faithful service. The 'pit in his stomach' has become so bad, he goes to the doctor, who diagnoses stomach cancer. Inside he thinks, "I knew there was something wrong with me, with my luck I'll probably die." Six months later, he passes away.*

This is a classic example of the degree to which thinking itself is the source of so much pain in people's lives. By unintentionally feeding negative thoughts with his precious life-force energy, the resulting stress contributed to creating favorable conditions for disease to emerge.

C.) **From the Connection to the Field** within, you merge your consciousness to the Infinite Consciousness to live Soul Purpose.

Example: *A young man named Ben Carson showed great promise in medical school. His major downfall was that he struggled with organic chemistry. The understanding of this course was indispensable to receiving his doctorate, and he would flunk out if he failed it. Though he studied feverishly, he was crestfallen to learn he had failed. His teacher saw such tremendous promise that, though it was against school policy, he decided to allow the student to re-take it again the next morning. Carson went home to study for his 'do or die' exam, said a prayer to God, and promptly fell asleep. He awoke in horror the next morning, having spent no additional time studying. The only recollection of the night before was a dream in which he was taking the re-test. He was amazed at the detail of the dream, down to remembering exact questions and answers. He dismissed it as irrelevant, and gloomily went to re-take the exam. He nervously opened the exam packet, and was astonished to find that the exact questions and answers he saw in the dream were on the test he now held in his hands. He passed the test, and went on to become a leader in the study of the human brain. Dr. Carson is currently recognized as the greatest living neurosurgeon in the world* (Rose, 2003).

Carson was totally committed to accomplishing his Soul Purpose. When you are doing all you can, the Field of Infinite Intelligence always plants the right idea at the right time. History is filled with hundreds of these stories, and I chose this one from a less popular historical figure because it is more believable. These people are no different than you are, and you have no less greatness than do they.

Now, please be honest with yourself: are you creating your reality from A, B, or C? You have a choice over which level of awareness you want to create your life from. But YOU MUST CHOOSE. By making no choice, that still is a choice...to do the old program. Remember—to do the same thing in the same way day in and day out, and *expect a different result,* is insanity. You either create your success, or you do not. Ultimately, the Law of Creation operates because of the power of intention, which is the seventh sense. Intention is the conscious or unconscious choice to create. Intention exists inside of human beings and is the divine spark of creative energy in the universe.

The truth is that most people create their whole life reality about 50% from A, and 50% from B, and only once or twice in their lifetime do they access and create a result from C, and when they do, they convince themselves it was just luck. You create luck, by taking total responsibility for creating your life through the willingness to connect to the extra power received from the Field of infinite abundance.

The Law of Responsibility

I choose to define responsibility in terms which differ slightly from the classic Webster's definition. For our higher purposes, responsibility is *conscious management of personal power.* With this understanding, here is the law:

The Law of Responsibility—I am 100% responsible for every aspect of my life.

Personal responsibility begins with the commitment to manage your own power more effectively. This is done first by being more aware of all inner dialogues, and then consciously aligning your power with highly successful strong-force attractor patterns.

At the mission-driven level of creating a new success reality, no one is to blame or at fault in any way for your success or lack thereof. **You** are completely and solely responsible. Lack of personal responsibility leads to blatant mediocrity and develops the failure habit of 'just doing enough to get by' which plagues most people and society. It is often heard in today's business world, 'it isn't my fault,' which leads to blaming other people and things as the reason one was not more successful. This is a violation of this important law, and here's why.

It is of critical importance that you stop playing the blame game. You are a creator, and when you blame something *outside of you* for creating your reality, you are unknowingly giving your power away. If you say and believe that the root cause of any upset is "out there" you are limiting and destroying your own ability to positively change the situation. By your own declaration, if the problem is 'out there,' then the solution is *out there,* meaning outside of you. You have unintentionally declared yourself to live as a plaything to outside forces. If you affirm that the responsibility for your lack of success is 'out there', then the ability to change it flows out of you into the 'out there.' THERE IS NO "OUT THERE" OUT THERE! Everything you experience is perceived from 'in here'—that is, inside of yourself. Life is subjective, and changes from person to person depending on each person's inner level of consciousness, combined with their belief system.

You and two friends may be listening to a song, and you declare, "I love this song! "Your one friend goes, "You're kidding me, right? I can't stand this song! "Your other friend says, "I could take it or leave it—it doesn't affect me one way or the other." The same song is playing, yet three varied experiences are perceived. Who is correct? The Truth is that each individual is subjectively right—for them. This is not at all saying that there is no right or wrong. <u>While perception is subjective, Truth is not</u>. Truth is infinite, knowable, and eternal. Right is that which ends suffering, wrong is that which creates it (Maharaj, 1973). By living in accord with the Law of Responsibility, your level of consciousness is raised by the Field, which increases your power output. The Field then guides you in making 'right' choices, words, and actions that benefit yourself and others. Decisions that were once confusing and difficult are made effortlessly and confidently.

A hidden secret that all wealthy people know is that having money is a tremendous responsibility. Therefore anyone who plans on having more of it must work in harmony with this law. Verification of this truth resides in the fact that most people are not wealthy precisely because they violate these laws. Jesus said, "to whom much is given and entrusted, much is required" (N.T. Luke 12:48).

By not taking full responsibility for every aspect of your life, you are causing a 'personal power outage'—dooming yourself to go from creator (strength/success), to creature (weakness/failure). So by taking responsibility, you change your response-ability. By operating in harmony with the Law of Responsibility one is automatically empowered by the Field to think and feel the following MDB success thoughts to a greater degree:

- No one can hurt my feelings, make me angry, get me to take rejection personally, or make me feel guilty unless I—at some level—give them permission. If I give them permission, I am 100% responsible.

The Law of Repetition

Successful people create success habits—unsuccessful people don't. Please read that last line several times. This whole book is about creating success habits, and it happens through application of this very powerful law.

The Law of Repetition—Repetition of an action or a statement firmly ingrains it as a habit in the subconscious mind.

Human beings are creatures of habit. You eat a rotating variety of the same ten meals for the majority of your life. You drive to work or school the exact same way each day. You wash the same body parts in the same order each time you shower or bathe. You watch the same TV shows, or type of shows—sit coms, sports events, game shows, dramas, soap operas—your whole life.

Ninety percent of your daily behavior is based on habits, and you don't think about it, you just do it because it's a habit. Your habits and beliefs are largely a product of your current paradigm. Thus, because our generation was predominantly raised with fear-based thinking, that has become our habit.

Most people act as if they are powerless over their habits and that they aren't changeable. This is untrue. You absolutely can change bad habits—and you must—to experience a new life result. Success habits are created by choosing a new success paradigm and then committing to make it a habit through constant repetition. Any time you create a new habit, it is uncomfortable and you will experience fear. Know this, so you are ready; being forewarned is forearmed. The key point is that if you know this, there is more hope that the fear won't derail your efforts before the new success behavior has become habit. Happy, prosperous people all know this powerful secret—**successful people create success habits, unsuccessful people don't** (Canfield, Hansen, Hewitt, 2000). Here are the power points to understand about habits:

- Your habits and belief systems are a product of your current paradigm.
- Up to 90% of your normal, daily behavior is based on habits.
- You absolutely can—**and must**—create new, empowering habits
- Your current habits will determine your future success—or lack thereof.
- Once a new habit is well-developed, it becomes your new normal behavior
- Habits are developed through disciplined repetition

As long as you intend on growing in your life, it will require you to branch out into new unfamiliar territory. When human beings are on unknown ground, fear is inevitable—it is programmed into our DNA (Jeffers, 1987). So you must be prepared, because with growth comes a little fear. When you commit to success in your life, you will have faced this fear enough that through the repetition of this habit you'll come to make peace with fear. While this may sound strange to you now, imagine how fantastic life will be when fear can no longer cripple you. You'll see fear like the sting of antiseptic on a small cut that temporarily hurts, but is of course acceptable for the greater good.

The Law of Attention

This law has an 'A' principle and a 'B' principle which are corollaries of each other.

Law of Attention: A. Energy flows where attention goes.
B. The only thing that can grow in my life is that which I give attention to.

The following story has this law as its underlying theme.

Pastor Smith's church sat next to an old abandoned farm. The once-beautiful property sat vacant and neglected for so many years that it finally decayed into a dilapidated wreck. One day farmer Brown and his family moved in and began fixing the house, barn, and surrounding property. Two years later the farm had been transformed into a picturesque home with a freshly painted barn, mended fences and neat rows of crops. One hot summer afternoon the Pastor rode by, and waved to farmer Brown and his wife as they sat on their lovely front porch. They waved back, motioning the Pastor to come over and have a glass of lemonade together. Pastor Smith took a long drink, and surveying their property said, "Farmer Brown, God sure has been good to you hasn't he?" At that, Farmer Brown raised an eyebrow and said, "You think so, eh? You should've seen the place when He had it."

At the core of what makes this story humorous is the underlying wisdom of the Law of Attention. Through constant loving attention, the farmer and his family brought out the latent beauty that was always inherently present in the property from the day it was purchased. This is the powerful hidden meaning in the story…God always supplies an infinite potentiality for things to be beautiful, meaningful, and successful—**always.** The reason so many people do not actualize this inherent success potential is because they focus on lack, what is missing, and what is wrong with their life. These things then grow because energy follows attention (Essene & Kenyon, 1996).

Whenever you give your attention to a thought, word, or action, your energy is sure to follow. Notice that when the thoughts words and actions are negative and fear-based, you can be certain that what grows from the situation will also be negative and fear-based. What really made the farm so beautiful was all the positive, loving attention and energy the farmer had given to it. When no attention was paid to it, weeds grew and entropy set in. Entropy is a state of degeneration that is marked by increasing degrees of uncertainty, disorder, and decay that are the inevitable results of violating this law. You are constantly 'planting seeds' in the field of life, but you must pay attention to the quality of seed, and, into which field you are planting. If your business or life results are in a state of decay, disorder, or uncertainty, you need to pay extremely close attention to where you are giving your energy, because the only thing that can possibly grow is that to which you give attention to.

Another way of understanding this law is to imagine you're looking to buy a new car. Let's say the dealer recommends a gold Honda Accord. You find one you like, test drive it, and then go home to think about buying it. As you're leaving the dealership, traffic is going by and you happen to notice a brand new gold Honda Accord pass by. Then on the highway, another passes you, and the next day you notice that a neighbor has been driving one for a month. At first you may wonder, "What's going on—did my interest in this car cause everyone to buy one?" Because you are giving energy (thoughts, words, actions) to it, your Attention is "tuned in" to gold/Honda/Accord consciousness—therefore seeing what was already there, that you had unconsciously been **editing out**. Those cars were always there, you didn't see them because you weren't tuned in to them, which is akin to tuning them out! What else might you unconsciously be tuning out of your life? Perhaps things like more business, better relationships, or greater joy? This is another aspect of the Law of Attention. If your attention is on negativity you are *editing out* the success that is all around you by negating it. For you, it simply doesn't exist! Therefore, reality is much like a Hollywood 'blue screen' that one's inner consciousness projects an idea onto, which then holigraphically takes outer shape as *my reality.*

Think about the computer, which is a relatively recent invention. All the basic physical components—the silicone, metals, plastic, and wiring—were always here in raw form on planet Earth for billions of years, right? What was missing—that once it appeared, made the invention inevitable? The *consciousness* that a computational machine capable of artificial intelligence was possible. These analogies confirm that all components to success are evenly present and available at all times (much like the Honda Accord and the computer were already here just waiting to be 'seen').

Can you expand your higher mind to imagine the latent potentiality that is present in your life right now, just waiting to be actualized? Your life-force energy is so precious, why throw it away on garbage beliefs, ideas, and situations? Here's how precious your life-force energy is: Imagine the richest man on Earth has been given only six months to live. What amount of money would he give to find a possible cure? *Everything. Your life-force is far more precious than any amount of money.* Living in concert with the Law of Attention teaches you how to not waste it, and to wisely apportion it into worthy causes.

Because energy follows attention, the key is making a habit of 'tuning in' to the most strong-force attractor ideas, people, and activities, while no longer giving any energy to the negatives. By doing so you are operating in harmony with this law, creating optimal conditions to actualize the latent potential inherent in every moment and situation.

The Law of Synchronicity

As with all the laws, this one was referred to in detail by all three of the great masters, and given modern scientific credibility by the great psychoanalyst and research pioneer of the mind, Dr. Carl Jung.

The Law of Synchronicity—There are no accidents, **all events** are important lessons happening in a meaningful timing.

Jung described synchronicity as 'meaningful coincidence.' One may view my story about the speeding ticket as meaningful coincidence, but with a higher awareness one easily sees the amazing correlation between what I 'vibrated' and what was 'attracted' to me in somewhat of a cause and effect relationship. Synchronicity, on the other hand, is an *acausal* (beyond cause and effect) connecting principle, based on Jung's theory of Collective Consciousness (Jung,

1968).

My speeding ticket story (pp.160-162) was created by my working in harmony with natural law through *free will*. Synchronous events are acausal—meaning there is no trackable cause and effect origin—and are sent by the Infinite Intelligence via *Divine Will*. Synchronicities are little gifts from God that are meaningful both in their timing (when they happen), and the underlying lesson (what Infinite Intelligence is teaching that I really need to listen to). It is simple to explain the phenomena using this analogy.

Your intelligence is tied into the Infinite Intelligence much like your individual computer is tied into the World Wide Web. You have an individual consciousness which appears to be independent from others, as is your office computer is separate from other office computers. But once you get internet access, the Internet links your computer to the World Wide Web, which is like a collective consciousness. Now, your individual computer is tied into a collective computer database by the phone or cable modem which sends and receives information via an electromagnetic signal. Similarly, your individual consciousness is always tied in to the database of the collective unconscious via the electro-magnetic Field. Your computer-like mind constantly uploads and downloads information via the electromagnetic frequency of thoughts, feelings, or even dreams.

As one of the founders of modern psychology, Jung analyzed thousands of patients from all over the world. He was stunned by the similarities of the dreams, visions, and myths that people from very different cultures had in common. This observation led to his theory of collective consciousness. This theory offers the idea that there is one consciousness on planet earth, and that the dreams, visions, and myths from these different cultures all come from this same place—a collective unconscious realm that ties us all together. He theorized that synchronicities, and even déjà vu (the feeling of familiarity in a situation or place you know you've never been before), were slits in the fabric of the conscious mind, revealing the collective consciousness beneath it that we all share.

Most of the people he analyzed were all in some state of mental and emotional crisis, and he noticed that in a large number of them a common theme existed. At the critical point in their therapy, a 'meaningful coincidence' often occurred that provided a breakthrough for the patient.

The most famous case involved a woman of staunch rational belief who was making little progress in therapy. The night before their session, she had a dream about a scarab beetle. Jung told her that in Egyptian mythology, a scarab beetle symbolically represented rebirth. He shared his belief that this was possibly a sign they were about to have a breakthrough. At that precise moment, they heard a tapping at the window; Jung opened it and in flew a green scarab beetle. She was so amazed at this synchronicity that she opened herself up to him for the first time and immediately showed rapid improvement. It was the only time in Jung's life he had ever seen a beetle appear at his window (Talbot, 1991).

I once led a workshop in Florida and had just explained this law in detail to a large audience of businessmen. During the morning break one of them came up to me and said, "I like most of what you shared this morning, but I must admit that I think this synchronicity stuff is crap." I smiled and told him how much I appreciated his honesty, and then we began a little small talk. In this small talk, he happened to ask my lunch and travel plans, and I said, "I'm not sure what I'm doing for lunch, and I'm hoping someone here will give me a ride to the airport. At that moment, an old friend, whom I didn't even know was in attendance, walked up and said, "Stay here and have lunch with us at the hotel, then I'll drive you to the airport, OK?" The first man was flabbergasted at this sudden synchronicity, and looked at me in shock. He confessed that this was particularly meaningful to him because it gave him hope that other things I shared that he had secretly doubted might also be real and true. Notice in this story both the timing—a synchronicity occurring at the exact moment he professed *disbelief in synchronicity,* and the lesson—his renewal of hope in himself as a result of it.

I recently was driving home from a workshop in downstate New York and had the sudden thought that if somehow a deer appeared in the road, I was going too fast to safely avoid it. I looked down to lower my cruise control speed significantly, and when I looked back up a split second later, the largest buck I ever saw was standing not twenty yards away directly in my path. I was going slowly enough to swerve, and though I still clipped the deer, avoided a major crash.

As these synchronicities occurred throughout my own life, I began to look at them as lessons that I could implicitly trust. There are no accidents possible in your life. Everything has meaning, and every person and event contains a very valuable lesson designed specifically for you. The infinite Intelligence is trying to tell you something important for your own growth in this way, and my experience is that if I ignore the lessons, they only get more intense. A lesson will be repeated until learned and each time it needs to be re-learned, it becomes more painful.

Chapter Nine

The Law of One

Law of One—There is only one power and presence in the Universe—God—the omnipotent (all powerful), omniscient (all knowing), omnipresent (always here) Source of unfailing Love and Abundance.

Your left hand and your right hand appear to be separate from each other, but they are part of one larger body. And so it is with all matter and energy as well. Physicists have mathematically proven that our universe is one big cosmic soup of intricately interwoven energy. This is precisely what the masters have been saying from the beginning.

Since all things are connected, whatever you do to others you are doing to yourself, because *we are each other*. Because there is only one Self here, everything you do, you do for—and to—yourself. The bodies are separate, but the minds are not!

Physicist Alain Aspect separated two photons that were part of the same light particle. As they drifted far apart, he measured the spin of one photon. As he did so, the other sister photon simultaneously spun in the exact opposite direction! The two photons were somehow still connected though separated by vast regions of space. His continued experiments proved that these photons could be on opposite sides of the universe, and yet when one was measured the other instantly registered interconnectivity (Talbot, 1991).

If you absolutely knew for certain that everything you do to another, you are doing to yourself, the concept of doing the right thing would take on new meaning. Our bodies are separate, but our consciousness is one. This separation mentality is called duality, and is an illusion.

People suffer enormously under the illusion of duality. Duality is the doctrine theorizing that there are two antagonistic forces in the universe, and that these forces are opposites constantly warring against each other in an un-winnable battle. This illusion has been called 'the polarity of the opposites.' Some familiar dualities include God/Devil, Good/Evil, Rich/Poor, Light/Dark, and so on. Buying into this illusion causes you to become dramatically weakened, and resolving it creates greater strength. A major advancement in power, integrity, and intelligence is realized when one sees that he is an individual aspect of a larger whole that is one thing. Duality splits your power in two. The effect of realigning your personal power through living the Law of One multiplies your life success results *exponentially* (Balsekar, 1989).

Here are three commonly held dualistic beliefs: Rich/Poor, Light/Dark, and Heat/Cold. Can you see how each example is really not two things in opposition to the other, but actually gradations along the same line?

Figure 1	Figure 2	Figure 3
Rich	Blinding Light	Boiling Hot
Wealthy	Brilliance	Hot
Affluent	Very Bright Light	Really Warm
Prosperous	Light	Balmy
Well-off	Muted Light	Lukewarm
Middle Class	Dim	Cool
Living Check-to-check	Gloomy	Chilly
Struggling Financially	Dark	Cold
Poor	Pitch Black	Bitter Cold

In figure 1, closely observe that there are not two things which are opposites—rich vs. poor—but in reality is one essential thing (prosperity) that is present to varying degrees. That which you call 'poor' is the ***absence*** of prosperity beliefs, *not the opposite* of 'rich'. Each example represents varying degrees of prosperity beliefs, or their absence, along one and the same line, not two opposing lines. Rich and poor are merely labels. Rich people have a high degree of prosperity beliefs, and poor people have an absence of prosperity beliefs.

In Figure 2 you again see one essence—light—and its absence, which is called dark. Can you purchase dark? You can purchase light—bulbs, matches, flashlights, etc. Light clearly has existence, and can be shined into any room. Can you shine 'darkness' into a room? No! It doesn't exist. Darkness is simply a word that has been given a meaning which describes the prevailing condition in the absence of light. Similarly there is no such thing as cold—there is heat, and its absence, gradating along one continuum in varying degrees (Hawkins, 2003).

The rich/poor duality deserves greater scrutiny as money is such a controversial idea in our world today. Transcending this illusion and acting in harmony with the natural laws of the Prosperity Paradigm is the path to success that all self-made wealthy people have traveled (Price, 1987).

We live in a stunningly abundant world. By making new choices, and by speaking and acting on these new choices, you raise yourself higher up on the scale of abundance. Abundance is the only reality—you merely manifest whatever degree of abundance you believe exists. Look at Figure 1 above and realize that whatever degree of outer abundance you currently experience is the exact degree of inner abundance thinking you possess.

Poor is the absence of abundance thinking and prosperity beliefs. You cannot *own* 'poorness'. It is not a condition that has any intrinsic reality at all, for it is merely the result of the absence of prosperity beliefs. There is no power in poorness, for it is the absence of power. Similarly, there is no power in darkness because it is the absence of light. How could the absence of something carry an opposite charge that might compete against it? This is precisely why poorness is such an insidious condition; it can only be eradicated when the 'poor' have the right amount of discontent, and are thus ready to be educated. Learning abundance beliefs, and how to use them in context is therefore critical to the evolution of the world.

Throughout history, abundance itself changed into various mediums of energy as power—food, shelter, tools, weapons, seeds, gold, doubloons, and eventually money. Wealth exists as a *state of being,* that leads to a lifestyle called prosperity consciousness. The absence of prosperity beliefs however, does become a way of being and thinking called scarcity consciousness.

You can see scarcity consciousness prevailing in certain areas in every major modern city in the United States. You cross a particular inner city street and you begin to see broken glass, boarded up and burned-out buildings, graffiti, and half-eaten fast food on the ground, etc. The exposed food draws rats and vermin. Young men congregate on street corners at all odd hours drinking alcohol out of brown paper wrappers. Regardless of ethnic origin, these people suffer from a prevailing scarcity consciousness. The poorness is not only in money, it is in the thinking. They are often times poor in education, communication skills, relationships, dietary habits, health choices, social skills, work habits—the *absence of prosperity consciousness* pervades all areas of their life. There are books galore that outline the exact steps self-made millionaires have taken to get rich, yet they aren't the secret. People who try duplicating those steps, but do so with a scarcity consciousness, fail every time.

Mission-driven beings live in a perpetual state of prosperity consciousness, and are often teachers of this state to others (Ponder, 1984). The MDB is consistently and highly advanced on all scales, leading to a beautiful natural balance in many areas of life. Many advanced teachers who achieve love mode transcend the need for money. Those who are not outwardly wealthy have intentionally given it up because they are the rare few whose dazzling inner wealth is a testament to their having accomplished the supreme goal of life on earth—enlightenment. Those in the financial services industry experience a huge leap in productivity when they transcend dualism by serving as teachers of Prosperity Consciousness to all.

Once you understand that we are all one, you will no longer want to succeed at the cost of someone else's success, for that would be 'cutting off your nose to spite your face.'

The major problem one suffers under the illusion of duality is that, if I am separate from others, then taking advantage of them seems justifiable and acceptable. Doing so seems acceptable out of self-interest, but there is really only one Self in this universe. This is the big difference between self-interest and **S**elf interest.

The essence of the Law of One teaches us that there is only one Self here, and therefore when you serve someone, you are really serving your Self.

Teachings of Jesus Christ—*There is one body and one spirit, just as there is one God, Father of all, Lord of all who works through all and is in all. Under his influence all the different parts fit together, so when each part works as it should, the whole body grows and builds itself up through love.*

Ephesians 4:4,16

Krishna—*Where all the subtle channels of the body meet, like spokes in the center of a wheel, there He moves in the heart and transforms the One into the many. Know God as all that is, and all that is not, the end of love-longing beyond understanding, the highest in all beings—know him as the One.*

Mundaka Upanishad 2:2,25

Buddha—*He becomes one with the *God-self when a man has risen above the duality of this world. He has become a force for good, working for the freedom of all. All that he had to do is done, he has become one with all life.* **Buddha actually used the word 'Brahmin' which I translate as 'God-self'*

Dhammapada 413,421,423

And from science:

Unified Field theory—The 'Theory of Everything' that explains all matter, energy, and universal forces using one coherent principle: Consciousness.

To clarify how 'Oneness' operates in commerce, observe the following example. For a salesperson, their car is important to their ability to make a living. Taking this apparently individual idea—*my car is important to making a living*—observe how it is interconnected within the framework of a larger whole.

Your car was sold to you by a person who made a commission from selling that car. That person worked at a dealership that made a profit as well. The dealership bought it from a manufacturer who makes thousands of cars, which keeps thousands of employees working and earning. The manufacturer also received compensation from your purchase. Your seemingly individual sale has already contributed in some way to benefit thousands of other people, but let's keep going. A car manufactured in the year two thousand seven has over one thousand individual inventions that, when combined, make it the great car that it is. From the engine to the headlights, air conditioner, stereo, windows, exhaust system, power steering, every individual invention adds a unique quality you derive value from at the precise moment of need. Each inventor made a fabulous living from that one invention. For example, take the person who invented windshield wipers, which every car uses. He, or his heirs, may still get paid a royalty for his invention, even today.

Your 'making a living' is, in fact, tied into everyone's making a living. While driving your car, you buy gas, oil, pay tolls—and at each step there is a monetary exchange in which your individual effort to 'make a living' is interconnected with millions of others also 'making a living.'

Continuing to look deeper, let's take one car part and follow it further to see the inter-connectedness of it. The engine block in your car is made of iron. The presence of the iron in that engine can be directly traced to the early metallurgists' inventiveness dating back to five thousand BC. Iron replaced bronze, as iron was more plentiful, durable, and easier to work with than bronze.

Bronze replaced stone because it served as a better substance to make tools out of. We've now taken the car and traced it back in an interconnected way to the Stone Age. I could keep going all the way back to the Big Bang but I will stop here to make the point perfectly clear. One invention goes all the way back to the beginning of creation, and everyone benefits from it. We are all inexorably linked together in all we do. We use hundreds of things critical to our life success on a daily basis, and each thing represents the Soul Purpose contribution of someone's entire life. Pens, cars, lights, toilets, vacuum cleaners, aspirin, ovens, beds, linens—the list is endless! The quality of your life is great because of the contributions of all beings living and deceased from the dawn of creation.

Our lives are an inter-connected web that grows exponentially successful when we take the time to see it from a higher perspective. There is only one thing present on Earth—consciousness—and it is awake to varying degrees in six billion human forms.

The cynic might say, "Inventors today are seeking innovations purely for making money." This clearly shows that the cynic doesn't know any inventors and hasn't done his research. Of course there is a thought of reward when one works, no matter what their trade, because everyone seeks to provide for their family and themselves. The difference with being mission driven is that the MDB knows that he gets what he wants by first focusing on the client's needs, and that *then* his own needs are met. The great salesman Zig Zigler said, "I always remember that I can have anything in this world I want, if I'm willing to help enough other people *get what they want,* ***first***.' Jesus revealed the same truth this way, *"the first shall be last, and the last shall be first"* (Matt. 20:16). When we put serving others first, in the long run we win to a greater degree than can be imagined.

The ego does not want you to put others first, and so it is at the core of sustaining duality. This is the true source of the chaos and suffering that prevails on Earth. The ego can justify any horrible behavior to fulfill its selfish, myopic desires. Until one becomes mission-driven, duality deceives each of us into believing *we are the ego,* separate and superior to all others. These so-called 'others' are secretly viewed as objects that exist solely to please the desires of the ego. Being mission-driven means transcending duality, which in turn helps you to transcend the ego. This is how the soul evolves into unity and oneness with the Infinite Intelligence of God, and in so doing, the planet may be able to enter an era of unprecedented peace and prosperity.

The Law of Two

One might ask, "why is the illusion of dualism so real, and if all things happen for a reason, then what is its purpose? " The answer lies within the Law of Two.

Law of Two—To know and experience a thing, the opposite energy must *appear* to exist.

Imagine you lived in a realm of continuous happiness, and had never experienced anything but that emotion. If someone came up to you and asked, "How do you feel today?" what is the only possible answer you could give? You'd say, "happy."

But then what if they said, "How do you know you're happy, for what if that which you've called 'happiness' all these years has really been a *state of boredom,* not joy!" How could you possibly know if they were telling you the truth?

The only reason you *know* happiness at all is because you've been *sad,* and realize the tremendous difference. Having experienced the absence of happiness—that which is called 'sadness'—made it possible for you to know, experience, and most importantly choose happiness habits. To ever feel any emotion, these two seeming opposites must *appear* to exist. This is the Law of Two, without which *you could never learn or experience anything.*

This then, is the Divine Paradox:

In the absence of that which IS NOT (Ego) that which IS (God)—cannot be experienced.

In the absence of darkness, you could never *experience* light.
In the absence of pain, you could never *experience* pleasure.
In the absence of cold, you could not *experience* heat.
In the absence of scarcity, you could not *experience* prosperity.

God, in infinite wisdom, sought for us to KNOW the magnificence of all things, but realized they could not really be EXPERIENCED in the world of relativity without the opposite energies as an option. This, then, is a Divine Paradox. Since God is all there is—without opposite—there can be no opposite of anything. The infinite Intelligence resolved this by creating 'the illusion of the opposites' called the Law of Two (Walsch, 1995).

Out of intense love for creation, God gifted us with the ability to not just *think* about God, but to *experience* the Infinite State Itself. *Thinking* about something is a far different thing than *experiencing* something. For any thing to be known, it **must** be experienced. When one is hungry, thinking about a cheese pizza might be nice, but only in eating the cheese pizza are you really fulfilled. *Thinking* about making love may be nice, but *experiencing* making love is indescribably superior.

A child born into major wealth often has no appreciation for his fortunate circumstances because he's never *experienced* earning. He has a sense of entitlement, oftentimes showing little appreciation for the great gift of monetary wealth his family has provided. Since he never spent any 'sweat equity' in earning the money, he cannot appreciate it at all. Having never experienced the seeming opposite to wealth, he in fact is not wealthy at all. He has *money*, but not ***prosperity***.

The Infinite Intelligence realizes that there can be no greater experience for a person than re-uniting with Itself, which is the supreme goal on Earth, called enlightenment. So for you to experience love, fear must be an option. Only when you have suffered sickness can you fully appreciate health. For you to relish in success, failure must be experienced. But in seeking to fully experience all these positive things, you immersed yourself in their illusory negative aspects to do so, eventually forgetting the Law of One. And since the belief in anything makes it so, humanity got lost believing in fear, disease, and failure.

The Fear/Love Principle

In the absence of fear, love cannot be experienced. We have been taught that the opposite of love is hate, but now that you see that opposites aren't real, recognize that the absence of love (not the opposite) is fear. It is the learned habit called fear that is the root of your inability to be more successful. **All negative emotions—doubt, envy, jealousy, anger, greed, worry, and suspicion**—all originate from fear. Let's look at the last two as an example—worry and suspicion. Everyone knows that worrying about a problem does absolutely nothing to solve the problem—it is a total waste of perfectly good energy. Yet almost everyone does it—why? They are programmed to fear. Worry is the fear of something going wrong, suspicion is fear of being taken advantage of, and every other negative quality is likewise a fear of something. Fear drains you of the energy necessary to be successful. It makes people confused, sick, paralyzed, unfocused and paranoid. Fear is behind all evil, and always ends up destroying peace and happiness.

Whatever discontent you are currently experiencing, and continue to experience, is because your mind is stuck in a repetitive pattern of negative fearful thoughts. We have been taught fear. Turn on the news and it is all fear-based and negative—we expect it. It has become our habit, and it is much more acceptable to believe in and publicly espouse than is love.

It is a simple fact that behind every thought, word, and action one experiences is the underlying energy of either fear or love (Williamson, 1992). The next time you are aware of your continuous inner conversation, take notice of this important fact. Fear is the fuel for your negative thoughts, love is the fuel for your positive thoughts, and you have no neutral thoughts.

The sad truth is that the average person's brain is mostly filled with negative, fearful thoughts. Fear of rejection, fear of failure, fear of being misunderstood, fear of not being smart enough, fear of success, and many others.

When you think of love, chances are you are thinking of the

emotion of deep and tender affection for another. I am not referring to love as a feeling, but rather as a choice you make, or fail to make, every moment.

LOVE—Choosing to become the greatest, highest, and most magnificent version of who I AM.

If your goal is to experience a balance of health, wealth, and happiness, this definition of love is the most powerful tool you can use to make it so. Most of us were **not** taught by our parents, schools, and society how to love in this manner. We have been taught a version of love that is an attachment to people or things that often becomes a bondage, which leads to resentment. This is why many new couples fear using the phrase 'I love you.' Its connotation is one of weakness, need-based bondage, and the end of joy in the relationship. This is not love.

Love is a style of living life—it is a way of being in the world.

When you continually choose fear instead of love, what else could you possibly attract but suffering and failure? This is no mystery. When you consistently choose love over fear, what else could you attract but positivity and success?

It is the underlying message of the movie Forrest Gump—a fictional film that resonated deep truth in the core of so many people. The character was a simple man of low mental intelligence—*but extremely high **emotional intelligence***—who continually chose love over fear, resulting in a prosperous life.

The Law of Choice

Every second of existence you are choosing between love and fear. This, then, is the Law of Choice.

The Law of Choice—All life success is preceded by a clear choice, followed by a committed plan of action.

Whatever area of success you are seeking—whether it is health, wealth, happiness, or career—the most important factor will be your ability to choose Love (Buscaglia, 1972). It is the choice to speak and act positively, enthusiastically, and creatively regardless of the situation or circumstances. It is the choice to be creative—***especially when you don't feel like it.***

To succeed in this world you need power. The more you love, the more you are rewarded by the Infinite Intelligence with a higher quality, and greater quantity, of Power. This is because Love opens the door to the Field of power, and fear closes the door to the Field of power. Notice how the following acronym for the word LOVE infers the infinite energy potential within the Field.

Limitless
Omnipotent
Vibrations
Everywhere

Looking at the lists below can be helpful in deciding which attractor patterns you currently associate with; which honestly apply to your life as it is right now.

LOVE- Strong Attractor Patterns	**FEAR**—Weak Attractor Patterns
Faith	Doubt
Confidence	Worry
Truth	Falsehood
Forgiveness	Resentment/Revenge
Peace	Belligerence
Compassionate	Condemning
Understanding	Critical
Patient	Disruptive
Funny	Derisive
Focused	Diffused
Disciplined	Procrastinating
Responsible	Blaming
Accountable	Making excuses
Kind	Cruel
Respectful	Demeaning
God	Ego

What difference might the single commitment to consistently choose love over fear make in your being happier and wealthier? Another scientific breakthrough will help clarify this point.

In 1961, research meteorologist Edward Lorenz of Massachusetts Institute of Technology was working on an experiment to predict probabilities in weather patterns. One night he discovered an equation that proved useful, yet required further experimentation. To forgo the tedium that was commonplace in this type of work, with his next experiment he took a shortcut. He rounded the equation variable .506127—a six decimal place number—down to .506, a slight change of only three decimal places, and continued the experiment. He assumed such a tiny change would make no difference in the outcome.

The result was so completely different; he originally assumed his computer had malfunctioned. But upon re-entering the full number he discovered the reason for the ENORMOUS difference in the two results. The infinitesimal alteration of having rounded off .000127 caused a completely different outcome. Because the permutation affected millions of other variables, its effect was more far-reaching than he could have ever known or predicted. The consequence of entering the exact equation contributed to proving that the wings of a butterfly in Africa affect weather patterns in South America—the now-famous Butterfly Effect (Gleick, 1988).

The point is that <u>an infinitesimal change at the beginning of a journey has profoundly different results later on down the road</u>. The seemingly smallest choice can have the most life-altering effects! When that choice is the monumental decision to replace the mental virus of fear with the high-consciousness energy of love, the results are profoundly positive and amazing! This is a further proof of the power of the fundamental ethic of the Prosperity Paradigm.

Remember God—Choose Love—Create Value.

Fear is not the opposite of Love, it is merely its absence—but Love is nevertheless always available and always choose-able! As an action step, the next time you're angry or frustrated, ask yourself...

What am I so afraid of?

This simple awareness will reveal new options in your life that were really always available. The next step is to put your hand on your heart and say…

If LOVE were in this room right now, how would Love have me act—what would Love have me say—what would Love guide me to do?

You will have a new and very powerful experience from using this teaching. The Law of Two is an important illusion designed to make the process of re-uniting with the Infinite Intelligence magnificent beyond normal comprehension. If you have the courage to remember this, you will immediately connect to the Field and transcend dualistic thinking. Failure exists only to experience success, sadness to give meaning to joy, and *fear is the unreal* that defines Love as real and knowable.

So now you know the Truth. And here's the most exciting part—once you wake up to the Truth and remember to habitually act on the Law of One, you no longer have to re-create fear to know love, or failure to know success. You are free to create your life as you choose without negativity wearing you down.

* * *

In brief review, the Law of One taught us that there is only God, it is all love. This means you. You have an immortal consciousness (your soul) that can never die. Your body will—but your consciousness or soul can never die—it is one with God. Energy can't be killed; it only changes form, which is proven by the physics principle called the Law of Conservation of Energy. This law states: *energy can neither be created nor destroyed, but merely changes from one form to another* (McCutcheon, 2004). As pure spiritual energy, you cannot die, you merely transform. God is playing a game called LIFE, and dreaming it through you. We explained that to truly know God, which is LOVE, the opposite energy must appear to exist, which is

FEAR. This created the Law of Two.

But here's the paradox—If God and Love is all that exists, then the only way to create the opposite energy was to create an illusion, and this illusion must appear to be very, very real. Hence fear itself is the following acronym:

False
Evidence
Appearing
Real

Much like a magic trick, in which a good illusionist convinces the whole audience that he made an elephant disappear, God created the illusion of fear so that we could fully experience love. Since God/Love is all that is real, but you could never experience it without the opposite energy as a choice, this illusion has to be extremely convincing. And fear is, isn't it? Fear is at the core of scarcity, just as love is at the core of prosperity. To experience consistent prosperity, this rift must be healed.

Throughout history, as fear became more dominant than love in people's minds, we forgot our Godliness, and developed a false self called the ego, which is also an acronym:

Easing
God
Out

So through habitual fear we unknowingly created a false self, called the ego, which continually pushes happiness away by easing God out. Since God is love, and love is the key ingredient to a balanced joyful life, most people repeatedly destroy success through what they have termed 'normal' fear-based thinking. It is actually self-defeating and abnormal. Now they have a bigger problem because they are self-deceived by believing that the cause of their failure has nothing to do with them. The biggest problem is the one I don't know I have. This is the habit deeply imprinted in the subconscious human mind, and even further ingrained in our DNA through thousands of years of fear, death, and failure.

If this universe is an ocean of Infinite Intelligence, you are one droplet in the ocean, *in smaller quantity but the exact same quality*. My great friend...here's how unlimited the potential within you really is—you are One with God, still sleepwalking. Wake up! Put your hand on your heart, and breathe three deep breaths. Now ask yourself if this story is TRUTH. Go ahead—ask God within...what does your intuition say?

Through this layer of fear deeply stored in human DNA that is perpetuated by our social programming, our subconscious mind has been polluted, and is therefore asleep to the truth. Being mission-driven is a lifestyle in which we co-create a spiritual discipline that acts like a divine alarm clock, waking us up to trigger and apply our sleeping potential. This potential is Soul Purpose, and everyone on Earth has one.

As you persist in following these teachings, you awaken to higher and greater levels of your true Self, which is God/Love. According to the great masters, this is a never ending upwards evolutionary spiral. So the thinking mind is the ego false-self that has no real power, and the God/Love aware mind is your True-Self power source. **Here is a very crucial point in this teaching. The Prosperity Paradigm is a spiritual discipline that awakens who you *thought* you were to your True Self, preparing the way for inevitable Enlightenment.** This state of ultimate prosperity and bliss is referred to by all three great masters. Jesus calls it the Kingdom of God, and says it cannot be realized by merely watching, but must be actively sought, inside you. He declares that it is already within you, not somewhere or something outside of you.

...The Kingdom of God does not come by watching, nor is it here, nor there. For behold, the Kingdom of God is within you!—***Jesus Christ*** (N.T. Luke 17:20-21)

Buddha again confirms the same idea, simply stating the process to attain the supreme goal of human life on earth, which he calls Nirvana.

*Avoid all evil, cultivate the good, purify your mind…and attain Nirvana—the highest goal in life.—**Buddha*** (Dhammapada 14:183-184)

Krishna is very specific about the enlightened state which he calls samadhi. He specifically refers to non-attachment (Chapter Seven) as a means of transcending both the noise of the mind—and duality—to achieve enlightenment.

*When your mind has overcome the confusion of duality, you will attain the state of holy non-attachment to things you hear and have heard. When you are unmoved by the confusion of ideas and your mind is completely united in samadhi, you will attain the state of perfection.—**Krishna** (Bhagavad-Gita 2:52-53)*

Similar passages exist in other religious texts like the Torah, Book of Mormon, and the Zend-Avesta.

One main purpose of this curriculum is to help create many enlightened millionaires and billionaires. This is important because of the enormous difference in how unenlightened people use money in contrast to the way in which enlightened people use it.

In the context of the three lower modes (fear, desire, pride), money is a medium of energy people hoard to primarily serve themselves. It is a mostly futile attempt to be happier inside by the purchase and accumulation of objects on the outside. Using money to fix his inner problem is like trying to repair a car with a blown engine by re-painting the body. Once 'the blush is off the rose,' the new toy that brought him happiness last week can do nothing to quell this week's inner emptiness.

But when large amounts of money are utilized by a mission or love-driven being, world-changing, magical things can happen. The Melinda and Bill Gates Foundation recently donated $258.3 million to eradicate malaria in Africa ("What Money Can Buy?" *New Yorker*, Oct. 2005). This curable disease currently accounts for the daily deaths of roughly three thousand children under the age of five on that continent. (Three thousand multiplied times 365 days equals over *one million lives* saved in a year.) Rick Warren, author of the book The Purpose-Driven Life, has given away ninety-percent of that best-selling book's profits to charities.

This is the power of what can happen when money is in the hands of enlightened people. Because enlightened people are loving on the inside, they are guided to use their prosperity in loving, meaningful ways on the outside. You can now see why it is so important to build the new habit of choosing love, for ***it*** is the key that opens the door to everything beautiful in life.

Four Ways to Love All

We have been conditioned to think of love as an emotion, but that is not the definition of love that applies here. Neither is Love something you give or take, love is something you are— it is a way of being and a lifestyle. At first glance this may sound like a new age frou-frou concept that implies weakness, but it is the infinite strength. It requires less effort to be a bully, mean, and hostile than it does to be gentle, understanding and peaceful. To be loving is far more challenging than being negative, but like anything else, when done long enough becomes habitual. It becomes a style of being that attracts people to you. This is because all human beings secretly crave love (Chapman, 1992).

The sticking point is that it is so difficult to love people when they are behaving unlovably. You can go beyond this stumbling block by realizing that you love as your style of being in the world, because of who YOU ARE—not because others deserve it.

Jesus, Buddha, and Krishna all say essentially the same thing on this topic. That, "if you only love those who love you," that is typical and unexceptional, for everyone always does that. This way of reserving love only for the people you deem 'lovable', is really not love at all. From whose viewpoint are people lovable? Who other than God is qualified to make that value judgment?

It is in loving the so-called unlovable people in the world that the great power arises from within (Matt. 5:46-48; Gita 10:8-11; Dhammapada 17:230-233). When we understand that life is a game, and that this game has an objective, life becomes much more enjoyable and winnable (Shinn, 1925). The win/objective of the game of life is this—**he who loves the most, wins**. It therefore behooves us to learn how to love the ignorant, vile and evil people in the world.

Most people do not believe you can be loving without compromising self-respect and safety. They equate being loving with being taken advantage of. This is untrue. The four levels of love teach us how to love consistently without compromising our self-respect and peace of mind (Young-Sowers, 1995). They are detailed in order, from those who are easiest to love, to those who are most difficult to love.

1. **LOVE THE ONENESS** in those who 'get' you and your deepest thoughts, dreams, and desires without question or effort. The amazing thing about these people is that they may be relatively new in your life, and yet the depth of connectivity between you both is obvious. They are kindred spirits to you and understand you thoroughly, as you understand them. It takes little or no effort to love these people as much as you love yourself.

2. **LOVE THE SHARED FRIENDSHIP** in those people who are good friends in your life, but do not 'get' you all the way. You know they are good-hearted, and that your life is far richer for their presence in it. But your deepest truths are not, and may never be, understood by them and are therefore questioned. Typically, these are relationships where social and light conversation works well, but more meaningful conversations fizzle. Appreciate the gift of meaningful friendship they bring, without requiring any more than that.

3. **LOVE AT A DISTANCE** those people who are great examples of how **not** to be, how **not** to treat people, and how **not** to be

happy and successful in life. These are very important teachers existing in your life as examples of how not to be in the world. In many cases, these people may be family members, old school or childhood friends, or co-workers who are clearly in your life to learn from. They are takers, and draining to be around. Learn to have impersonal, concise communication in a short polite manner covering whatever necessary pragmatics are required with no extraneous small talk—then move on.

4. **LOVE THE GOD FIBER** in those people whose behavior makes it impossible to find any redeeming human qualities whatsoever. These are the criminals and evil ones of this world, who serve as the contrasting point that allows 'good' to be an earnable experience. These are the Osama bin Laden/Saddam Hussein type characters that God put here to play a role you are glad you do not have to play. You see the same earthly flesh and blood 'fiber' of God weave through them as through you—*not loving them for **who** they are, but rather '**that** they are'.*

These last two levels are the challenge. When these kinds of people arise in your conscious awareness—don't think about them or their deeds because doing so invariably initiates fear and loathing towards them.

Learn to separate their *becoming* from their ***being***. The *becoming* is the negative karmic role certain characters perform in the Divine Play called life. The ***being*** is the "God Fiber' that is inside of the *becoming,* hidden by the cloak of the ego. Could there have been a Jesus Christ without a Judas? Judas had a very difficult, but necessary *becoming* to play in the life of Jesus.

Applying this ethic at a more day-to-day level, when your children are behaving badly, you learn to separate the behavior from the child so you can say to them, "You, I love—but your behavior, I don't love." You still love them by separating the child's *becoming (behavior)* from their ***being*** *(essence).*

The Law of Three

In the mid seventies, psychologist Dr. Richard Alpert traveled to India on a quest to verify the deeper levels of the God/Love aspects of higher mind. Alpert had such a profound mystical rebirth from working with the guru he met there, he took the name Baba Ram Dass, symbolic of his new level of spiritual awareness. His life-altering journey resulted in what is now considered to be a metaphysical literary classic entitled Be Here Now. The simple message is that by being totally aware, completely present and focused in the 'here,' you can access your own unique *point of power* to create your highest personal reality. The three word title alluded to a unique combination of three qualities that, when combined, accessed the Field of personal power that this book describes in detail.

Be—A state of focused awareness
Here—The focused awareness is in this particular point in space
Now—Not stuck in the past, not worried about the future, totally and fully present
Combining these three ideas into one principle, a formula emerges -

One's personal power is multiplied when you are totally present in this particular space with a state of focused awareness.

This is an excellent example of the Law of Three.

Law of Three—All 'Powers' in this universe appear as the intersection of three different energies.

Notice how each of the following powers expresses itself as a triad.

Christianity—Father, Son, Holy Spirit (Jesus was an incarnation of God as the son)

Hinduism—Brahma, Vishnu, Shiva (Krishna was an incarnation of Vishnu)
Buddhism—Yin, Yang, Tao (Buddha was an incarnation of the Tao—

the Way)
Science—$E = mc^2$ (Energy = Mass x Light^2)
Time—Past, Present, Future
Space—Here, There, the space between (everywhere)
Form—Solid, Liquid, Gas
Humanity—Physical, Mental, Spiritual

Notice that each triad has one main topic (in the above examples in bold) made up of three qualities containing a highest, a medium, and a lowest potential. This does not mean that one of the three qualities in each triad is better or worse than the other. Is a tall tree better than a medium or small tree? Not necessarily. What it does mean is that in each instance, **one out of the three serves as the most advantageous starting point for you to realize a goal in the fastest way.** As an example, with <u>time</u>, which has the three qualities of Past, Present, and Future, the highest point is the present. If you decide your goal is to create a better future, the greatest plane of potential is accessed in the '**Now**.' With <u>space</u>, the highest plane of potential is in the **'Here.'** With <u>humanity</u>, the highest plane of potentiality is the '**Spiritual.**'

Recognize that there are three aspects to being human; we are spiritual, mental, and physical beings simultaneously. Those who believe themselves to be merely a physical being are predominantly programmed to be reactive. Reactive people wait for something to happen, and then respond with old patterns that are mostly based in fear. This is extremely limited, in that re-actions are merely old actions done over and over—hoping for a different result that rarely comes. Those who believe themselves to be predominantly a mental being are operating at a higher level of power, that which might be termed proactive. Proactive people act first—taking the initiative instead of waiting for something to happen and then responding. Being proactive is far more powerful then being reactive, yet still not operating at the highest level of potential. This is true because, without the consistent presence of an advanced teacher or coach, the decent desire that compels proactive behavior can quickly erode into selfish desire.

Being creative is the entrepreneurial style that compels you to bring value creation to the business world in unique ways. Through a very specific process of spiritual discipline, the MDB can increase his power and draw on a higher creative power from the Field. Review the table below to further understand the Law of Three and how it pertains to creating from a higher plane of potential:

Process	State	Ethic	Essence	Realm	Business Style	Business Model
Being	God-Self	Work Mission	Soul	Spiritual	Creative	Interdependent
Thinking	Ego-self	Work Smart	Mind	Mental	Proactive	Independent
Doing	Animal-self	Work Hard	Body	Physical	Reactive	Dependent

Physical Plane—REACTIVE—In this business style, people wait for something to first happen, and then respond in a fear-based manner. Some only work hard when threatened with a serious consequence, and then work only enough to solve the problem temporarily. The physical being is almost completely *dependant* on others for work and money. Self respect and self-confidence are often shaky because he is not working in his Soul Purpose, and the hidden feeling that he could be doing better is always present. This is the level at which most human beings who are asleep to their higher spiritual nature are stuck. Separated from their true source of power, the business world is seen as hostile and cold, as are most wealthy people. This misconception makes the reactive person grateful to not be in any higher business mode, which supports their rationalizing the inner decision to play small. (Fear and Desire Mode)

Mental Plane—PROACTIVE—The person using this style is taking the initiative to move towards success from a place of choice, which initially creates greater financial success. At first this is great, but it soon becomes draining because this man is still swayed by the effects of the ego-thinking mind. The mental being sees himself as *independent* of others, therefore adopting a separation mentality. This often evokes feelings of being alone and unsupported, which causes underlying negative tension. He continues his proactive style without realizing there has been a shift that is imperceptible to him. A negative tension is now underlying his work, and what he calls proactive is now a pushy feeling that is received by clients and even partners as an arrogance or coldness. In sales people it can reveal itself as the 'chase vibration.' This is verified by his repeatedly calling the same customers who don't return his calls because he is acting like a business predator and the client feels like the prey. The lion is also proactive, but the zebra will always run. (Desire and Pride Mode)

Spiritual Plane—CREATIVE—Through spiritual discipline, this entrepreneur's style is interdependently focused on building the success of ***others***. His success is interwoven with many others through strategic alliances and a history of giving more than getting. As you adopt this style, other entrepreneurs want to go out of their way to reciprocate back ***to you*** the phenomenal value they received ***from you***. *Interdependence* promotes ultimate prosperity as the whole community appears to be contributing to your success. This person knows they are evolving upwards because they are being pulled by a higher power. (Mission and Love mode)

Acting in a spiritual way is always serving the highest good of all concerned. Spiritual contemplation allows us to transcend petty problems and focus on the learning and growth inherent in every life challenge. Speaking in a spiritual way draws people to you because human beings are attracted to that which uplifts, and are repelled by that which drains.

Spiritual choices naturally flow from choosing the loving thing to do—especially when it requires tough love—in a situation in which it's easier to be negative or passive. The higher power guides you to deal with confrontational situations that once flustered you in all new ways. When others say tactless things out of anger, you recognize their attack as a cry for help. This assuages the need to take a defensively hostile position. In those situations, an obvious truth is revealed to your inner awareness—which is; if someone uses lies and hostility to intentionally injure me—I have *nothing* to defend. By not 'feeding in' to these situations, they will no longer 'get to you,' and your inner power will continue to evolve and increase. A judicious calmness and composure is then made available so that you can effectively speak a hard truth in a soft way. You learn how to be pleasant while speaking about the unpleasant situations that occasionally occur in business, family, or social settings.

The Interdependent Business model

As it pertains to commerce, the Law of three appears in the three differing business models used in America today. None is better or worse than the other, but only the Interdependent business model allows for people to live Soul Purpose and become wealthy in the highest sense of the word.

1. **Dependent**—You work for someone else—trade *time* for money—have little freedom and little control over earnings. Working for long periods of time in this model often results in self-esteem issues.
2. **Independent**—You work for yourself and are self-motivated—trade *talent* for money—have more freedom and more control over earnings but eventually feel alone, unsupported and having to re-create business on a daily basis.
3. **Interdependent**—You create strategic partnerships with other entrepreneurs—*leverage* your combined talents and systems to increase money—have greater freedom and control over pay.

Dependency is a model in which one man creates a valuable product or service, and then hires a well-paid board of directors, who hire teams of workers who trade time for money. The typical idea is to pay the workers as little as possible, while hoping to get as much productivity out of them as they're willing to give. This creates obvious discontent in the workers, some of whom stay out of fear, while others leave knowing there must be a better way.

I learned this model as a teenager when I worked at a locally-owned family restaurant. After a year of faithful service I asked for a raise. The owner put his arm around me and, with a smile said, "kid—the job pays what it pays—you're a good boy—you'll figure it out." Without laughing in my face, he was telling me that if I wanted more money I was in the wrong place. It also taught me that bussing tables was not a very unique talent and that I needed to educate myself. He was right, I did figure it out, but it took a while.

After more schooling, I found myself earning far more in an independent business model. In my twenties I became a salesman for a home improvement company, and because I was blessed with God-given people skills and integrity I did very well. It was a straight—commission outside sales job. I realized that any day I chose to give myself a raise, all I had to do was study the great salesmen and apply their success principles with my customers. I did so, and led the company in sales for three years in a row, progressively making more money each year. What was troubling was that I felt that I was not building upon anything of my own—that I had to continually re-create success every single day. Soon, discontent again set in, because my spirit was whispering to me that there was definitely something bigger that I came here to do. Simultaneous to that realization, I discovered a dark secret about the company that convinced me they were not operating from integrity. Upon leaving this company, interdependency was utilized.

Interdependency is more powerful than the other business models for several reasons. First, it empowers everyone in the partnership—even support team members—to experience greater fulfillment because it allows everyone to live their soul purpose. It's obvious that people do better work when they're doing what they love and are rewarded well for doing it. In our company every support team person owns a small percentage of the overall earnings of the company. They not only enjoy what they're doing more, but they are directly compensated for making a greater contribution to the overall enhanced success of the Prosperity Paradigm.

When I finally committed to living my Soul Purpose, I sought out my highest integrity friends and proposed creating a strategic partnership. I already had an existing client base of people who liked me and trusted me. I noticed that each of my entrepreneur friends also had a valuable service every one of my clients would eventually need. Each one had a great service and system, and also had an existing client base. We created a mutual admiration society in which the total exceeded the sum of the parts. Looking back, the reason it worked so well was that I had chosen the highest integrity people I knew who were already committed to being Mission-Driven.

This model also maximizes the power of leverage. Combining forces with other Mission-Driven beings allows you to leverage:

1. **Other People's Experience**—Everyone in our network knew something about business that I previously didn't know, that they shared with me, and from which I benefited.
2. **Other People's Money**—By combining financial resources we were able to do projects any one of us could not have afforded to do alone.
3. **Other People's Ideas**—Every team member was creative in slightly different ways—so they each brought unique ideas about advertising, marketing, research, and a myriad number of other crucial business topics.
4. **Other People's Time**—They were willing to cover for me admirably when I was away on vacation, out sick, or taking a free day.
5. **Other People's Energy**—They picked me up and inspired me when I was down—as I did for them—and we gladly allowed each other to ride the others' coattails when necessary.
6. **Other People's Clients**—We created an internal switch for referring business to each other when the need arose—which it somehow did more often, once we made that commitment.

The father of what is now modern architecture was the ancient Greek engineer Archimedes, who said, *"Give me a lever long enough, and a place to stand, and I'll move the world."* He was referring to the power of leverage to create greater success momentum.

I have heard many entrepreneurs tell me they tried this approach, but that it didn't work for them. After doing an organizational x-ray of their company, I almost always discovered the same reason it hadn't worked. The hard truth was that they were not mission-driven beings—they were operating from fear, desire, or pride, therefore drawing the same kind of partners to them. Of course this kind of selfish partnership cannot possibly prosper on a consistent basis. Negativity caused their team to crumble, as it always does—and rightfully so.

Other so-called success networks of people who are not mission-driven invariably collapse. Here are some examples of how and why this may occur. The examples shown below include six- team members in each strategic partnership. A mathematics equation follows each example to give a numerical illustration of the direct proportion in value created to dollars earned.

Fear-Driven network: Team members talk about success but no one believes in themselves, much less each other—so no referrals, time, energy, money or any other resources are shared. With fear at their core, they drain each other instead of inspiring each other. This has the opposite desired effect of the original purpose, and energy is subtracted causing the scarcity paradigm to be reinforced. Every time the idea of networking or strategic partnerships arises in the future each former member says, "I tried it but it doesn't work."

Mathematical energy principle of *Subtraction.* The six team members actually subtract energy from each other:

1—1—1—1—1—1 =—**$60,000** (Fear subtracts group energy—negative paradigm is reinforced—money invested is gone when the group disbands or company goes bankrupt)

Pride-driven network: These networks are often populated by fairly successful earners who are willing to try a new idea only for the sake of money, but lack understanding of the true principles required to succeed using interdependency.

Pride causes this team to view money as the asset—instead of seeing that the true asset is people. This blinds each member to the concept that creating value first for others will eventually result in more money. This network contains people who want to *receive* the benefits of greater business, without the willingness to *give* referrals to the right strategic partner. These men are so habitually committed to their own success first and foremost (independent), that they developed the habit of rarely giving referrals.

Dollars may be made in the short-term because of the initial energy boost that occurs by putting money-makers together, but often fizzles quickly because of violation of the following interdependent success principle. Because of a lack of understanding the Law of Vibration and Attraction, they fail to realize that the more they give **to** each other, the more opportunity they will receive **from** each other.

Mathematical energy principle of *Addition*

1 + 1 + 1 + 1 + 1 + 1= **$60,000** (A little extra money but no velocity of value—hence, the alliance is eventually viewed as not worth it and the group disbands.)

<u>Mission-driven network</u>: By *living* your mission, you attract others with impeccable integrity who are also committed to being mission-driven. By *becoming* the right partner, you draw more of the right partners. This synergistic partnership model turns clients into partners and partners into clients.

Everyone in our network realized the others had something great, and utilized each other's business processes and products. We gave each other our own business, and received value from each other's great services and products. Because we had personally experienced the direct value each member offered, we wanted to refer each team member to all family and friends. As we did this, we collectively experienced something astounding. By *giving* more referrals, we began to receive more great referrals from all points imaginable.

You will experience the same. By *giving* more business you receive more great business. This behavior is so valuable to mission-driven professionals that they want to reciprocate and send value back to you. It becomes a competition to see who can create the most value for each other—not the least. Because of the exponential multiplication of power that happens at this level of understanding and operating, you increase the velocity of value.

Mathematical energy principle of *Multiplication*

$6^2 = 6 \times 6 =$ \$360,000 (velocity of value exponentially multiplies group energy and income).

Chapter Ten

The Morass of the Mind

Creating from the spiritual realm requires you to understand the formidable barrier that is the intellect. To unravel the Gordian knot of the mind, we must be able to see the obstacles to success that it presents us with. Being exposed to the obstacles, then removing them, greatly increases favorable conditions to experience prosperity.

Think these next two questions through slowly and carefully.

1. Can your eye see itself? *(Please take the time to think this through for a moment.)*

2. Can the tongue taste itself?

Much like the eye cannot see itself, nor can the tongue taste itself, <u>the mind cannot clearly perceive itself.</u> Only from your true essence—Spirit—can the mind be clearly seen. The spiritual realm is a vantage point above the mental realm. From this higher realm you are able to clearly see the complex attack thoughts of the ego-thinking mind, and unravel them to go beyond. It has been said that the mind makes a terrible master, but is a wonderful servant.

Normal thoughts are often chaotic and destructive, while spiritual thought is creative and empowering. For those who are trapped in the lower two realms—that of 1.) the physical, or in 2.) the mental—thought can be tremendously distracting, uncontrollable, and draining. Thoughts generated from these lower realms come from what has been referred to as the ego-thinking mind. The actualization of latent potential increases greatly when one goes beyond these realms to create from the spiritual realm. Thoughts coming from this highest realm are generated from what can be called the Aware Mind.

There are three categories that all thoughts fall into:

1. **Physical realm** (Animal Instinct)—This quality of thoughts are the animal instincts which hypnotically compel one to run after and fulfill physical sensory desires and avoid perceived physical dangers.
2. **Mental realm** (Social Programming) These thoughts involuntarily push into your screen of consciousness in a mostly random chaotic way—dominating with fear, doubt, and worry.
3. **Spiritual realm** (Infinite Intelligence/Field) The quality of these thoughts are creative ideas that serve all. They are Self-Evident truths which exist in a specific frequency of the Field that can be 'tuned into' through a process of spiritual discipline.

When a person believes himself to be merely a physical being, his thinking processes are dominated by involuntary thoughts centered on fulfilling physical sensory desires. Thoughts of conquest, preening, shopping for new clothes, sex, sports fantasies, getting intoxicated via drugs or alcohol—all are examples of the quality of thoughts that dominate this person's screen of conscious awareness. It is important to understand that this process is involuntary. It occurs beyond the person's control, for as the young soul is evolving, it must do these things to create discontent. At this level of evolution, the 'seeds for discontent' are planted as the individual is being conditioned to make its happiness dependent on external things. All of these thoughts are based upon fulfillment of physical sensations, which cannot possibly be consistently met, therefore discontent is inevitable. This is simply a part of the human journey—not to be judged—but rather to be viewed with compassion and understanding.

Trapped in the realm of the body/mind, these involuntary thoughts propelled by the ego are mainly based in fear, doubt, and worry. **Thought becomes tremendously creative *only* when one commits to transcend the mental realm and live as a spirit—in a body—who has a mind.**

A major advancement in joy and achievement occurs when you break free from the imprisonment of being stuck in your mind. The mind is like an inner amusement park filled with thrills, spills, and chills that is the source of almost non-stop noise and annoyance. If it weren't for the forced unconscious peace of sleep, the cacophony of the average person's mind would drive them insane. In most people, it currently is the cause of great suffering.

Many personal development programs can be effective when the goal is achieving beyond the limitations of the physical realm by creating from a higher plane—in this case the mental realm. This is powerful for, while the body is a great gift, it is the realm of lowest potential with far more power available in the mental realm. These programs can work well when they are applied to specifically help break free from painful or unresolved memories of the past. They also prove useful when applied to produce results beyond that of only the physical realm. They work by making one aware of, and forgiving, fear-based past memories that stunt creativity. Once you are released from a hurtful past memory, you free up wasted power to create anew, and your personal productivity and happiness can bloom. While valuable in the short term, they can only operate until the point at which one must rely on the mind to lead the way, and then they often fail.

To illustrate this point, let's look at someone—a construction worker—who makes his living at the level of the physical realm. The construction worker uses his body to make a living, and while it is honest, honorable work, this career has limited pay and longevity potential. He 'works hard'—but after a while his sore body, lack of creative input, and limited pay make him eventually feel *stuck in his body*. He is discontented.

Deciding he wants to earn more, he chooses to 'work smart,' and changes careers to one that uses his mind—let's say he chooses a career as a financial planner. He has shifted realms of power from the physical to the mental, into a higher realm of potential in which pay and longevity are greatly increased. Financial planners have been known to work well into their eighties, and some earn millions of dollars a year. He begins studying the stock market and financial trade magazines and enrolls in night school to eventually get a degree as a Certified Financial Planner. Five years later he has a thriving book of business, and looks back in amazement at his old salary of $30,000 a year in construction compared to his current salary of $150,000 a year as a financial planner.

He has used his mind as the way out of the limitations innate to the physical realm, but may have unknowingly adopted the belief that the mind is the way out of every dilemma. While he is earning more, he has reached a false ceiling in his productivity, is overweight, unhappy, and argues with his wife and/or kids. Why? He has now become *stuck in his mind*. The quandary of the mental realm is that the mind convinces you that it is the pinnacle of human existence. Everyone stuck in the mental realm secretly believes his beliefs are right and superior to others. That which was once the way out, has become the next impediment to be transcended.

The mind is an endless fear, doubt, and worry mechanism that one moment is happy, the next moment is sad. One moment it's focused, the next moment it's confused; it starts humming a song, then thinks you're having a heart attack, then thinks about politics, then asks "is someone at the window?" It berates you for not focusing, then worries about money, then fantasizes about a vacation…

Its content is mostly chaotic and random, with short bursts of focused concentration, intelligent reasoning, or clear decision-making that are quickly followed by lapses back into nonsensical babble. Unfortunately, the 'short bursts of clarity' are the exception, and 'the babble' is the rule.

The mind can be exhausting and unreliable. It is actually a great relief when one has this deep truth finally revealed.

It is this way because <u>the thinking mind is the ego</u>, and the ego has two functions, both serving a great importance in the overall scheme of Reality.

Function One—Survival of physical form. The ego-thinking mind is the reptilian brain which thinks like a clever animal—mostly with fear, confusion, and worry about the next thing that might try to eat, kill, or threaten its survival. It is excellent at surviving—which is a good thing—but the 'fight or flight' response that is its main feature causes exhaustion and suffering, and limits productivity and prosperity (Selye, 1978).

Function Two—To make one's life unhappy, unsuccessful, and/or painful enough for the inner Spiritual being that you really are to wake up and say *"**no more**—there must be a better way."*

On the one hand, without the ego there would be no potential to survive and grow—but on the other hand, those who are hypnotized by the ego become sleepwalkers who perpetrate horrible things under its guise. Sleepwalkers are immature souls who refuse to wake up even though something inside of them is telling them that there is so much more possible in their life. All sleepwalkers exist in a state of self-deception. They know something is terribly wrong on planet Earth, but have resigned themselves to live 'small' lives, and thus doom themselves to an unhappy existence by refusing to wake up to their higher purpose.

Signs that one is a sleepwalker are repeated patterns of alcohol abuse, legal or illegal drug abuse, watching too much television, excessive gambling or video game playing, mocking and laughing at others, over-eating, and a major intolerance of others' perceived incompetence. Their ego is still too strong, and therefore resistant to awakening.

Like iron filings inexorably drawn to a magnet, ego-desires exert an irresistible force over the sleepwalker. Much like the iron filing has no choice but to go to the magnet, the desire-drunk human animal sees no choice, magnetized to fulfill its negative karmic destiny. This is a programmed aspect of Function Two—the negativity creates so much pain in the sleepwalker that they eventually seek a way out of the pain they created—and awaken. For those who refuse to awaken, the pain becomes so great that 'misery loves company,' and they set out to destroy joy in the lives of others. Oftentimes this destruction is masked behind the guise of religion, as in the case of the World Trade Center disaster. Nowhere in the Koran is it written that suicide is acceptable for any reason, yet the ego hides behind anything to accomplish its evil intent (Dawood, 1956).

Every terrible thing in this world, and all pain or failure you create and experience in your life is due to the exact same reason—**misidentification that I am the ego-thinking mind.** The ego-thinking mind is a corrupt, selfish, brutal animal wearing a mask of civility. **It** is at the core of 'man's inhumanity to his fellow man.' Go into any prison, and this is obvious—but the aware mind can easily see it in the boardroom today as well. Being mission-driven corrects this grandiose error. It is precisely because the whole world is connected through commerce and business, that the MDB can have such a profoundly positive effect world-wide. Through Awareness, and then careful conscious choices, the MDB replaces the flawed software program all human beings are born with.

From Homo-Sapiens to Homo-Spiritus

Remember that the brain is the *hardware* of the computer-mind, yet it is the *software* that has the endless fear, doubt and worry program of the ego-thinker installed. This is because the pre-frontal cortex (genius) did not *replace* the reptilian brain (killer) at the base of your skull—*it was added to it*. So your brain is like Einstein with a gun (Hawkins, 2003). Homo-Sapiens is a brilliant animal that, when confused enough by the ego, can justify anything to get 'its' way. It can justify destroying a business, cheating on a spouse, ignoring its children, stealing from clients, killing people, raping the environment or any other heinous behavior to attain its selfish narcissistic desire. If you are stuck in the 'mental realm,' which most readers probably are, you are under the illusion of the ego. Using the ego-thinking mind to solve a problem is like trying to heat a house in winter that has all its windows open. The open windows leak the energy out as quickly as it comes into the room.

Homo-sapiens is a servant to its ego-thinking mind and doesn't even know it. The sleepwalker doesn't know he's sleepwalking, and is therefore in danger. The software program of fear doubt and worry is on the back end of virtually every thought, and, though painful, is viewed as being normal. When its needs or desires aren't met it goes into a default mode of 'Fight or Flight.' Default modes are what any system uses to reset its program in a power outage, much like your alarm clock blinking '12:00' repeatedly when the power goes out in your home. The stunning truth is that the human mind automatically defaults to negativity, and until you change it, your chances of living true prosperity are slim.

Like any other creature, the brilliant human animal called homo-sapiens wants to attack, or run from, a situation or person when it is not getting 'its way'- that is simply its default mode. The ego is continually comparing itself to others, while criticizing the same person it compared itself to.

In any sales-driven industry, it's common for a sales-person to feel 'belittled' when a colleague makes a huge sale (comparing), then secretly call the colleague a 'schmuck who got lucky' (criticizing). So he suffers each end of the equation, both the comparison and the criticism. How does he suffer it? Drained energy! Your energy is the most precious commodity you have. This results in *anxiety and envy,* ("I should've made that sale—he's better than me") on the front end—and *guilt and shame,* ("I'm really jealous of him because he succeeded and I didn't") on the back end. Both result in a weakened energy field.

Homo-sapiens is a five senses reality creature who thinks that if he can't see, hear, taste, touch or smell something, it must not exist. This limitation is false and results in the erroneous assumption that *seeing is believing*. It is followed by the even deadlier belief that *perception is reality in the mind of the perceiver*. This too is false. Your five senses perceptions tell you that you're living on a flat world—is that true? They tell you that all solid material objects are inert and dead, but when viewed through an electron microscope even the chair, table, and lamp are made up of particles and waves in a state of constant movement. These same perceptions tell you that you are walking upon a planet that is still and unmoving, but the Earth is actually hurtling through space at great speed, and is also spinning. Five senses reality is limited, and perception is often misleading. Only *essence* is Reality. The Law of One, which has been previously outlined, explains what this real essence is.

Using the Prosperity Paradigm is obviously far more than a great way to make more money. It is the path to a new branch off the evolutionary tree of life. Careful study of the table below can be useful in raising your awareness to the Truth of what is possible in your business and in all aspects of life as one evolves from homo-sapiens to Homo-Spiritus.

Ego—self (homo-sapiens)	**God—Self** (homo-spiritus)
1. Thinking Mind	1. Aware Mind
2. Fear, Doubt, Worry Program	2. Love, Faith, Knowledge Program
3. Fight or Flight (Default mode)	3. Remembers God (Default mode)
4. Comparing & Criticizing	4. Accepting & Understanding
Results in feeling...	*Results in feeling…*
Anxiety, Envy, Guilt, Shame	*Reassured, Joyful, Peaceful, Calm*
5. Uptight, Easily angered	5. Easy-Going, Patient
6. Fear/Desire/ Pride-driven	6. Mission/Love-driven
7. Blames others	7. Learns from others
8. Is Controlling	8. Is Non-Attached
9. Primary Focus—Achieving/Attaining	9. Primary Focus—Awareness/Teaching
10. Animal self: 5-senses reality *creature*	10. Sacred Self: Multi-Sensory *Creator*
a. Sight, Smell, Hearing, Touch, Taste	a. Intuition, Intention, Imagination
1. "Seeing is believing."	1. "Believing is seeing."
11. Relies on Externals for Joy	11. Joy/Success internally created
12. Sees itself as separate and alone	12. Sees itself as inter-connected, all one

You, the entrepreneur of the 21st century, have the greatest opportunity in modern history available to you through your potential business success. This is the opportunity to use your business to uplift yourself and humanity into a new species of existence—a higher version of beings who see each other as one, and are totally invested in helping each other because *we are each other*. This is what can be called Homo-Spiritus. The next book in the *Paradigm* series will be entitled

The Spiritual Paradigm, and will explore this theme in greater detail.

Intuition and Ego -Delusion

Homo-Spiritus is the Love-Driven being described in detail in Chapter Eight. Re-reading that section, and also contemplating and remembering the twelve qualities of Homo-Spiritus as described above, are very important to moving forward with your Soul Purpose. Some well-known examples of current Love-Driven beings are Oprah Winfrey, musician Stevie Wonder, and author Dr. Wayne Dyer. The Love-Driven person has discovered—and, through living his mission, developed—the higher senses of Intuition, Imagination, and Intention. These will be described in greater detail a bit later, but are cited here because a basic comprehension of Intuition is necessary.

Most people typically think of intuition as a lucky hunch. I have come to know it as a higher sense that we all possess, but must nurture to use with confidence. As you become acquainted with intuition you will gain a greater familiarity with it that can be trusted. Much like a blind person's other senses become more powerful, the spiritual being's intuition becomes more powerful with practice. It has nothing to do with luck, and rarely has to do with personal gain. To use it for personal gain actually disconnects one's ability to use it, unless it is to ward off danger.

Intuition is the ability to clearly see the loving guidance that Infinite Intelligence is always showing us. A main feature of intuition is that it always guides you to do something kind, and in service, for others. Those deluded by the ego rarely, or never, act on this guidance. They backslide deeper into a fear-driven life because of ignoring it. Because of the corrupt software program of the ego-thinking mind, Homo-Sapiens exists in a state of ego-delusion. To act on this extraordinary opportunity to evolve into Homo-Spiritus, a deeper understanding of the innate deception that results from ego-delusion is necessary.

Ego-delusion is a condition of self-deception caused by a problem one does not know, or refuses to admit, one has. The alcoholic's foremost problem is not that he drinks too much liquor (which is *the result* of the actual problem), the problem is that he has a disease called alcoholism. He is an alcoholic—and this disease always results in misery, family suffering, and is progressively fatal. Since he doesn't know or can't admit it, he never seeks help. He continues to rationalize his aberrant behavior, destroying his life (and the lives of those he loves) in the process. This is why it is said that "knowing the problem is two-thirds of the way to solving it." All of humanity in fact has this same dilemma as the alcoholic.

We are deceived by the lower self that the cause of all our problems is *out there,* when in reality it is ***inside of us. It is the limited animal consciousness of the ego itself.*** Buying into this ego-delusion erroneously causes one to self-inflate their own position of being right, while incorrectly condemning others as being wrong. Observing a very simple, but true, story may be helpful. I have changed the names of the actual participants for obvious reasons.

Tom and Monica discovered they were having what they called a 'change of life' baby, due to Monica's age which was forty years. Tom was an attorney with a demanding schedule and responsibilities, while Monica worked as a team leader at an software company. Monica began having severe morning sickness. One morning as Tom was watching her vomit, he received a clear guidance to assist her by holding her long hair back while she got sick. This loving guidance also told him that this simple act would help her feel better by 'doing whatever he could do to share in every aspect—both good and bad—of *their* pregnancy.' But due to the influence of the ego, Tom ignored acting on it, and turned away while rolling his eyes. Monica happened to see him do so, which made her feel slightly worse. She began to cry, as feeling misunderstood was added to her feelings of nausea. The raging hormones that accompany being pregnant were also making her feel dizzy. Because of his ego-self betrayal, Tom thought," she's totally over-reacting and making it far worse than it really is—what a baby." Then he thought, "I've puked lots of times in college, what a weakling. What's the big deal?"

After washing up, Monica emerged from the bathroom white

as a ghost, and Tom unsympathetically said, "are you OK?" Because the ego was running his mind, the next thought that popped into his head was how *considerate* a man he was for asking her this question despite what a baby she was being. He thought, "I'm a *good husband*!" Monica answered his question by saying,"no, in fact I think I may call in to work and take a sick day today." Now Tom thought "she's really exaggerating and using this little thing as an excuse to be just plain lazy." Fighting the urge to raise his voice, he said, "I went to work with 102 degree fever just last month!" He then thought of how strong and *dedicated* he was to both his job and to the marriage, while perceiving his wife to be the total opposite. Feelings of *superiority* coursed through him as he thought, "Did I marry a bad wife?" He feels a little *sorry for himself* that this may be true.

Now, let's look **Truthfully** at the consequences of Tom's decision to ignore the loving Intuition from his God-Self.

Tom's Intuition: *Help Monica through the nausea by holding her hair back*

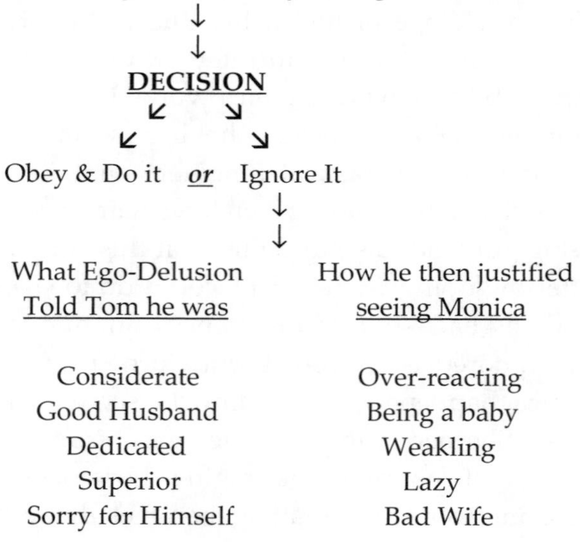

Do you see the incredibly complex ramifications caused by following the ego-self's decision to ignore the loving intuition? Was Tom really being considerate, a good husband, and dedicated? Did he really have any possible reason to feel superior or sorry for himself? No. In fact just the opposite is the Truth, right? And even more twisted was the way in which he came to view his wife after ignoring the loving guidance from his intuition. Was Monica really being a baby, over-reacting, and acting like a weakling? Was she really lazy and, worse yet, a bad wife?

Most importantly, **when** did Tom experience all these false perceptions about himself and his wife—*before or after* the ego-delusion? Stop right now and re-read that last question and deeply think it through—because it's crucial. After, right? *Before* he ignored the guidance things were fine—but *after* the ego-delusion, they were not. Tom felt totally justified in feeling that way, didn't he? The ego-deluded being no longer sees the other person as a human being; he sees them as an object (Arbinger Institute, 2000).

This is how the ego de-humanizes others as mere objects that are either causing inconvenience, or as pawns to help it get its way. By the way, dear reader, at some point in this human journey we are all Tom. How many acts of ego-delusion might we be going through on a daily basis? Recognize that these acts compound one upon the other very quickly, with increasingly negative consequences.

Now, imagine how differently things might have been if Tom had immediately obeyed the guidance and did the simple act of service and loving kindness for his wife? Let's look at how, by listening to one's higher sense of intuition, the situation might have changed. The scenario now looks like this:

Tom is aware of the guidance of intuition and holds Monica's hair back. It's not hard to imagine that while doing so, he might've gotten a visceral sense of how badly the nausea and raging hormones made her feel. The resulting compassion might've prompted thoughts of how big a sacrifice she was making to go through a pregnancy at her age. Monica had worked very hard to build a fine career for herself, and was recognized by all who knew her as successful. Knowing that her career would be adversely affected, he might've then considered how giving and brave she actually was to face the rigors of raising another child at her age. It's not a stretch to believe he may have come to think of her as being strong, and deserving of a day off. Had he followed the Intuition one could truly say he was being helpful, considerate, a good husband, and dedicated. Observe the difference…

Tom's Intuition: *Help Monica through the nausea by holding her hair back*

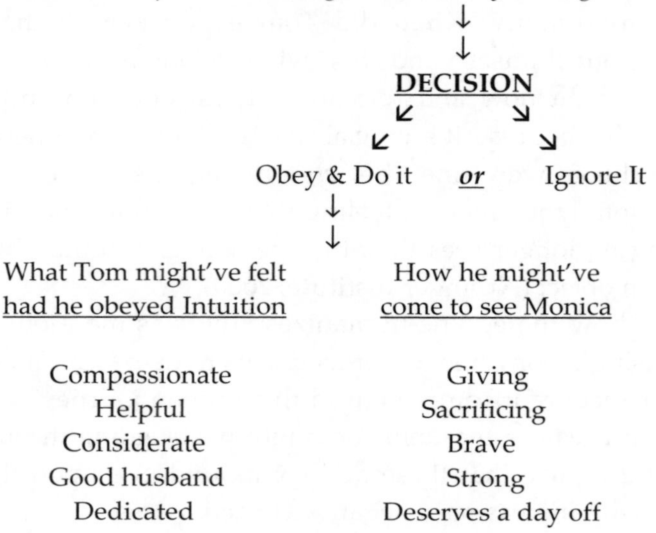

Within us, intuition is continuously whispering ideas of how to serve and be kind to others (and ourselves) in ways that would make life better. Just by following one simple guidance from his Higher Self, Tom would have experienced a profound shift in how he and his wife felt that day. Instead of seeing his wife as an object causing him to be inconvenienced, Tom might have felt the satisfaction that comes from the joy of helping another—especially one you love.

All great masters have said that all answers lie within, and these answers can be directly accessed through development of intuition. It takes time to practice rising above the ego-delusion of the lower self, which is most directly done through spiritual disciplines.

Through higher insight, you recognize people stuck in lower evolutionary states with compassion, instead of anger. You can see they are simply suffering the self-imposed prison of the ego-thinking mind. It is natural and easy to choose not getting angry at the sleepwalker simply for being asleep. This process is called recontextualization, which is an important spiritual technique of the MDB that will be further explained in Chapter Nine.

The Way Out

What lies beyond the thinking mind is the aware mind. It is mostly silent, and is an amazingly powerful creative tool because it operates at maximum efficiency with almost no wasted energy or motion. It is the commitment to AWARENESS that is the first conscious decision you must make. An effective starting point is reached by asking better questions of the Infinite Intelligence, for all the masters say to "ask and ye shall receive." The way out is ascertained by first asking the question, "Who am I?" (Maharshi, 1988).

Later on, this monumental question is often followed by "Why am I here?" Next, "Where am I?" Start with the first question only—it is the proverbial '*Open Sesame*' to the Field.

Buddha said the well-worn adage, "*when the student is ready, the teacher will appear*." As you repeatedly ask these questions, the answer will come in the form of new teachers, opportunities, and internal guidance. You will become aware of the development of what I call the 'Internal Compass.' It is inside of you right now, whether you are aware of it or not. It is your soul—and it is continually receiving guidance from Infinite Intelligence. Through faith, you will be willing to look and see that it is speaking to you even now. Most do not hear it because the mind must reach a certain level of stillness for this intuition to be clearly heard. This is what is meant by the saying, 'still waters run deep.' The still mind allows for the deep guidance of the higher aware mind to be heard. Since the mind is so noisy, it is usually not heard, and therefore most people assume that on the rare occasions they followed intuition, it was only a lucky hunch. This internal compass is always pointing in the direction of your, and others, highest good, and is yours to use by simply asking. All students show their readiness to realize higher evolutionary states by asking better questions. Continually ask this first question. As you do, carefully watch what shows up in, or disappears from, your life—for nothing and no one will be irrelevant. The appearance of this book at this exact time period in your life is the answer to an inner question, for sure.

Upon asking this first great question, the way to proceed opens by showing you *who you are not*. You will begin to see "I have a body, I am not my body." Again, while the body is a great gift, to equate the essence of that which you are as *only the body* is to critically limit your potential. Secondarily, it is important for you to recognize, "I have a mind, but I am not my mind." If you were the mind you would be able to control it and shut it off at will—which you cannot. After many years of meditation I subjectively experienced this great gift. I was having a particularly frustrating meditation, with frequent mental noise and interruption. I was frustrated and annoyed because I felt that with all the practice I'd had up to that point, I should have been able to silence the mind at will. But this day it seemed impossible. In frustration I put my hand on my heart and said, "Thank you God for this gift—show me the lesson!" Sometimes I would do that and nothing would come for days or even weeks, but this time it was instant. The most amazing thing is that it wasn't even guidance; I simply became aware of an obvious truth that had always been present. The awareness was: "you didn't start the mind—and you can't stop the mind. You can't shut your mind off because ***you are not it***."

This is a major turning point in one's soul work. It cannot be merely an intellectual musing. For real growth to occur, it must be subjectively experienced. In other words, as an intellectual concept it is interesting—but as a self-realization it is literally mind-blowing. The 'answers within' are drowned out by the noise of the mind—that is precisely why so few people hear them. When the mind becomes still, the answers that were always there are revealed and heard.

The mind is a great gift—but only when it is harnessed and used properly. Like a controlled fire that is set to burn out harmful, nuisance weeds, but if used improperly, burns out of control and destroys the whole forest, the mind is to be carefully monitored. The power of realizing that you *have* a mind, but *are not* your mind, allows you to create the space in which you learn how to master the mind. This is the purpose of meditation, which is the most thorough means of doing so. The space created in meditation, which I call **the GAP**—**G**od-Self **A**wareness **P**oint—allows 'You' to objectively view thoughts. Then you must selectively and judiciously choose which ones deserve your precious energy. When you cease giving your precious energy to negative thoughts, THEY STOP HAVING POWER OVER YOU. You then learn to transcend the ego-thinking mind, which is the great gift accomplished by all too few.

'You' are a Spirit, living in a body, who has a mind. *You are a Spiritual being having a human experience,* not a human being having a spiritual experience. Again, I am aware this contradicts many other courses that tout the 'powers of the mind' and teach how creative your thinking is. It has been previously explained how and why with certain people these trainings can be effective, but they cannot work if you are stuck in the mental realm—as most readers are. Many religions also fail to raise adherents to a spiritual level because they hide behind the guise of being spiritual, but are mental manipulations *in the name of God* that often lead to unhappiness. If you continue to use the mind to get you out of something 'it' got you into, you're only banging your head against the wall.

This is evident when you are trying to think of something on 'the tip of your tongue,' but the harder you try to think of it, the farther away from your memory it goes. Thinking harder only pushes the answer away. When you're trying to solve a problem by commanding yourself to "Think! Think! Think!," nothing comes. Then, the next day you might be doing a simple chore like walking the dog, and the answer pops into your mind from out of the blue. Notice that thinking often pushes answers away, but releasing oneself from the mental realm of thinking allows you access to the spiritual realm of **Awareness**—where all answers exist right now. This is the revelation I experienced that day in meditation.

Finally, to transcend the ego-thinking mind, it is imperative to recognize the following points:

- I must see that 'I' am not the thinker, the ego is the thinking mind, and that my thoughts don't mean anything.
- I must release the belief that thought is always creative, and that thinking is pleasurable.
- I must release the belief that thoughts are valuable, and that since "I'm thinking them, they must be right."
- I need to see that "I'm never upset for the reasons I think—I'm upset *because* I think."

1. 'I' am not the thinker, the ego is the thinking mind, and that my thoughts don't mean anything.

Reflect back over the past few years to a time when you were driving your car across a really high bridge, having a perfectly normal day with nothing going wrong. You were half way across the bridge when the thought crossed your mind, "You could slip on this bridge, crash through the guardrail, and fall to your death." Have you ever had that thought? (Please stop and think about it.) I bet you have. Where did it come from? You certainly didn't choose to think it. You were having a great day, so why did it happen? It arose from the ego survival animal that is looking for, and often times fantasizing about, any possible way you can be hurt even when there is no actual threat. This situation confirms that the ego is the thinking mind, and you are actually the observer of thoughts. Does that which your ear hears belong to your ear? Does that which the eye sees belong to your eye? Similarly your thoughts do not belong to your mind because your mind is the focal point for thought—but not the thinker—therefore the thoughts cannot be yours.

If you were to continue on with the 'bridge scenario' you'd have just viewed the thought, then made a choice to give it energy or not. If you gave that kind of negative thought your energy, you'd possibly begin to breathe shallowly, experience rapid heartbeat, dry mouth, sweaty palms, and actually begin to panic. This kind of scene is often what happens in panic attacks. If, on the other hand, you simply dismiss the negative thought by saying something out loud like, "That's not going to happen," the thought dissolves instantly.

The thought itself means nothing until you give it energy—only then does it take on meaning.

2. Release the belief that thought is creative, and that thinking is pleasurable.

Thinking is highly over-rated, for it is *conscious choice* that contains the real power. Consciousness is the Unified Field of God, from which all life springs. Consciousness is the Aware Mind.

During short moments of clarity thought can be creative. The problem is due to the unruly nature of the mind in which most automatic thought processes are experienced as disorganized, random and distracting. Given that most readers are seeking to accomplish greater goals in life by reading this material, being confused and distracted is not very conducive to doing so. This is why learning to silence the thinking mind while gaining access to the Aware Mind is of great value. Can you imagine the peace and productivity that is possible from having a still mind?

You must also relinquish the belief that you derive some pleasure from thinking, because for the most part thinking drains—not gains—energy.

Imagine you're having a great night's sleep, but you are awakened by the urge to go to the bathroom. All you want to do is relieve yourself, and resume sleeping, right? So you use the bathroom, go back to bed, and without warning you begin thinking about the next day, or something that is troubling you. Now you can't go back to sleep. That's pleasurable? Intentionally surrendering the desire to think expands the efficacy of the techniques outlined in detail in Chapter Ten, so as to tap into the aware mind.

3. Release the belief that thoughts are valuable, and that since "I'm thinking them, they must be right."

The mind predominantly operates on opinion, speculation,

assumption and supposition. These are fantasies which have no essential reality or value, as they are rooted in guesswork and judgments, not wisdom. Opinion is rarely based upon knowing anything, and is mostly formed when the ego assumes it knows something it has incomplete information about. Ego-delusion uses opinions to gain control and feel superior by arguing a convincingly polarized viewpoint that it has heard about, but has not experienced. To ***know*** anything can only occur from experiencing and/or 'being it'-all else is simply conjecture. To believe one knows 'all about' a topic without experiencing it is a grand error. To know all about Mexico does not make one Mexican.

All the pride-based dualism of the world demands your taking sides and leads to the vanity and positionality of opinion and negative judgments. This feeds the perpetuation of the thinking mind which can rationalize and justify anything to feel more powerful. For the ego to be right, it has to make someone else out to be wrong. The energy boost one feels from offering opinions and judgments satisfies the ego-thinking mind, which then sees itself as special, admired, superior, and worthy of respect. The aware mind *knows*, the ego mind *thinks it knows*.

4. I'm never upset for the reasons I think—I'm upset *because* I think

All pain in life arises from misidentifying with the essential nature of that which you really are. When you erroneously misperceive your Self as the 'thinker', you get sucked into chaos. It has been repeatedly stated in this curriculum that you are the being above the thoughts—who has the ability to look down on them. **You have a mind, but are not your mind—you are existence itself—you are the I AM.** If you really are the spirit (the God-Self) in the body, and if there really are no accidents in the universe, then nothing can ever really go wrong in your life. Do you see this critical Truth?

The ego has a vested interest in keeping the 'thought game' going because the ego, like any animal, does not want to die. The death of the ego is the birth of enlightenment. The way that the ego insures its survival is through thought control over ***you***—*the real being*.

Therefore, the ego constantly needs to be in control and have things go according to its expectations. But when things do not go 'as planned,' what does the ego-thinking mind automatically fire across your screen of consciousness? A series of very painful, fear-based negative thoughts like: *This stinks! I'm so frustrated I could scream. I hate people! I wish I could run that car right off the road! I'm going to give her a piece of my mind! I'm outta here—I quit!* Then it rehashes and exhaustively replays the negative scenario over and over until the point of near-madness.

What is really happening here?

Within each of us, the basic structure of the ego is more or less the same. It is misinformed, self-serving, unloving, vain, and totally attached to viewing itself as morally superior and above all, right. It believes it is the sovereign lord of the universe.

Therefore when something does not go **its** way, the ego blames others, even constructing ludicrous and insanely bizarre mythological scenarios to protect its vanity. It causes emotional pain with its crazy thinking, which it deftly convinces you is a result of some outer cause. It is the ultimate illusionist—waving the left hand to get your undivided attention while the right hand steals your watch.

Since all events somehow occur in accordance with what might be termed ***Divine Will***, when its expectations aren't met the ego is basically telling God: *"you screwed up God. It didn't go my way and I wanted it to—it was supposed to. This event wasn't supposed to go Thy way—it was supposed to go my way."* It creates an inner hell, and in extreme cases it decides to take the whole world to hell with it. (Enron, 9/11, the Third Reich, Jonestown Massacre) The startling truth is that when you fall prey to the ego-thinking mind you are, ultimately, fighting God. This is precisely why the ego has been accurately termed the satanic influence on Earth.

The true cause of all pain in life is the noise created by the ego as it barks negative thoughts as a temper tantrum because it did not get its selfish desires fulfilled. It is the thinking itself that is the greatest source of pain in these instances, not the fact that things didn't go as planned.

You are never upset for the reasons you think, you are upset because you think. Because most people believe their mind to be the basis of existence, there may be fear associated with the idea of transcending it. I can assure you that it is totally safe. You'll lose no memories or acquired wisdom; you'll only lose the fear, doubt and worry that are preventing you from applying this wisdom at a much more meaningful level. Once you recognize that thinking itself is the source of your pain, you will be empowered by the commitment to transcend the ego-thinking mind.

Chapter Eleven

The Differing Aspects of the Ego

The aware mind emerges free and uncluttered when one rises above the thinking mind. This awareness has been referred to by countless geniuses who have reached this level, which is accessible to anyone willing to take the first step. Pro golfer Tiger Woods speaks about clearing his mind before he strikes the ball, having noticed that when he is playing his best, he is not thinking at all. He becomes aware of the shot needed, first imagining it happening perfectly. He then relaxes, and frees his mind, trusting his God-given well-rehearsed swing (Woods, 2001).

The ego is perceived to be only the brash, loud, pushy aspect of people that thinks it is better than others. But that is only one aspect of the ego, which reveals itself in two distinctly different patterns of distortion. The two aspects are the 'masculine' ego and the 'feminine' ego, and everyone has both aspects present to varying degrees.

When people use the word 'ego' in everyday conversations, the meaning refers to the masculine aspect of the ego. It is the self-inflating aspect of the ego which believes it can out-think, out-fight, out-run, out-work, out-earn anyone else. This aspect dominates the mind with thoughts that tell you, "I'm superior to ________." The masculine ego constantly wants adulation, to win, and to be exalted. This quality of the ego is primarily found in men, but can also be dominant in a smaller percentage of women. These women are 'type A' strong-willed people. It is the alpha trait that compels physical intimidation when necessary to assert and prove domination. It also prevails in manipulative mental behavior designed to fulfill hidden agendas. In common vernacular this is called playing 'mind games'. This commonly recognized aspect of ego undermines one's ability to connect to the field, because it doesn't honor or respect anything outside of its own limited self-interest.

One transcends this aspect via conscious humility, which is the last thing the masculine ego wants for itself. Being humble**d** is far different from being humble. Being humble is empowering, and being humbled is painful. Being humble**d** happens as a consequence of the unconscious pride of the ego, while being humble is the act of leading with conscious humility. Conscious humility is an intentional way of being in the world, so that pride doesn't 'kick in' and cause you to fall again and be humbled. This is what Jesus refers to when he says "He who would be exalted will be humbled, he who would be humble will be exalted "(N.T. Matt 23:12).

The 'feminine' aspect of the ego is the self-negating aspect. It undermines joy and success with thoughts that tell you 'I'm not _________ enough.' This distortion is at the core of the massive self-esteem issues that influence so many Americans. It destroys confidence and self-love, insidiously weakening the individual to believe in their dark side while undermining belief in their inherent higher potential. It is predominant in a higher percentage of women, while prevailing in a lesser percentage of men. It is at the core of the victim mentality that is so destructive and pervasive. In this person, Soul Purpose can barely even be believed much less seriously considered. This part of the ego convinces people to become infatuated with playing the victim. What do they get out of it? They get the perverse inner *energy boost* that comes with seeing oneself as the victim. The archetype of the *poor m*e loves to wallow in their victimhood because of the attention and 'inner juice' they derive from playing that bizarre role. This unknown aspect of the ego obviously undermines one's ability to create a higher reality.

Being radically positive transcends the feminine aspect of the ego.

The limitations of the mental realm are predominantly based on these two tendencies of the ego. The way to transcend it to the spiritual realm takes place via the Awareness to choose Radical Positivity with Conscious Humility.

The ultimate in conscious humility is making the Love of Truth more important than the need to 'be right.' The ultimate in radical positivity is making the Love of God more important than the love of thought.

If you choose to experience an enormous spike in consciousness and personal power...

- **MAKE THE LOVE OF GOD MORE IMPORTANT THAN THE LOVE OF THOUGHT**

and

- **MAKE THE LOVE OF TRUTH MORE IMPORTANT THAN THE LOVE OF BEING RIGHT**

Earth School

One of the most painful things about being human is the tendency to repeat the same mistakes over and over. Of course, each time it repeats it becomes more painful. We see this tendency with people who have many relationships, but none work. We see people have many jobs, but none offer satisfaction. This occurs because we must begin to connect the dots, and cease violating Truth Principles.

A simple way to express these truth principles is via the Earth School concept. If the enlightened masters are correct, it appears that we live in a school called Earth. If you take the time to look at life from this perspective, you will see this is an extremely useful truth. Every person and event contains a valuable lesson. All lessons will be repeated until learned. Every time a lesson is ignored as irrelevant, this re-learning process requires the lesson to repeat in a more intense fashion. In other words, every time it has to be re-learned it becomes more painful (Silva, 1977). By the continuous remembrance that you are in Earth School, a miraculous shift will occur in your life. You focus on learning instead of blaming. This is a miraculous breakthrough indeed, and a huge test that must be passed.

As stated earlier, perceived negatives exist in all our lives to wake us up to Higher Possibilities—these negatives are the Lessons. This is precisely why every true teacher recognizes problems as opportunities, for without them you could never grow or evolve. The Law of Synchronicity explains that they happen to all students in an extremely meaningful timing, and serve as a transformational teaching device perfectly designed by the Infinite Intelligence. These lessons are simply part of the curriculum in Earth School, and this is a required course. Free will determines when, not if, one takes the curriculum. Free will does not allow you to write the curriculum—it only exists in relation to the timing, attitude, and persistence you bring to your life (Schucman, 1992). Your life is the classroom.

When you were in college there were certain required courses you had to take within a four year time span. You could choose when, but not if, you took them. If you failed the course, and graduating was the goal, that course had to be repeated. In a more random fashion, Earth School operates similarly. The Earth School curriculum contains several key components which are revealed throughout this book, and when successfully completed, may result in Enlightenment. If you apply any of them, they most certainly will result in greater happiness.

Because most people are in ego-delusion, they ignore the lessons as irrelevant, choosing to instead take the negative situation as a personal insult. Hence, most human beings walk around on the defense, just looking for reasons to be offended. This causes them to blame, instead of learn. The lesson must then be repeated, and the student unknowingly destines himself to the merry-go-round of painful repeat performance mistakes. As this continues throughout life, he eventually becomes resigned to his fate of playing small, wondering why others experience prosperity and joy but not him.

The ego is causing the pain, while very convincingly projecting that the source of the pain is due to forces outside of us. 'Sane' people take the pain caused by ego-delusion and internalize it, but in doing so destroy inner joy and belief in themselves. (This equates to being trapped in the Mental Realm which has been previously discussed.) 'Insane' people take the pain caused by ego-delusion and externalize it onto others, feeling justified in destroying others' lives, because misery loves company.

This syndrome is at root of the scarcity belief system most people live by—a paradigm that holds the Earth and her inhabitants in a state of war-like misery. If one were in a war zone in which the idea is sheer survival, to abide by the scarcity paradigm would be wise. If, however, one is living in an area where physically surviving is not threatened but thriving is the goal, it will greatly expand your life success to implement the Prosperity Paradigm.

On Earth, as it is in any other school, to advance on to the next grade you must pass tests. It was like this for all of us in middle and high school, and college—to prove that you knew the given course knowledge you had to pass the exam. This is an ancient model created by enlightened teachers who, recognizing Earth as a kind of school, used this model as the prototype for modern academia of today.

Learning the Source of True Happiness

It only makes sense that if you want to learn to speak French, you go to French class, to learn business you take business classes, and to learn joy and success, you must study joy and success. Joy and success are feelings, and as such are non-linear. Human beings live in a linear world, so this presents a problem. How do I experience that which is non-linear in the world of the linear? The quandary is that you cannot *own* joy, success, satisfaction, or fulfillment because they are intangible feelings.

I was sharing this concept with a wealthy client recently and he said, "You're wrong—my Mercedes brings me joy and makes me feel successful." I said,"Really? If you went out to the parking lot right now and found a huge dent in your driver's side door how happy would you be with your Mercedes? "He said thoughtfully, "I guess I'd be miserable and upset." It's not tangible things that bring you happiness, it's the specific meaning *you give* to those things.

When you re-examine, then re-create your core beliefs, you get the magnificent opportunity to give greater meaning to the things you choose to be.

By re-creating the greatest, highest, and most magnificent beliefs as to who You Now Choose To Be, you can live a life of prosperity.

If you cannot own joy and success because they are non-linear, how do you bring them into the linear world? Spiritual work. The MDB is on a spiritual quest—that is his mission—to make the world a better place for his having been here. Instead of blaming others, he takes responsibility for all things existing in his life. He learns from every negative, and by doing so rarely repeats the mistake. He then takes the valuable lesson he learned and files it away as a success tool to be used whenever a similar situation arises that caused the lesson to be learned in the first place. As one repeats this crucial success habit, the different 'tools and skills' he acquires go with him for the rest of his life. By doing so, the MDB never stops growing and learning—and most importantly achieving greater victories in the process of doing so. Ask any successful business person and they will tell you that learning from mistakes is critical to one's evolution. This is a huge test—which repeatedly comes up in the business world—that the MDB passes each time it arises. When you learn instead of blame, you will also pave the way to live in greater peace, joy, and true wealth.

Adding the earth school idea to the Prosperity Paradigm can be simply outlined as follows:

1.) We live in a school called Earth.
2.) Every person and event contains a valuable lesson.
3.) The greatest lesson we came to learn is choosing love over fear, especially when we don't feel like it.
4.) A lesson will be repeated until learned.
5.) Every time a lesson needs to be re-learned it becomes more painful.
6.) By learning from a perceived negative, we instantly transform it into a positive lesson.
7.) This is a required course based on the Golden Rule—and free will only determines when, not if, you take it.

The Golden Rule is an ancient gem of wisdom that is included in every central text of the world's most well-known religions:

Christianity *Whatever you wish for men to do for you, do likewise also for them; for this is the law and the prophets.*
Matthew 7:12

Buddhism *Hurt not others in ways that you yourself would find hurtful.*
Udana-Varga 5,1

Hinduism *This is the sum of duty: do naught onto others what you would not have them do unto you.*
Mahabharata 5,1517

Confucianism *Do not do to others what you would not like yourself. Then there will be no resentment against you, either in the family or in the state.*
Analects 12:2

Islam *No one of you is a believer until he desires for his brother that which he desires for himself.*
Sunnah 40 Hadith of an-Nawawi 13

Zoroastrianism *That nature alone is good which refrains from doing (to) another whatsoever is not good for itself.*
Dadisten-I-dinik, 94,5

Judaism *What is hateful to you, do not do to your fellowman. This is the entire Law; all the rest is commentary.*
Talmud, Shabbat 3id

Taoism *Regard your neighbor's gain as your gain, and your neighbor's loss as your own loss.*
Tai Shang Kan Yin P'ien

The essence of the Golden Rule operates because it is a scientific fact based upon the Law of Vibration and Attraction. Remember that the energy you vibrate out into the world with your thoughts, words, and actions is instantly attracted back to you. When you vibrate goodness, you attract good people and events—if you vibrate nastiness, you attract nasty people and events. Every kindergartner is taught this Golden Rule, and knows it to be true—so why don't we use this in our lives consistently? Because we are conditioned to believe that when our expectations and goals are not fulfilled, the normal reaction should be one of anger, frustration, and disappointment.

Now—think through this next concept very carefully—because this behavior is so detrimental to achieving new goals in your life. When you set your sights on a specific goal being accomplished in a specific time frame, but it does not happen, you have been conditioned to emanate what kind of energy? Negative, right? But if the Law of Vibration and Attraction is true, and you are vibrating negative energy, what are you attracting back to you? More negative people and situations. Does the extra negativity that you then create help you accomplish the original goal? Of course not! This behavior only produces more resistance and difficulty.

Embracing the Earth School belief system will teach you to view negatives as lessons. This great shift in behavior then allows you to emanate positive energy in the face of a negative. It attracts ***positive people and events*** to you to help you solve the problem. At first glance this may appear to be a small point, but making this new pattern a habit is absolutely crucial to becoming happier and increasing the likelihood of success.

Non-Attachment

Of all the spiritual disciplines that I've taught people throughout the years, this is the one that students have received the most benefit from practicing. It is as surprisingly unknown or misunderstood, as it is valuable. It is misunderstood by being thought of as indifference. Non-attachment is precisely the opposite.

Almost all pain in life comes from unfulfilled expectations, and expectations are attachments. Forming attachments to things going 'my way' is a major limiting belief/teaching contained in the cultural rulebook of scarcity consciousness. Attachments cause tremendous suffering. It is a learned phenomenon that, when unlearned, frees up a vast amounts of power, time and energy.

Attachments ultimately turn into **addictions**, for in truth, they are one and the same thing. "I'm attached" is a nice way of minimizing a deeper truth which is this—*"if things don't turn out the way I expect them to, I'm going to give myself permission to freak out!"* Expectation turns into attachment, which then turns into an addiction. Most everyone in the world is struggling with addiction in one form or another—to things like money, power, sex, food, control, alcohol, drugs, being right—the list goes on and on. Addiction is an enormously damaging habit that is the root of so much pain, and overcoming it is a big test in this curriculum. Non-attachment is the spiritual discipline that can heal this pain.

We all have this habitual need for things to go our way, to be right, for events to occur in a specific timing, and we form these attachments in an inner hidden way. Most of the time, people aren't even aware they've formed an attachment to something. **Addictions/attachments occur when we make our happiness dependent on something outside of us**. Practicing non-attachment is the way to unlearn this limiting belief. Non-attachment teaches us how to make happiness an 'inside job.'

Non-Attachment is the ultimate form of caring, in which you consciously free yourself from outside forces beyond your control that are weakening and draining you. It is a practice that takes discipline and awareness, and it is often misconstrued by people to mean indifference. This is the furthest thing from the truth. Figure 1 will be helpful in understanding this point more clearly.

Figure 1

The Scale of Caring

-10	**0**	**+10**
Indifference	**Caring**	**Non-Attachment**

In Figure 1, the emotion of caring is the zero-point—it is our baseline. Indifference is the ultimate form of not caring about people and things. It is the calculating coldness of the killer, rapist, or thief—and is the core emotion of the criminal mind. Thus, it is minus ten on our imaginary 'Scale of Caring.'

When we care ***too much*** about someone or something, we create a negative tension that transmits an energy signal which attracts the worst negative scenario directly to you. The husband who is so attached to his wife becomes intensely jealous and mistrusting, *which causes her to no longer want to be around him.* He doesn't realize it, but he drove her away. The salesperson who wants the sale so badly that his demeanor becomes anxious and 'red-hot' for the client to buy does the same thing. He makes the client uneasy and suspicious, actually *preventing* the sale from occurring. He can't see it, but his desire/need for money pushed the sale away from him. The athlete freezes under the pressure of playing in the championship, because he is so attached to winning that it weakens him, making him ineffective in his biggest game. When good, caring people become attached to an external thing or event to make them happy, they unknowingly push the desired reality away!

Non-Attachment is a plus ten on our 'Scale of Caring.' Again, it is the ultimate form of caring, in which you consciously free yourself from outside forces beyond your control that are weakening and draining you.

Let us observe what the three great masters of Truth say about this powerful idea:

"...let those who have wives be as though they had none—and those who weep, as though they had not wept, and those who rejoice as though they had not rejoiced, and those that buy (act) as though they did not possess anything. And those who make use of this world should not abuse it, for the fashion of this world is passing away"
- Teachings of Jesus Christ (I Cor.7:29-31)

"Let us live in joy, never afraid among those who are selfishly attached. Let us live in freedom even among those who are bound by selfish attachments. Selfish attachment brings suffering: selfish attachment brings fear. Be non-attached, and you will be free from suffering and fear."
- Buddha (Dhammapada 199, 212)

Perform work in this world with Self-awareness and without selfish attachments—alike in success and defeat. Seek refuge in the attitude of non-attachment and you will amass the wealth of spiritual awareness. Those who are motivated only by the fruits of action are miserable about the results of what they do."
- Krishna (Bhagavad Gita 2:48-49)

All three are very clear—be a person of action in this world but do not attach to external things, people, or events as the sole source of your happiness. Whether weeping or rejoicing, successful or not successful, staying non-attached allows you to live in joy, free from fear and suffering.

The first step to implement this practice is to realize the Truth—that your desire/need for a certain outcome forms the attachment that results in pain. Secondarily, you must replace that desire/need to control the outcome with the realization that you cannot control any outcome. Can I control whether you read the rest of this book? Can I control if you use any of the tools given to help you become happier and wealthier? I can't control anything that you, or any other person or thing in this world, does. To you sales people reading this: When making prospecting calls, can you control what the prospect does? Can you make them meet with you? Can you make them believe you? Can you make them show up on time for an appointment? Can you make them buy? Can you make them pay you? Can you make them give you referrals? No, no, no, no, no, and NO!!! You can barely control what YOU do—how could you possibly control what someone else does? Control is a total illusion.

All you can do is create **"favorable conditions"** for something to occur. The greatest sales people in the world are the best at creating favorable conditions for their clients to buy. The greatest athletes create favorable conditions to win the big game. The greatest teachers create favorable conditions for students to learn. Non-attachment conserves the energy one exerts by being attached/addicted, so the extra power they re-capture can then be used to create the utmost favorable conditions for life success.

This is the truth behind why goal setting works only to a certain point, but often becomes an impediment for you to take your business/life to the next level. At the beginning of one's career, goal-setting gave you a 'track to run on,' acting as the treasure map to get from point A to point B. Back then, by using goal setting as an empowering belief, you reached the goal and you felt great. But as time went on, and you were taught to always set higher goals, you began not reaching them, right? Then the pain kicked in, you began to 'force' your business, and goals became attachments, and therefore painful. Goal setting is beneficial when moving from the realm of the physical to the realm of the mental. But most readers of a book like this are stuck in the mental realm, where goals have become debilitating. To take it to the next level we must transform your goals into ***preferences***. Non-attachment teaches us to use preferences as Spiritual Focal Points. Replacing goals with preferences allows you to focus power only on that which you *can* control, instead of wasting power on things beyond your control.

Non-attachment teaches you to recognize those things that are beyond your control before they cause you pain, and to instead focus your attention and power only on that which you can control. This is the essence of the message contained in the world-famous poem The Serenity Prayer, which has become a mantra to those who are in the highly successful program known as Alcoholics Anonymous:

> God grant me the serenity
> to accept the things I cannot change;
> courage to change the things I can;
> and wisdom to know the difference.
> —*Reinhold Niebuhr*

Reviewing these steps in sequence can be helpful.

<u>Steps to Practice Non-Attachment</u>
1.) **Drop the need to Control:** Recognize that the need to control outcomes forms attachments, which always result in suffering if the expected outcome goes unfulfilled.
2.) **Realize Happiness is an Inside Job:** Remember that control is an illusion, that by making my happiness conditional upon external things, I set myself up for pain.
3.) **Control the Controllables:** As best possible in all situations, be clear about that which is beyond my control, and focus all efforts only on that which I can control, to create favorable conditions.
4.) **Drop Wanting, Focus on Preferring**—Know that you create the utmost favorable conditions only by replacing *needs, wants,* and *desires* with **<u>preference</u>, choices, and creative actions.**

Preferences are **spiritual focal points** that allow for a plan of action without the pain of attachment. This allows for the acceptance of whatever God brings us to be understood and accepted as being for the highest good of all concerned.

Recontextualization

No truth exists without context being clearly set. Things, people, and ideas all constitute that which we call *content*—while situation, setting and intention creates *context.* Recontextualization is another spiritual discipline that few people know of. It is intentionally shifting the context of any perceived negative event, so that by seeing it as a lesson, you are empowered rather than weakened. The amazing thing is that regardless of however dire the content is, you have the ability to shift the context at any time you choose. By doing so, any negative event can be seen and experienced in a higher light so that one never loses their inner peace

Author Steven Covey was on an early morning subway train in New York City. There were very few people in the car at that early hour, where he sat quietly while others read or dozed. At one stop, a father and his sons boarded the train. The boys proceeded to destroy any semblance of tranquility through their wild behavior, while the father sat in a trance-like state seemingly oblivious to anything they were doing. Everyone in the subway car was annoyed and, as if speaking for the all the passengers, Covey could no longer stay silent. Trying to mask the resentment he felt he said, "Sir, your children are really disturbing a lot of people. I wonder if you couldn't control them a little more?" As if slowly snapping out of a trance the man said, "Oh, you're right—I'm sorry. We just came from the hospital where their mother died, and I guess we don't know how to handle it."

The justified resentment Covey felt the second before instantly melted in the realization of the context of why the man was lax and spaced out. Now Covey could truly *understand*—and instantly recontextualized the whole scenario. Feelings of sympathy and compassion overflowed as he asked the man,"Your wife just died? Oh, I'm so sorry! Can you tell me about it? Is there anything I can do?"

* * *

The great understanding one gains by making a habit out of practicing recontextualization is this:

True understanding is realizing that hostility and resentment are never justified.

People are always doing the very best they can, with what they have, given the conditions of their life. No one ever does anything inappropriate given their model of the world. When someone's behavior is aberrant, by leading with understanding we can *shift the context* from one in which we feel justified resentment, to one in which we instead realize, "though I could do better, *this is simply the best* ***they*** *can do.*"

Recontextualization is a paradigm shift from fear mode to love mode. By doing so, we see people's behavior as the best they can do at any given time. We are then spared the suffering of complaining, blaming, and stressing out over a situation that can only be made worse by adding our negativity to it. In making our own paradigm shift, we set the miraculous precedent that then makes it possible for others to follow in our footsteps.

Remember, no truth exists without context being firmly set. In the story above, the behavior of the father and sons served as *the content*. Covey's initial annoyance was the result of a misunderstanding of ***the context***. Once he understood the true context, compassion flowed freely. By going out of our way to show other people compassion and understanding, we can go through any negative situation peacefully. We can't control the content of any situation, yet the power lies in our ever-present ability to change the context. When the content is something we do not prefer, shifting the context allows us to stay peaceful and powerful. This shift is called recontextualization.

Chapter Twelve

Internalizing Prosperity via A.P.R.I.L.

This chapter reveals how to delete old programming and replace it with the Prosperity Paradigm by applying a series of spiritual disciplines. This process can be easily remembered by using the acronym A.P.R.I.L., which stands for:

A -Awareness Commitment
P -Pattern Interruption
R -Reality Statement
I - Instant Prayer
L -Love Meditation

Awareness is the always the starting point.

You simply cannot change that which you are unaware of, therefore awareness is key. Imagine being pulled over by a police officer while driving, having no idea why you were stopped. He says "Do you know why I pulled you over," and you say, "No, why?" He asks you, "Did you know that your left tail light is out?" When you honestly respond, "No officer, I had no idea," he lets you go with a warning to fix it as soon as possible. Why? He knows you can never fix what you are unaware is broken.

There are four levels of Awareness:

Level Four—**<u>Unconscious Incompetent</u>** ***(no growth possible)***

The unconscious incompetent is totally asleep to the truth about life on Earth. He *doesn't know* (unconscious) that he is *ignorant* (incompetent). At this level growth is not possible. He also doesn't know that he worships his ego as the sovereign lord of the universe. He secretly believes his view of the world is always correct, and that everyone else is to blame for the inner pain he experiences. (Either the greatest saviors, saints, and geniuses [whose message is essentially the same] in history are correct, or the ego is correct—but both cannot be correct.) This person cannot be helped or coached until the ego guidance he follows causes the required amount of suffering. The Infinite Intelligence always allows him to then glimpse the truth at the moment of greatest suffering—and that truth is the realization that *he himself* is the problem. If he can transcend the ego at that moment to admit this TRUTH, the Holy Spirit raises him to level three of Awareness. If not, his life continues to get worse.

Level Three—**<u>Conscious Incompetent</u>** ***(growth now possible)***

By simply admitting 'I don't know, but I'm open to learn', a profound shift occurs. The most telling shift is in humility, for *he knows* (conscious) that *he doesn't know* (incompetent). It is at this level that 'the student is ready', and right on cue, 'the teacher appears.' Personal development programs as well as spiritual paths spring forth in perfect harmony with the will of the Divine and the individual's karmic merit. He has surrendered to a Higher Power, which is the first step to breaking free from the torture he felt at the previous level. This is a great breakthrough, for it is here that true soul work begins. The increase in awareness frees the individual to evolve, learn, and grow.

Level Two—**<u>Unconscious Competent</u>** ***(growing)***

As one develops the success behaviors and spiritual disciplines into daily habits, this level is often attained without the person even realizing it. With his eye thoroughly fixed on the mission, he is not fully aware (unconscious) of the heights he is climbing and the success path he is paving (competent). Humility and non-attachment have forged a new inner being to the degree that he doesn't even know that he is no longer the student, but is now the teacher. The term 'unconscious' is appropriate because despite the obvious growth, this being is still vulnerable to pride, and intermittent backsliding into fear and doubt because of it. This pitfall can recur if he takes sole credit for the success without internally—and in the right context, externally—acknowledging the Higher Power. It is also at this stage of awareness that immense growth can occur if one has the great blessing of aligning with an advanced teacher.

Level One—**Conscious Competent** ***(helping others grow)***

This being is more than a teacher; he is the rare advanced teacher who is in Love Mode (Chapter Three). This is a higher mind state of constant awareness (consciousness), in which the Divine uses his body as a conduit of truth (competent). The personal will has been surrendered and his life has been dedicated to the service of God.

Awareness Commitment

The doorway to the spiritual realm is awareness. Awareness begins with the commitment to turn your senses inward to look within at all inner conversations. As has been previously mentioned, these conversations arise unsolicited, and have been referred to as the 'ego-thinking mind.' This is an important function of consciousness, because without the ego-self, the God-Self cannot be experienced. So the ego plays a necessary role in evolution and creation, and is not to be demonized or condemned. We must simply become aware of it, and begin to view it as the inner pet that it is.

For any of you who love dogs, the following analogy can help further explain. Once in a while your dog gets sick, and vomits or defecates on your favorite carpet or floor because the poor thing just can't help it. Do you kick and beat the dog? No. Though it is frustrating to have to clean the mess, you love and nurture your pet back to health as best possible.

Similarly, the ego is an inner pet that is not meant to be vilified and beaten. It is the inner animal (reptilian brain) programmed only for flight or fight—therefore by fighting it, you are nurturing it to grow stronger. Doing this is simply using ego to attack the ego, which merely reinforces it. Trying to conquer the ego by fighting it is like attempting to extinguish a fire by throwing gasoline on it.

Awareness teaches us to observe the ego as an inner pet that is sick and in need of nurturing and love. Instead of being endlessly pushed around by thoughts, instincts, and impulses, awareness trains you to become the Observer/Chooser. As you become more aware, you will begin to notice an endless stream of thoughts, fantasies, projections, assumptions, suppositions, opinions, speculations and meaningless banter.

The mind is like an inner TV with hundreds of stations vying for your attention, that you will come to observe as mildly entertaining, but mostly pedestrian and trite. Taking nothing personally, practice watching with a keen non-attached eye. You will learn to sift through the mind's fear-based commercials, horror shows, victimizing passion plays, and banal inner situation comedies. Just like you switch off the TV when you're bored or it's time to sleep, you learn to *switch off* giving your energy and power to the negativity of the ego's thoughts.

At this beginning point, you are learning to observe the fear, doubt, and worry continuously churned out by the ego—without taking it seriously or personally. It is not you, it is simply your inner pet barking and puking in your head. Without getting angry or taking it personally, you will learn to *catch it* at its game, and eventually experience the power surge that comes from transcending it. Once you no longer allow fear-based thoughts to zap your energy, you will have a greater energy reservoir to draw from. You then channel this higher creativity into the positive empowering ideas that were always there, obstructed by the clouds of ego. Once you remove the clouds, the sun of empowering ideas is always shining.

This leads to the increased consciousness referred to in the second chapter of this book, and it starts with the Awareness

Commitment. Again, with an increase in consciousness, the Field gives you more power. As you emanate more power into your external environment, the people around you react favorably as they feel the magnetic love energy coming through you from the Field. Many will be internally guided to participate in whatever value you are offering, provided it is for the Highest Good of All Concerned.

Make yourself a promise to take none of these observations personally, because doing this work will absolutely bring out the ego virus so it can be healed once and for all.

Therefore, a word of caution to the serious seeker who intends on using this Knowledge diligently. **When you declare your existence to be a life based in 'love,' all that is 'not love' rises up to be healed and eliminated. A lifetime of fear, doubt, worry, and limiting beliefs begin to arise out of the subconscious mind where they lay buried. As they surface from the subconscious mind into your conscious awareness, the truth is momentarily overwhelming. The ugliness of the inner reptile can be frightening and depressing, which is exactly why spiritual work is difficult. In fact, most people quit spiritual work for this very reason: it brings out all the flotsam and jetsam of being human. <u>This is normal—so stay the course!</u>** This phase will pass fairly quickly, and will be replaced by higher connection to the Field.

Observing a pragmatic scenario of how a higher awareness commitment works, specifically in business, can be helpful.

Figure 1

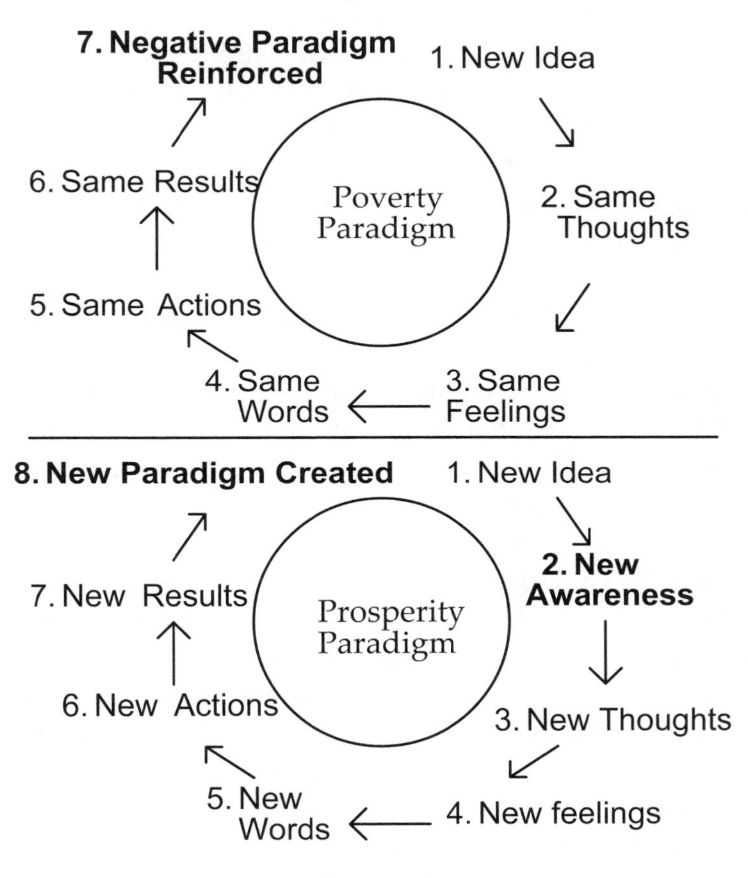

Figure 2

Imagine that you came up with a new idea about marketing your business in a way that will create a great service and huge potential revenue. In **Figure 1**, this exciting new idea (1) is processed through one's current awareness, which contains limiting beliefs, habits, and mindsets. The engine of your mind's existing paradigm takes off and runs, initiating a series of thoughts. This same thinking (2), which is habitually fear-based, creates the same old feelings. The feelings (3) are typically frustration, entanglement, disappointment, and fatigue. They drain you, depleting the joy and strength you had previously felt about actualizing the new idea. These feelings affect your words (4) and actions (5), limiting your performance, often manifesting as the same old result (6). This result is the same one you always got, and is probably not realization of the new idea. Unfortunately the negative paradigm, that actually stored and gave rise to the limiting beliefs, is then reinforced as being true (7). This is insidious, because the next time a great idea arises, the same negative paradigm fires in your mind saying, "don't bother, it'll never work." This is the anatomy of the death of one's dream, and exactly how hope dies.

Now observe **Figure 2**. The exciting new idea (1) is processed through a new level of super-conscious awareness (2), releasing a flood of new creative thoughts (3) into your realm of possibility. Instead of draining the initial joy and strength you felt, they raise your power another notch higher as you are enthused by the power of the Field. These new thoughts inspire new feelings of courage and inspiration (4) which compel you to take new action. You begin to speak (5) and behave (6) differently, and your internal energy level again increases. Your activity and performance is more focused, to the point, and emanating a higher frequency. These new actions (6) then actualize as a NEW RESULT (7). Most importantly, this new result verifies your belief in yourself, and you internally construct a new paradigm (8) which motivates you to repeat successful behavior over and over again.

Awareness is recognizing yourself in a higher way; not as the body, and definitely not as the mind, but instead as the observer/chooser of your thoughts. You are observing good and bad thoughts as if they are not yours, from a non-attached position above the fray. Imagine you're standing on a bridge carefully watching a river pass beneath you. You see beautiful things (flowers) and disgusting things (dead bloated fish), but none of it is allowed to ruin the happiness of the moment. The thought-stream flows similarly. It contains beautiful and disgusting thoughts. The disgusting thoughts are fear-based, and the beautiful thoughts are love-based.

You, as the observer/chooser, must see the fear thoughts and surrender them to God as they arise. If you do not, you will give these thoughts your energy and fear will continue to destroy prosperity and happiness in your life. These thoughts will continually arise over and over until you finally do surrender them.

Choose to give your precious power only to love-based strong force attractor thoughts, and soul purpose will be revealed with greater joy and potential wealth as the result.

Pattern Interrupt

Being aware of negativity is oftentimes enough to help you change it, and you are able to follow through with some positive behavior. Despite this, there are certain times when awareness of the negativity is not enough to heal or transcend it. This is when using the second technique called Pattern Interrupt becomes important. This technique helps you, in those really difficult times, to break the bondage of fear perpetrated by the ego.

Pattern Interrupt is a word, phrase, or action that is performed in a moment when the temporary illusion of fear is causing anxiety to dominate your life. Pattern Interrupt words or phrases work most effectively when they are spoken out loud, except when to do so is socially inappropriate or might cause another harm.

It has often been said that insanity is doing the same thing in the same way over and over, but expecting a different result (Robbins, 1991). Pattern Interrupt will help you shatter the old paradigm's grip on you. This will free you to create a new result in your life. What negative patterns must be broken through for you to go higher in life? Here are some examples:

Use PATTERN INTERRUPT to eliminate old feelings of:

Fear, doubt, worry, suspicion, envy, jealousy, greed, defeatism, racism, intolerance, anger, rationalizing, blaming, vengeance, resentment, cruelty, hatred, lust

Use PATTERN INTERRUPT to eliminate Limiting Beliefs like…

I can't do it
I don't have what it takes to succeed
My personality and habits are unchangeable
Money is a necessary evil
Wealthy people think they're better than others
The more money you have, the more stress you get
I come from fat people—I'll always be fat
My gene pool determined my fate and I'm stuck with it
My life path is set in stone and I'm helpless to change it
I'm unhappy because of my parents/family
I'm not smart enough
I'm not good-looking enough
I'm not educated enough
I'll never recover from _______ (death of loved one, traumatic event, illness, etc.)
I use fear to motivate me, why would I want to get rid of it?

How does the concept of pattern interrupt work? With your new-found commitment to awareness, you are going to observe many inner negative thoughts, beliefs and mindsets. Though they have probably been a part of your psyche for quite a while, you will just be discovering *what was always there* undermining your efforts for years. The moment you hear them, you must say the pattern interrupt word out loud immediately (Skinner, 1953). Below are highly successful examples of pattern interrupts:

Suggested Pattern Interrupt Words/Phrases

Stop
Next
Switch
No way
Reverse
Back Up
I Can Handle It
Not Me, Not Now
Thanks for Sharing
Control, Alt, Delete
Cancel Error Thought
What would Love do now?
Remember God—Choose Love—Create Value

Now imagine a scenario where fear is dominating your mind, and you become aware of it. If the word STOP were your chosen pattern interrupt, you must instantly say **STOP!** out loud immediately. If you work in an office where it is impractical and/or unacceptable to be shouting out loud every few hours, a pattern interrupt action may be more practical. Below are examples of pattern interrupt actions:

Suggested Pattern Interrupt Actions

Wearing a Prosperity Paradigm bracelet on your wrist & snapping it
Carrying and staring at a family picture for five seconds
Tapping your temple three times
Internally counting to ten slowly
Taking the three deepest breaths imaginable
Holding an object that has special meaning, ie. necklace, photo, crucifix, ring
Repeating your pattern interrupt word internally ten times slowly

Using pattern interrupt reinforces a higher knowledge that

things are ok, and that you are in the process of making meaningful changes that others before you have used to create joy and success. It has the immediate scientifically observable effect of changing neuron activity—first in your brain, then in your body, and ultimately in your personal energy field.

Once a thought is given energy, it then creates a feeling, and this feeling causes informational chemical messengers to flow throughout almost every cell in your body. These messengers either heal and inspire (loving strong-force)—like interleukin-1 and endorphins—or stress and drain you (fearful weak-force)—like adrenalin and cortisol. Using pattern interrupt has the effect of increasing ***measurable power* in the form of chemical information messengers** which enable you to go beyond old self-imposed boundaries into the Prosperity Paradigm (Pert, 1997).

Reality Statement

Whether you realize it or not, people are always setting favorable conditions for creating their own reality. Most people think, believe, speak and act as if they cannot do so, and this negative paradigm manifests as their reality. This is because the natural laws continuously concentrate and expand your choices, words, and actions into reality. We are going to apply this truth for your highest good right now. We do so by marshalling all of the natural laws into one technique that will change your life magnificently when/if you use it. This technique is called a Reality Statement.

A reality statement is a series of words, usually five to seven sentences long. This reality statement must be extremely positive, written in the first person, (I am, I know, I choose, I create), and always in the present tense. Phrases like—I will, I might, I could, would, or should—*can* ***not*** *be in a reality statement*. Everything must be written in the NOW—even (and especially) if it's a goal that you have had a hard time believing can happen. The lack of belief **is** the bad habit that must be dissolved, so that a new reality can become impregnated in the subconscious mind.

Your statement must be said out loud a minimum of three times a day for a full fifty-two days. You cannot say it too much, but three times each day is the minimum. The Reality Statement is said for fifty-two days straight because it takes twenty-two reversals of a habit to break a habit, then thirty more implementations of a new habit to make it a reality in the subconscious mind.

To better understand how this works, let's take the habit of smoking cigarettes. Smokers have a little chemical messenger in their brain called a nicotinic 'receptor,' which non-smokers do not have. We're not born with this receptor; it develops through the repetition of habitual smoking. After a smoker has been awake for a short period of time, this little chemical messenger 'fires.' The smoker receives this firing as the thought, "I think I'll have a cigarette," and they light up. The nicotine receptor fires after each meal, it fires when they get in the car, it fires after sex, and it fires more than normal during high alcohol consumption times. When two addictive habits collide, they often reinforce and multiply each other's negative effects.

If a smoker stops smoking for twenty-two days, something extraordinary can occur. Right around the twenty-second day, the 'receptor' begins to disappear. It dissolves into the nothingness from whence it came. The smoker is not free from the habit yet. He has broken the old habit, but he has yet to create the *new habit*, which is equally important. The new habit must be input for the ensuing thirty days to truly become a locked-in pattern. Without a new habit, people revert back to their old, long-standing patterns all too easily. Saying the reality statement for twenty-two days breaks the habit, and continuing to say it for the next thirty days creates the new pattern as a habit. So, to fully modify an old pattern, a new paradigm must be reinforced for a minimum of fifty-two days. This is what a reality statement does.

It is like a prescription. If you have an ear infection and the doctor says take three pills a day for a certain number of days—and you don't do it—you can't be surprised if the infection lingers. This is your success prescription. If you don't do it you can't be surprised when fear and failure linger.

Some people who have worked with affirmations think this is the same technology—it is not. Affirmations are a *mental* exercise, reality statements are a ***spiritual*** discipline. They are created from the highest realm—that of the spiritual—to awaken the God-Self, which is the infinite power in the universe. This is why each statement begins with the phrase, "Thank you God for..." Because every thing you need to be happiest, healthiest, and wealthiest is evenly present and available right now, this phrase acts like a vibrational bridge to connect you to it—providing it is for the Highest Good of All.

It is a physics fact that in one cubic centimeter of empty space there is more latent energy than in all the matter in the universe combined (Bohm, 1980). This is evidence of the infinite power of the Field. **The reality statement combines Intention with Conscious Choice and, using the magnetic power of the Spoken Word, creates favorable conditions to manifest the latent potential from the Field into actualization.** That last sentence may require a leap of faith to accept, but I promise you will come to know it as an experienced truth when you say the reality statement.

An important disclaimer: reality statements cannot be used to manipulate the lives or actions of other people; they can only pertain to your life. It is against Spiritual Law to try to do so, and violating this principle can have negatives consequences.

The reality statement engages all the Natural Laws that were previously discussed. For reference, they are:

1. Law of Vibration and Attraction: Humans constantly emanate energy via thoughts, words, and actions—whatever energy I 'vibrate,' I instantly 'attract' people and events in harmony with that dominant vibration.

2. Law of Creation—I create favorable conditions for reality to actualize. Reality is created through my choices, words, and actions.

3. Law of Responsibility: I am 100% responsible for every aspect of my life.

4. Law of Repetition: Repetition of an action or a statement firmly ingrains it as a habit in the subconscious mind.

5.Law of Attention: A. Energy follows attention. B. The only thing that can grow in my life is that which I give attention to.

6.Law of Synchronicity: There are no accidents, all events are important lessons happening in a meaningful timing.

Through faithful repetition of the statement (Law 4), you are creating a new reality (Law 2) by vibrating, then attracting (Law 1), greater success. Success is synchronous, not accidental (Law 6), and is the result of taking total responsibility (Law 3) to align your attention (Law 5) with strong-force attractors.

This specific reality statement has been used thousands of times by various students with highly beneficial results.

REALITY STATEMENT

I AM now connected to the only true source of Infinite Prosperity—**GOD**, the essence of All That Is. Thank you God for raising my awareness to see the abundant opportunities that are all around me right now. This awareness bestows new vision upon me. This new vision empowers me beyond old fear, doubt, and worry to create a new life of Financial Freedom. I no longer allow any person, thought or event to steal my joy from me. If ever I feel fear, I instantly put my hand on my heart and say, I REMEMBER GOD, CHOOSE LOVE, and CREATE VALUE. Love itself now eliminates all forces that once weakened me. Prosperity Consciousness inspires me to focus solely on creating value for others. Through this value creation, limitless abundance flows to me in the form of money. This reality now manifests in harmony with Thy Will for me, Amen.

Again, this statement works best when said aloud three times a day for a full fifty-two days. Typically the first week of saying the reality statement is joyous, empowering and fairly easy. This is because the excitement of doing something new and fresh inspires you to consistently repeat it. The second week becomes more difficult, as the newness wears away. By the third week, it becomes painful and difficult to continue saying, and here's why. Old paradigms do not go down without kicking and screaming. This is another aspect of the ego—it does not want to die, and therefore cleverly convinces you to give up on doing that which threatens its survival. Much like a trapped rat that leaps at your throat, the ego's old habits and paradigms will attack to survive. Saying this reality statement represents the beginning of its demise. How does the ego attack? By encouraging you to revert back to your old habits.

Think about a poor child who is suffering abuse from its mother. When the authorities finally arrive to take the child to safety, the child cries, kicks, and screams for its mother. Though the authorities' actions are clearly for the sake of the child's highest good, the mother is all it knows, so the child fights to stay with her. This represents the ego fighting to keep you thinking in scarcity and fear. This is the inner struggle many people experience while saying this first statement. If this occurs—don't stop—it is normal, and is a sure sign that the process is working.

To maximize efficacy and ease of saying this statement, the following action steps are strongly urged:

1.) Type up the reality statement on your computer so it's about the size of a business card, but big enough so it's easily readable. Copy it three more times so it appears a total of four times on one 8.5″ x 11.5″ piece of paper and print it out.

2.) Have the whole sheet laminated, then cut the 4 copies into separate cards. Put one in your wallet/pocket, one in your car, one on your nightstand, and one in your office.

3.) Commit to read the Reality Statement a minimum of 3x a day out loud, preferably once in the morning, then at noon, then before bed.

4.) Remember to persist repeating it for a full 52 days—the first 22 days break the old paradigm, then the next 30 days input the new paradigm

5.) Saying your Reality Statement is a difficult discipline that will challenge the ego, and therefore expect resistance. If you forget to say it for a day or two, forgive yourself, and then begin saying it with a renewed level of commitment.

6.) Remember that living your Soul Purpose is a unique gift realized by all too few people. By saying this Reality Statement you are creating favorable conditions to discover your Soul Purpose. Commit to being that one person out of a thousand who actually completes the program.

Instant Prayer

Historically, people have used prayer as an invocation to a higher power for the alleviation of suffering in a painful situation. What is prayer? In short, it is talking to God. It is an attitude of the heart with which we communicate with the Infinite Intelligence, invoking its Higher Power to lessen suffering. The effectiveness of prayer as a medical intervention has been clinically studied in depth for the past twenty years, and the results are quite conclusive and irrefutable. Prayer works. Science knows prayer works, but much like certain medicines, it just doesn't know precisely how. Many scientists do not ascribe to the efficacy of prayer as an intervention because they cannot prove *how* prayer works—only *that* it works.

The mini-battle that has been going on for the past one hundred years between science and religion is based on the lower mind of the ego that is threatened by the supposed 'other side.' Those who might be termed low-consciousness, whether scientist or religionist, fall prey to the dualistic fear generated by this lower mind. Each secretly believes his own rigid view of the world is the only right one, therefore editing out any other possible Truth—even if it is verifiable and duplicable. High-consciousness beings are unthreatened by, and love, New Truth—for the higher mind embraces scientific and spiritual realities as one and the same thing. The higher mind embraces these truths not as a weakening invalidation of a previously cherished illusion, but rather as a welcome addition that increases

Knowledge. To this author's understanding, science has never proven one thing that contradicts the teachings of Jesus Christ, Buddha, or Krishna. If anything, quantum physics has verified the realities of the mystical realm of the spiritual.

There are more than one-hundred and thirty scientific studies on the power of prayer as a healing intervention. Over fifty percent point to prayer having a beneficial therapeutic healing effect. When certain strict parameters were followed, efficacy rose to roughly eighty percent—alluding to the indisputable power of prayer to favorably alter reality (Dossey, 1996).

The clinical trials and double-blind studies provided amazing and tantalizing Truths. These prayer studies were done using a variety of living organisms, from people (both well and sick) to mice, on human DNA, and even plants and bacteria. The variety of test subjects was important so as to determine what effect the patient had on the experiment. In other words, did prayer work only with regards to the healing of *people*? Or did it work in a wide range of contexts with a variety of living organisms that could have no conscious interference (test subjects or their families might pray for themselves—mice, plants and bacteria do not).

This was also done for another reason. Some researchers theorized that prayer was working because the prayed-for patients knew they were being prayed for, and that they were not healed by a higher power, but rather by their own belief that they *might* be healed. This result is called the placebo effect—that one's own belief can heal—and it has been proven. Even though the higher power of God accounts for the placebo effect in people, the predominant scientific view of God is as an *outside* influence, not an *inside of everything* influence. To see if it was only the placebo effect, studies were done using distant prayer. If patients were being prayed for at a distance and didn't know it, and still got better—that would be a significant discovery. It would point to the intercession and existence of a Higher Power. Distant, intercessory prayer is therefore cited in the following studies.

Hospitalized (heart disease) patients were prayed for at a

distance without knowing they were being prayed for, while a 'control group' in the same hospital ward (other heart-diseased patients) went un-prayed for. Roughly eighty percent of the prayed-for group had shorter recovery times and a return to 'normal' life, while the control group did not fare nearly as well (Byrd, 1988). Distant prayer was again tested in a double-blind clinical study of AIDS patients. Prayed-for AIDS patients had significantly more favorable results than the non-prayed for control group AIDS patients (Sicher et al, 1997).

Mice were prayed for to resuscitate quicker after having been anesthetized. The prayed-for group awakened significantly faster than the control group (Watkins, 1971). Bacteria were prayed for to grow faster, and then even to grow slower—and both outcomes occurred in significantly altered fashion according to the desired reality that was prayed for (Nash, 1982).

The following parameters in the prayer studies repeatedly showed the most duplicable, favorable results.

1.) **That those who prayed all believed in a Higher Power based in Divine Love**. In all religions, the main underlying principle is that 'God is Love.' It is of great importance to realize that this unique version of Love is an ineffable, Divine Love—known as Agape in the western ethos, and Prema in the Eastern philosophies.
2.) **That the prayer was heart-felt, sincere, and authentic**. Authenticity was the key ingredient. All pray-ers believed that the desired reality they were praying for was possible due to the Love emanating from God. They also deeply believed their prayers were real, would be answered, and made a difference.
3.) **Praying to the 'God/Love of Your Understanding'.** The data concluded that no religion has a monopoly on God. Regardless of the pray-er's religious background, or the specific name of God used, results were consistently favorable (when steps 1 and 2 above were followed). Specific studies cited here included the following religious practitioners: Born-Again Christian, Roman Catholic, Episcopalian, Protestant, Buddhist, Jewish, Native-American and other Shamanic traditions, and healing traditions including several modern day

schools of healing (Benor, 2000).

4.) **No one specific religious prayer style proved to be more or less effective.** Whether one spoke out loud or not, was eloquent or not, spoke any specific language, was experienced or inexperienced, mattered not. The tactical points were utilizing a Higher Power based in Love, and, as best possible, being heart-felt and authentic (Dossey, 1996).

5.) **'Clarity of Intention' greatly altered outcome.** Intention has previously been referred to as the seventh sense. The prayer study cited here seems to prove the power of intention as a spiritual sense.

Spindrift is an organization that published an exhaustive study of the effects of prayer on a variety of subjects. They also studied two kinds of intention that was intrinsic to all prayers. One type of prayer intention was for a specific goal to occur. This, they called *goal directed prayer*. The other intention was for the 'Highest Good' to occur—this they called *non-goal directed prayer*. In goal directed prayer we are praying for a specific outcome according to limited human beliefs and intentions. This type of prayer tended to produce results that followed the belief system of the person praying.

In the studies using non-goal directed prayer, the effects were startling. Results were produced that tended to enhance the lives of the test subjects in ways the pray-er could have never known to pray for. When this type of prayer was used, best-case scenarios tended to manifest for the test subjects in areas the person praying had no possible knowledge would be beneficial (Klingbeil, 1993). In the Lord's Prayer, Jesus taught followers how to pray by using *non-goal directed prayer* via the famous statement, "Thy Will be done."

Reality Statements are non-goal directed prayers, always ending in the same way: this, or something better, now manifests in harmony with Thy perfect will for me—Amen. Please re-read the first Reality Statement a few pages back. Notice that the intention allows you to tap the Infinite Field of the Prosperity Paradigm so that God can create what is in your highest good. This is so important in that few people at their current levels of awareness actually know what their highest good is. This is the meaning behind the adage, "be careful what you ask for because you'll probably get it." Socrates spoke this point thusly: "Man always chooses only that which he believes to be the highest good—the problem is, he simply does not know what that highest good is." This is precisely why it is critical to understand the Teachings of Truth from the great masters, and to realize that scientific experimentation in the natural world verifies their teachings.

Instant Prayer is a technique that is similar to a reality statement, but contains a property which distinguishes it as unique. A reality statement is a fifty-two day, three-times-a-day prayer that never changes about that particular topic. Instant Prayer is a spontaneous prayer that may constantly change, depending on one's specific situation. Here is an example. Let's say your reality statement is about self-esteem, but four weeks into saying it you have a temporary money worry. The studies suggest it is wise to say an 'Instant Prayer' that addresses the money worry. Data shows that it is most effective to pray using the above parameters that tended to consistently manifest the highest reality. All prayers that begin with 'Thank you God for,' and end with, 'this reality now happens for the Highest Good of All'—appear to have powerful results. You simply insert a sentence that is extremely positive and depicts the greatest solution as if it is already here right now. As an example.

Thank you God for eliminating all money worries right now. I am a value creator—experiencing infinite abundance in harmony with Your Highest Will for me. This reality now happens, Amen.

At a sub-atomic level, quantum physics has determined that an atom can be either a *particle* or a *wave,* depending on the position and expectation of the observer (Talbot, 1991). All matter, even human beings, has both a physical existence (particle) and spiritual existence (wave). This may be evidence that goal directed prayer is particular (particle prayer manifesting human tendencies), and non-goal directed prayer is wavelike (wave prayer manifesting divine tendencies).

Faith is an important aspect to using this technique. Many people don't believe, or have faith, that a concept like this can work. Your disbelief can destroy the effect of the prayer before it happens—so, as best possible, suspend disbelief and negative judgment for prayer to have maximum efficacy. Practice doing so as often as possible.

Chapter Thirteen

Love Meditation

The lower mind is fear, and is thus based in force. The higher mind is love, and is thus based in power. Meditation provides the most thorough means by which a person can experience transcending the lower mind. The significance of doing so can be intellectually explained, but explanation pales in comparison to the magnificence of living the event. When the mind is transcended, happiness is ninety-nine percent guaranteed. The term 'Love Meditation' is symbolic of this understanding.

Meditation has erroneously been misperceived as weird eastern mysticism. Yet all people have experienced its benefits without even taking notice. Have you ever sat staring out a window, not focusing on anything in particular, in a peaceful state of being 'spaced out'? This might've happened to you while sitting in the car waiting for someone, watching traffic and people pass by in a state of non-attached awareness. No problems or worries exist in this place—it is peaceful, blissful, and calming. Then something snapped you back into normal consciousness, and you resumed the normal pattern of thinking without noticing how good it felt to take a break from lower mind. This preliminary experience is like dipping your toe into the ocean—when it comes to the enormity of the power that can be accessed through meditation.

As we go deeper into the purpose of meditation, it is important to reveal an odd truth. Human beings are meant to occasionally experience depression. It is part of the purpose of ego, as has been previously explained. Repeated experience of depression states occurs to compel us to seek the higher potentiality of a relationship with the God-self, versus sticking with the ego-self. Depression compels us to seek the higher meaning of life and ultimately our Soul Purpose. From a spiritual perspective, depression is a spiritual opportunity. In what is quickly becoming a Prozac society, Americans are using either meditation or medication to address this issue. Many people medicate with alcohol or illicit drugs on a daily basis, while many others use anti-depressants. We can either use these psychotropic drugs as a temporary solution to a chronic problem, or we can use a spiritual discipline to solve it once and for all. If we continuously and only medicate, it appears that we miss the spiritual opportunity.

This is not a position against using anti-depressants under a doctor's supervision as a temporary, or in severe cases, permanent, measure. The wisdom of modern pharmacology has been a blessing to many, and definitely has its place. It is a fact that in a certain percentage of people the physiology of their brain does not make enough seratonin for them to function happily (Hawkins, 2005). But this condition is the exception that makes the rule. Clinical depression is far different than short-term depression, which is meant to be part of the human experience.

This curriculum is promoting a long-term solution that has worked for thousands of years. Meditation is the spiritual discipline that people seem to struggle most with. This is because you confront the chaos of the ego-thinking mind face-to-face. Its job is to derail your efforts towards meditating, and in most people, it is successful. Prayer is speaking to God, meditation is listening to God. If you listen to God, the ego dies. It therefore considers meditation as a threat to its existence. This results in the ego turning up the volume on the intensity of the thought process. It is similar to changing stations on your radio, and encountering loud static until you tune in to the new station. You are moving from the lower ego-mind to the Higher God-mind. It is possible to listen to God, to become aware of God's Divine Will for us, and for our lives to evolve.

Watching the mind in meditation is like walking into a giant ten thousand square foot warehouse that is totally empty, except for two men unexpectedly arguing in one small corner. Where does your attention go, and what does it become engrossed with? The argument. In meditation we are aware of the argument (as noisy thoughts), but finally realize we cannot stop it. It is really none of our business, for the two men arguing in the mind represent the twin aspects of the ego—which are fear and desire. By intentionally playing the role of the Observer/Chooser we merely witness it, and then choose to shift our attention to the G.A.P—the **G**od-Self **A**wareness **P**oint.

This GAP is like a high-speed internet connection which links your individual computer to billions of other computers and trillions of bits of knowledge in cyberspace. Meditation links your individual consciousness to Infinite Consciousness. In meditation we are the Observer/Chooser—observing the noise, but choosing instead to focus on and expand the space to connect with the Infinite Intelligence of the Field. By doing so, we create a direct connection to the God Field, which is the initial intention of meditation.

This is a monumental accomplishment in the soul's evolution—choosing to turn around and look at the vast empty space in the warehouse of the mind, instead of being obsessed with fear and desire. In the warehouse of the mind, you must learn to focus on the power of the space, instead of the chaos of the thoughts. Soon we realize the space is not empty *(a vacuum),* but rather it is full *(a plenum)* of possibilities. As you master this inner space, you can then manifest your Soul Purpose in your outer space. Once we realize the inner space is filled with Love, we can then externalize that Love into our work. We can then fill the outer space with anything—a dance studio, an office building, a bookstore, a metal fabrication shop, an artist's loft—it is the doorway to an infinite realm of creative possibility.

Meditation connects you to your imagination, which is the genesis for all invention throughout history. This is precisely why

Einstein said "Imagination is far superior to knowledge." (Einstein, 1941) He called this realm the 'quantum realm of probability,' but in simpler terms, it appears to be an *Infinite Field of Possibility*. It is via this connection to the Infinite that your Soul Purpose can be downloaded as you mediate.

Another intention for meditating is that it enhances your ability to become familiar with, and then consistently use, the higher senses.

- The Sixth Sense is INTUITION—Spiritual **Sight** (Higher Awareness)
- The Seventh Sense is INTENTION—Spiritual **Purpose** (Higher Context)
- The Eighth Sense is IMAGINATION—Spiritual **Creativity** (Higher Possibility)

The higher senses operate in the following manner: Intuition leads to Intention, which leads to Imagination. So your awareness (Intuition) leads you to Remember God/Choose Love/Create Value which becomes the highest context (Intention) for your life. This choice activates the will, which arises as the decision to meditate. This decision initiates the connection to the creative ideas emanating from the Field. This creativity (Imagination) is a continuous source of the fully formed ideas from which all artists, scientists, and inventors receive their inspirations, visions and dreams.

Imagination is the sense through which soul purpose is revealed. A misnomer that is often taught in certain beliefs systems is that we can do anything, and that we are limitless. We are only limitless within the framework of our soul purpose; in all other areas we are actually quite limited. The acceptance of this truth comes with great relief and certitude. If we were limitless, I could decide to fly unaided off a building. No matter my belief system, that is not going to happen without physical peril or death. Or I could decide to become the greatest golfer in the world, but in truth no matter how hard I tried, since that is not this author's soul purpose it is not to be either. And yet all of my life, at a deep level, I knew I was always destined to become that which I am. As I continued to educate myself and apply the spiritual disciplines, clients sought me out and the mission evolved in ways that I pictured only in my imagination. The more consistently I meditated, the greater my ability to focus my concentration on any endeavor, whether creating a business plan or synthesizing the knowledge read from a book into life application. Remember, we are only limitless within the framework of our own soul purpose.

Through meditation, the noise of ego-thoughts is transcended so that we become aware of the soul purpose already fully formed. A pragmatic way of looking at it is to understand that the mind is ninety-five percent silent, and only five percent noise. You are merely focused on, and therefore entranced by, the noise. The intuitive proof that the mind is ninety-five percent silent and only five percent noise can be explained thusly:

Imagine waking up bright and early on a summer day and going outside to enjoy the morning, before anyone in the neighborhood awoke. What might you hear—quite probably a symphony of birdsong, right? You hear them so clearly because everything else is silent and still. The ninety-five percent background of early morning silence allows you to hear the five percent birdsong very clearly. But you do not acknowledge the existence of the silence, without which the beauty of the birdsong would be lost. If there were a construction site next door with thirty dump trucks at work you'd never hear the birds. The silence is context, the birdsong is content. It is the silence that allows you to hear them so clearly, and so it is with your mind. You are simply hypnotized by the five percent—you're ninety five percent on your way to oneness with higher mind! In meditation, we discover the power of the ninety-five per cent silent space that is the G.A.P.

While there are many different names and styles associated with meditating, they all condense down into two basic forms. One is a direct, active form, and the other is an indirect, passive form. They are tremendously beneficial, both to your health and towards creating conscious contact with the name of God you prefer and the style you understand.

ACTIVE
The first form of direct active meditation involves repetition of a phrase, or visual image over and over. Here are the steps:

1. Commit to twenty minutes daily.

Start out with a commitment to at least ten minutes in the morning and ten minutes in the evening. Wear loose fitting comfortable clothes and sit in a comfortable chair with your back straight. Choose a place where you'll be undisturbed by phones, people, etc. It is recommended not to meditate in bed. Practicing in the same location is preferable to building a long-term meditation practice.

2. There is no right or wrong

This is a spiritual discipline in which the rules differ from any other activity. It is the only life exercise where there is nothing specific to accomplish—there is no goal to 'do.' It is spiritual exercise to experience yourself as a Divine Being, not a human doing. Just showing up to do it is the win.

3. Close your eyes and follow your breath.

Close your eyes and begin breathing deeply. Follow your breath inward, listening to the symphony of your breath. In meditation, the focus on breath is important because it is the gift of life itself. The ancient holy sages believed each inhale was a new spiritual opportunity from God, and each exhale symbolized all that no longer served you, and as a kind of death in itself. Thus, the Latin word *spiritus* means 'breath' and is the root of the word spiritual. Focus deeply on elongating your incoming and outgoing breath.

4. Silently repeat your mantra.

Mantra is a Sanskrit word which means 'thought seed.' Meditating allows us to plant new seeds in the garden of life via repetition of a mantra. Pick a phrase (mantra) that inspires you or one that resonates within you as the right one. After a minute or two of deep, focused breathing, begin repetition of your mantra over and over. Silently repeat the first half of the phrase on the inhale breath, and then finish the last half of the phrase on the exhale.

5. When thoughts intrude, bless them, and go back to repeating your mantra.

Remember the ego must try to derail your efforts. It does so with a barrage of random meaningless (or even meaningful) thoughts. Some days are worse than others, and this is absolutely normal, so don't judge it, just watch it. It may take you a moment to even realize you're in thought. If you do find yourself thinking, just passively say 'bless you' or 'thanks for sharing' and go back to mantra repetition. Have a blanket handy as the body may get chilly. Tearing of the eyes is not unusual.

6. Mustering all possible power, fix your awareness firmly on the mind and watch it unrelentingly.

Before ending your meditation, concentrate every iota of your power on peering directly at the mind. It will stop instantly. Just stay fully present with fixity of focus, not exerting undue effort or struggle. The mind will be stunned into peaceful alignment and you will experience true peace and freedom. With practice, you will be able to hold this still point longer and longer. Just experiencing it at first is startlingly joyful and inspirational. This is the **G.A.P.**

7. When finished, take time to re-enter your day carefully.

Sit quietly for a minute to allow a gentle return to normal consciousness. Then open your eyes, sitting still for another minute before rising.

Suggested Mantras

I am one with the love of God—Non-denominational Spiritual
The Lord is my shepherd—Protestant or Catholic
I am one with my Father in Heaven—Mormon
Thy will be done Lord—Christian
Om mane padme hum—Buddhist

Ya Baha'u'lluh Abha—Baha'i Faith
La illaha il Allah—Sufi/Muslim
Om Shivaya namah—Hindu
Sh'ma Yisroel—Judaism
I am that I am—Unity

How to Practice

If you chose the mantra *I am one with the love of God,* you would repeat it this way (thinking the first half of the mantra while inhaling): ***"I am one with,"*** (then thinking this second part of the mantra on the exhale)—***"the love of God."*** As you repeat this mantra non-verbally, continue deep breathing. After five to ten minutes, you'll feel the mind get very restless—and this is where most people quit. If you can stay with it a little longer, the mind will begin to settle down. At that moment, look with intense focus directly at the mind. Be the unwavering witness, peering with the light of awareness at the mind. It will stop completely, and you will experience the **G**od-Self **A**wareness **P**oint. There will be stillness and complete peace. Once you find it, you will never lose the ability to reconnect to it again.

In meditation, you are like a jet plane taking off in a torrential rain storm. As you begin to meditate, there may be uncertainty—just like the plane taking off in the rain. The jet climbing through the rain, wind, and thunder is much like the noisy thoughts of fear, doubt, and worry one experiences in meditation. Then the jet enters the cloud layer, and in meditation this represents the G.A.P. This point is the leap of faith as you move from ego-self (below the cloud) to God-Self (above the cloud). When you are flying through clouds it is bumpy and turbulent. The pilot is visually blind, and flying on instruments only—he is flying on faith. Suddenly the jet breaks out of the clouds and enters a magnificent field of crystal clear blue sky in which the sun is brilliantly shining.

It is interesting to note that the blue sky is there even though you don't see it when you are beneath the clouds. Similarly, soul purpose exists even though you may not directly see it.

There are other tools to help transcend the thinking mind that can be useful during meditation. These may include a sacred picture or object, music, incense, or other aids that initiate transcendent energy. Highly visual people are often guided in reaching deeper meditation by unrelentingly fixing their focus onto an external object of symbolic Divinity. You may have a favorite picture of Jesus Christ, Buddha, Krishna, or Shiva; a Torah or a Lotus or the Sacred Heart, or some other image sacred to you. For people who have no such image, another object can work just as well. It may be a nature scene, a flower, or even a candle. Some religious practices forbid this, but do allow some aspect of traditional chant or repetition that takes the student to deeper levels of consciousness.

These are the pragmatic details for practicing meditation, but the more important idea is the commitment to stay with it. Some days may be frustrating, some days may be revelation, but showing up every day is the win. As you develop a fixity of focus utilizing higher mind, you have created the connection to the Field of the Infinite. By committedly creating a singular focus, you emanate a strong high-frequency vibration that develops spiritual Will. The Will is an unstoppable power, in that Will and Faith are of the Spirit, and are the two important essences that complete the transcending of the mind. The mind does not 'do' Faith, nor does it comprehend the Will.

It has been said that **Faith** equals **Belief** minus **Evidence**. The reason the mind doesn't understand faith is that the intellect is based upon logic and is therefore linear. Because faith is non-linear, the intellect views it as illogical and naively irrelevant. Will is similar in that it is an aspect of the spirit. As it gets stronger through the spiritual discipline of meditation, your ability to be more disciplined in other life areas is strengthened tremendously.

This has been confirmed via spiritual healing groups like Alcoholics Anonymous. Through connecting to their Higher Power via fellowship, prayer, and meditation, the willpower of individual alcoholics is exponentially increased. With a renewed faith and an increased will, the ability to heal the fatal disease of alcoholism was finally discovered. The same will occur for you, including the discovery of your Soul Purpose, as you commit to practice meditation.

PASSIVE

This second style can be best understood as a contemplative, indirect form of meditation. Instead of practicing one-pointedness via central focus, one practices shifting awareness to a peripheral focus. The peripheral focus is a pure devotion to being present in the here and now, and to nothing else. Awareness of all things, people, and objects becomes heightened—with a diminished attachment to any observed thing being any way other than as it is. Everything begins to be seen as perfect—exactly as it is—requiring no interference from you at all. Just noticing this becomes a revelation of stunning significance. One can walk through life in this contemplative state without losing any ability to operate at the highest levels. This is what is meant by *Love Meditation*.

Imagine sitting in your living room staring out the picture window at the trees and garden. You are not focused on any one thing, but you are nevertheless acutely aware of all things in your peripheral vision. A bird flies by and you see it without turning to follow its flight. The cat crawls on your lap and is allowed to do so without any movement, resistance, or effort on your part. The wind severs a branch from the tree, yet no worry crosses the mind about it causing damage by hitting the house. The telephone rings but is not seen as intrusive or annoying. All is understood as always being in its right place. Waves of reassurance are received from the Infinite Field that God is indeed Love, and therefore always sending that which is in the Highest Good. The awareness of the perfection and totality of all existence is suddenly realized, and even this monumental idea requires no comment or movement. As the Divine Oneness continues to be experienced, a level of rapturous peace descends with the gentleness of a feather, and the power of a billion suns.

With practice, one becomes the witness, and then eventually becomes the awareness itself. Witnessing eliminates the personal illusion of perception, replacing it with Spiritual Vision. The illusion of *me* slowly dissolves into the realization of the ***I***. This is how the ego-thinking mind is transcended.

The Ultimate Wealth

This book refers to five predominant modes of human consciousness, citing LOVE mode as being the highest. This was intentionally done because the great majority of human beings cannot fathom the ultimate mode of human potential. Until being exposed to a work like this, there is no reference point to verify this mode exists, nor that it has any relevance.

Love is the second highest mode to Enlightenment. What is the value of attaining such a state? It is the ultimate wealth, in which the human being has transformed into a Divine Being. The energy Field of such a Divine Being counterbalances the collective negativity of seventy million beings in the lower modes (Hawkins, 1995). What greater gift to give the world than to truly save the world in such a manner? The enlightened state is the mode of the Christ. It is what Jesus referred to when he said, "these things I have done, you shall do, and greater. "

The enigma of why Enlightenment is so rare and elusive is that it cannot be sought or attained. *Seeking it pushes it away.* Trying to seek enlightenment is like fishing in an empty pond. The process of 'seeking' alludes to searching for something you don't already have that exists outside of you. This essential misperception locks the experience up inside of you, making it unrealizable.

Enlightenment is the most natural condition of human *Being*, and is the essence of that which you truly are on the inside. It is a process of Self-Realization. The essence of You is already enlightened, but is deeply covered up by layers and layers of false perceptions; fear, limiting beliefs, and the illusion of the mind as who you are. These many false perceptions form the essence of the scarcity paradigm. They include perceptual errors about what is really important, who you truly are, what the purpose of life on Earth is, what love really is, the Godly context of wealth creation via money, and so many other layers of false beliefs. These misperceptions obscure the true essence of that which you are—GOD itself manifesting in a human body. Again we see the dualistic split-mind conundrum: '**I**' is hidden by 'me.' If the

Law of One is true, and God is all that there is, then what else could *you be?* This is the state of ultimate wealth, for when one **is** the Source of All, one *needs* nothing. What could you possibly need when you are fully complete? Money, fame, cars, houses, bullion—all are tinsel and twigs compared to the wisdom-consciousness of the enlightened master.

There is an unmistakable feeling of grace and intense spiritual power you receive by being in the presence of an enlightened person. It is such a rare phenomenon that whole religions have been created around such rare beings.

Money is not power, wisdom is power. Wisdom is applied knowledge. This curriculum has made it abundantly clear that there is a radical difference between *knowing about,* and ***knowing***. How, indeed, can **K**nowledge be known? I have enjoyed the grace of studying with two enlightened masters in this lifetime—one Eastern Indian and one an American. Both confirmed that the way we truly know anything is as follows.

Four Levels of Cognition

This section is included for you to understand the enormous difference between *Knowing* (essence) and *knowing about* (perception). Cognition is the process of **K**nowing in the broadest sense, including personal experience, current awareness level, degree of spiritual evolution, and a clear understanding of essence vs. perception.

The predominant worldly error is that people mostly expound perception (hearsay) as essence (Truth). Beginning at levels four and three, this error is revealed. It is then resolved via the explanations contained in levels two and one.

4. Hearing 'about something' via media (books, television, radio, newspaper, Internet and movies)

This level refers to your coming into impersonal contact with a particular idea or story about something via media. The error then perpetuates as the information is regurgitated with the individual's own slant and polarized opinion. It is from this error that the ego game called the 'polarity of the opposites' arises. It causes fear to spread like wildfire. Information is often chaotic, random, and misleading whereas Knowledge is clear, centered and purposeful.

Of great misfortune is the habit of espousing information as truth simply because it appears in a newspaper, book, magazine, documentary, or on the Internet. The latest study of the information found on the Internet shows that approximately fifty percent is false (Hawkins, 2005). The gullibility of the general public was revealed when actor Orson Welles performed his story *War of the Worlds* as a radio skit. Listeners who tuned in after the disclaimer in the intro was read thought it to be a real alien invasion ("Many Flee Homes to Escape" *New York Times,* 1938). After the movie Psycho was released, many women and people were afraid to take showers alone for years. The media has gone from *reporting* the news—to *creating* the news.

In the early sixties media professor Marshall McLuhan wrote that the 'medium is the message.' He stated that each medium, from newspapers to TV, often crossed the line from reporting the news to creating the news. His premise was simple—how can any reporter be truly *objective* about anything when each of us is the *subject,* seeing it through our own eyes and biases? Our own opinion is then layered on top of the event, coloring it with the filter of our own experiences and partialities. The ego feels superior as it spouts vehement opinions, assumptions, and speculations about world events it has no clue to the veracity of.

You do not ***know*** any truth by reading or hearing about it. You may know *about it,* but only ***know it*** via direct experience or by becoming one with the object of cognition (Father, Wallace, Schultz, Grey, F.O.R. papers, 1975).

3. Hearing 'about something' via the vicarious experience of another person

For the most part, this is not 'knowing' at all. Sharing others' unverified opinion of things as Truth is a very damaging and hurtful practice. It perpetuates falsehood by labeling something according to another person's experience or perception of it. Perception is not reality, only essence is reality. The accuracy of this level is much like the parlor game in which what is whispered into the first person's ear is humorously distorted by the time it comes around the circle and out of the eighth person's mouth. Most of the time what was originally conveyed is not even close to what is finally verbalized.

The Natural Laws prove that others' experiences are specifically meant for them—not necessarily you. They serve as personal lessons that they themselves had a hand in creating, by the way they treated others. The Law of Vibration and Attraction determines whether one experiences positivity or negativity. The Law of Synchronicity dictates the perfect timing of all events in the universe. If good things are happening, they were self-created, and so too with perceived bad things. Whether someone is complaining about or bragging about another person, their own experience is sure to be unique from anyone else's. How often does the re-telling of any story include all the subtle contextual nuances that give accuracy and meaning to anything?

How then, do you trust something you hear to be true?

Consider the source. When you are with high-integrity, high-consciousness people, you'll notice an enormous difference in the power level and value potential of their conversation. Unless you have direct experience with the object, (be it a person, place, or thing), place little importance on what you hear. Listen politely, reflect deeply on who is sharing the information, but be very discerning before you believe or promote it as Truth. Unless you are hearing information from a loving, high-consciousness being, take everything at this level with a grain of salt. When we base our beliefs upon the perceptions of another, we infuse grandiose error-thoughts into our mental realm software.

Two clients spoke to me of a certain man (we'll call him by the fictitious name of Mr. Smith) on the same day. Client one saw Mr. Smith give a keynote speech to a large group of financial planners and thought he was a great, inspiring man. Client two had also once thought Mr. Smith to be great, until investing several hundred thousand dollars with him in a real estate deal that went sour. Client one thought he was a great guy, and client two thought he was a thief, and each asked what I thought of Mr. Smith. Since I had never met the man, I said, "I don't know—I don't think about him at all." Anything I might have said other than that would have arisen from the bias of my ego, which distorts perceptions. These perceptions are then typically spewed as fact, but are really unsubstantiated opinion. I no longer allow this to happen. By not taking sides, my mind stayed uncluttered, unbiased, and free to have its own experience. More importantly, I stayed in a positive, love-based state of vibration instead of perpetuating negative judgments with incomplete information.

This technique is called *Recontextualization,* and has been referred to previously in this text. I shifted the context by realizing that these very different experiences of the same man were exactly as they should be—for each of my clients to learn from in the highest way. Each of my clients' experiences with Mr. Smith were specifically meant for them and therefore, synchronistic and ultimately, perfect. This enabled me to stay in the present and connected to the aware mind and to the power of the Field.

Levels Four and Three are based in scarcity consciousness, while levels Two and One are based in Prosperity Consciousness.

2. Personal experience with the object

This level is the beginning of KNOWLEDGE, in which one knows from personal experience. It is the first of two that engage the engine of the God-Self, while the previous two levels operate from the ego-self.

Human beings are constantly walking into the unknown every second, without a clue of certainty as to what the next moment may bring. The ego is most easily transcended by admitting this great truth—*I don't know*. Most people are simply afraid, and/or too egoistic, to admit it. I spent the first half of my life saying, "I know this, I know that, I *know*, I ***know***…"—in reality I knew nothing. Only when I finally declared, "I know hardly anything" did my life hit bottom, then immediately begin to shift upwards. The ego thinks it knows, but it knows very little of importance. Only God knows. Each person in the whole world thinks of himself as the ego, and as secretly right about everything. The stunning Truth is that ***we're all wrong***—and only God is right. This is why humility is such an essential aspect of any course that leads toward love and enlightenment.

Hearing and talking about a thing—without direct, personal experience of it—has virtually nothing to do with Truth in any way. Before I went to France, I had heard that the French were mean-spirited national chauvinists who disliked Americans. My own experience was the exact opposite, and I was treated with warmth, kindness, and friendliness when I visited there. If you have believed the common stereotype about French attitudes, your own ego may have been ruffled upon reading that last statement. Have you ever been to France?

Opinions and labels are worthless garbage based on vanities of the ego. Notice that your ego-thinking mind constantly labels everything almost automatically, and has non-stop opinions based on social programming—and nothing else. Those ideas and words are meaningless error thoughts. No truth exists without context, and personal experience is the only context by which anything can be ***known***.

All the so-called 'known stereotypes' of American social programming, i.e.: *Italians are greasy and involved with the mafia, Jews are cheap and only help other Jews, Blacks are lazy and untrustworthy, all lawyers are scumbags, the wealthy think they're better than others,* etc.—have all been personally experienced as falsehoods by this author. My Jewish friends are very generous and have treated me as their family. One of my greatest life teachers happens to be African-American, and there is no harder worker that I trust more implicitly than he. Throughout my life, all these negative labels and stereotypes—when I was open-minded to personally experience their targets—proved to be false.

I began to, and still do, practice *skillful faith* and *skillful doubt*. When you hear something from a questionable source, practice skillful doubt—which is a process of open-minded skepticism. When someone does or says something that just feels wrong, practicing skillful doubt is trusting your inner intuitive warning, which guides us to be open to truth—but to first act with cautious wisdom. When you're not sure, err on the side of caution. If what that source is sharing turns out to be true, it will eventually be revealed to you—at the perfect time. When knowing the truth about the universe in which we live becomes important to you, you can trust that you will eventually know the Truth. The greatest sign of faith is practicing skillful doubt. Any Truth, when challenged, will reveal itself as truth by whether or not it functions in the universe. Challenging a belief before you know it as Truth means you are actually considering using it. Skillful doubt is this challenge. Practice skillful doubt, instead of blind doubt—which is doubting everything.

Practice skillful faith, instead of blind faith—which is believing everything.

When hearing something from a reliable high-consciousness source, I practice skillful faith. Skillful faith is a process in which I *believe* something is true, but I do not yet *know*, so I practice judicious optimism. When information a person is saying feels right intuitively, remain open to experiencing it—but until you do so—you don't **know** it. **Until you know it, be careful about speak of it**. Be willing to apply the information, knowing that the Natural Laws will verify it as Truth or falsehood by whether it functions or not. The experience is then stored in your memory as Knowledge. Appropriate and consistent application of this Knowledge is then termed Wisdom. Notice the huge difference between information, Knowledge, and Wisdom.

With the development of this new habit, I began to recover energy that had once been wasted on upholding falsehoods. Being negative drains and wastes so much precious energy. Once the habit of spewing information as Knowledge was broken, a powerful truth was discovered. I had only perpetuated false social programming so that I could be accepted by a group of people who were really miserable. I spoke stupidly only to gain their acceptance. How ironic that I was seeking approval and love from others who were intolerant and unloving—therefore incapable of giving the love I sought.

Understanding this point will help you to drop labels and opinions, and seek open-mindedness and direct personal experience. It will also help you to quickly align with a higher soul group of people who are committed to love and joy. This will build your inner strength with true Knowledge, and greatly enhance your ability to create value for yourself and others.

Previous personal experience with someone or something will also change as you grow and evolve. The first time I read the Declaration of Independence was in high school. I thought it was boring, unintelligible, and dreary. Twenty years later, I read it again and found it to be interesting and informative, but strictly utilitarian. This year I read it and I hung on every word. I deeply pondered Thomas Jefferson's state of mind as I found myself enthralled, inspired, and humbly grateful. As **you** change, your access to deeper levels of the world changes. Thus, even if your first encounter with a Frenchman was experienced as an occasion of rudeness and arrogance, and you stored that experience as an example that confirmed the old stereotype, you may have later experiences that contradict that stereotype…even with the very same Frenchman. The difference could be in his behavior, or in your growing insight. Have you ever had a person you initially doubted you would like turn out to be a valuable friend or teacher? By practicing open-mindedness to previous experiences, *value can always increase.*

While this level is the first of the four levels that comes from choosing the God-Self, experience is still the secondary path to *K*nowledge. The primary path is Oneness.

1. Becoming one with the object of cognition—pure subjectivity as the I AM.

Living the Prosperity Paradigm has resulted in this author experiencing happiness approximately ninety-nine percent of the time. Any other trace negativity is continually surrendered to God as it arises. Love is who I am, yet I am unenlightened. It may or may not occur, for it cannot be chosen, nor is there any attachment to it. The last step is gifted only by the Grace of God.

Therefore I am truly not qualified to speak of this level at all. What I can say is that enlightenment is the final test in Earth School. Everything written prior to this point I have personally experienced as Truth. From this point forward I am quoting the masters. You may choose to believe it, or not, and either will be the perfect choice for you.

The ultimate path to ***K***nowledge is to *become one with it.* Enlightenment is a unified state in which the Knower becomes one with the Known, healing the split mind dilemma (dualism)—resulting in a state of Unity with ***K***nowledge itself. The enlightened being knows all because he is all. He knows himself as pure subjective presence, and since no objects exist as separate entities, his consciousness unites with ALL THAT IS.

When Moses received the ten commandments he asked God to declare himself, and the response was, "I AM THAT I AM." The enlightened one has merged the God within (subjective realization that I AM) and the God Without (the TOTALITY of ALL THAT IS). He has become one with God as the Totality of Subjective Unification—the 'I AM' subject—united with ALL THAT IS. The known, the knower, and the Knowledge become one at last. He is home. He has been perfected, and problems cease to be possible—he is awake, and complete.

Through an enlightened master, every living thing is uplifted without knowing why. Peace is felt by all conscious beings, and no greater value than this can be known.

To these rare Souls, the ego is dead. As one master said, *"The solution is in the realization that you already are what you are trying to become. It's in the seeing that there could never be a 'me' to be enlightened. All there is—is 'I'- the seeker is the sought."* The Universal ***I*** has replaced the individual ***me***. The eternal essence 'I' is life itself—consciousness as pure subjective Self-realization. The 'me' to which he refers is ego—a false self that has no permanent existence, therefore is an illusion. This is why Buddha called enlightenment Nirvana, which literally translates as 'blowing out.' It refers to extinguishing the ego, which then allows the full radiance of the Divine to shine through unimpeded. It is the I AM. The enlightened being IS everything, therefore needs nothing. It has been referred to as the unending Bliss of Self-Conscious Existence.

Nothing can disturb him—for He IS Love, Light, Laughter, Limitless, Forever—Free.

This is the ultimate wealth.

Epilogue

At the beginning of this curriculum three levels were outlined that defined how the process of prosperity works.

1. Understanding the New Paradigm—Shifting Beliefs from scarcity to Prosperity.

2. Internalizing It—Changing my behavior to create habits of abundance.

3. Externalizing It—Living the Mission by creating value everywhere I go, resulting in more money earned.

We at the Prosperity Paradigm have a mission statement for our company.

Our sole purpose is to help you discover and live your Soul Purpose.

To serve this mission, we have created the Prosperity Paradigm Symposium series, which we invite you to attend. Each symposium reveals specific principles, tools and techniques to build a life of Financial Freedom. Please visit our website, www.theprosperityparadigm.com, to see where the next symposium near you is taking place.

Also, if you received value from reading this book, please think about sharing this message with others. If there is someone, or several people, who you care about that need this message, give them the gift of a copy of this book. As you create this kind of value for others, they, and all of creation will surely reciprocate that kindness in some way back to you.

May the blessings of great health and an outrageously fulfilling life, be upon you—and also upon all people whom you love.

Appendix A

THE PROSPERITY PARADIGM PRINCIPLES

1. Collective human behavior/beliefs do not qualify those behavior/beliefs to be TRUTH.

2. No truth exists in this world without context being clearly set. (Material things are meaningless unless they are used to uplift people - how a thing is earned and used gives it meaning.)

3. The highest context of human existence is to Remember God, Choose Love, and Create Value

4. Discovering and living one's Soul Purpose expands the greatest possibility for people to create value for others.

5. In a world of seeming cause and effect, value creation is the cause, money is the effect.

6. When making a buying decision, the primary factor is understanding the value proposition and the secondary factor should be money.

7. Money is a useful tool of exchange, but people and wisdom are the true assets.

8. Wise stewardship increases personal power, thereby increasing one's ability to receive more abundance in return.

Reference Texts

Alpert, Richard. *Be Here Now*. San Cristobal, NM: Lama Foundation, 1971.
Arbinger Institute. *Leadership and the Art of Self-Deception*. San Francisco: Barrett-Koehler Publishers, 2000.
Balsekar, Ramesh S. *The Final Truth*. Redondo Beach CA: Advaita Press, 1989.
Beaulieu, John. *Music and Sound in the Healing Arts*. Barrytown NY: Station Hill Press, 1987.
Benor, D.J. *Science, Spirit, and the Eternal Soul*. Vision Publications: 2000.
Benson, Herbert M.D. *Timeless Healing*. New York: Fireside -Simon & Schuster, 1996.
Bohm, David. *Wholeness and the Implicate Order*. New York: Routledge Classics, 1980.
Brackenridge, Douglas, and Lois Boyd. *Presbyterians and Pensions*. Atlanta: John Knox Press, 1988.
Briggs, John P., and F. David Peat. *Looking Glass Universe*. New York: Simon and Schuster, 1984.
Buscaglia, Leo. *Love*. New York: Fawcett Crest, 1972.
Byrd, Randolph C. "Positive therapeutic effects of intercessory prayer in a coronary care population," *Southern Medical Journal* 81, 1988
Canfield, Jack, Mark Victor Hanson, and Les Hewitt. *The Power of Focus*. Deerfield Beach FL: Health Communications Inc., 2000.
Capra, Fritjof. *The Tao of Physics*. New York: Shambala/Bantam Books, 1976.
Castiglione, Robert. *LEAP*. Castle Lion Publishers, 2005.
Chapman, Gary. *The Five Love Languages*. Chicago: Northfield Publishing, 1992.
Coleman, D. and Murray A. Straus. Alcohol abuse and family violence. In E. Gottheil, ed., *Alcohol, Drug Abuse and Aggression*. Springfield: Charles C. Thomas, 1983.
Coelho, Paulo. *The Alchemist*. San Francisco: Harper Books, 1995.
Covey, Stephen R. *The 7 Habits of Highly Effective People*. New York: Fireside/Simon & Schuster, 1990.
D'Annunzio, S. excerpt from *Transcending the Ego*, a Sunday service given at Christ Church Unity, Rochester NY, April 9, 2006
D'Annunzio, S. *The Divine Nine Series Tuning Forks*. Rochester NY: The Sound Healing Center, 1994.
D'Annunzio, S. *Music For Healing*.Rochester NY: The Sound Healing

Center, 1996.
D'Annunzio, S., Q. Crawford, and J. Ransone. *A Double-Blind Study of Ethical Behavior as the Determinant Factor in Business.* Baltimore: 2004.
Dawood, N.J., (translation*) Koran 4:29*, London England : Penguin Classics, 1956
Denmeade, Michael. *Double-Blind Study of the Effects of* Music For Healing *on Alzheimers's/Dementia Patients*. Mt. Ascutney Hospital: 1997.
Dossey, Larry. *Prayer is Good Medicine*. San Francisco: HarperCollins Publishing, 1996.
Dyer, Wayne W. *Real Magic*. San Francisco: HarperCollins Publishing, 1992.
Dyer, Wayne W. *The Power of Intention*. Carlsbad CA: Hay House, 2004.
Easwaran, Eknath. *The Baghavad Gita* (Translation). New York: Vintage/Random House, 1985.
Easwaran, Eknath. *Dhammapada* (Translation). Tomales CA: Nilgiri Press, 1985.
Einstein, Albert. *The World as I see It*. New York: Citadel Press, 1956.
Einstein, Albert. 'Imagination' Quote, excerpted *from Science, Philosophy and Religion, A Symposium*. New York: The Conference on Science, Philosophy and Religion in *Their Relation to the Democratic Way of Life, Inc.,*1941
Eker, T. Harv. *Secrets of the Millionaire Mind.* New York: HarperCollins Publishing, 2005,
Elias, M. "High Pressure Jobs not always the Worst." *USA Today*, 8/18/05
Essene, Virginia, and Tom Kenyon. *The Hathor Material*. Santa Clara CA: S.E.E Publishing, 1996.
Father, Wallace C.P., D.R. Schultz, and C.Grey. *Foundation of Revelation Papers*. San Francisco, 1975.
Gallup Organization Poll. DEC 1994. Quoted in George Bishop, "*What Americans really believe,*" Free Inquiry, 1999, pgs 38 to 42.
Gandhi, Mahatma. *The Essential Gandhi*. New York: Random House, 1962.
Giblin, Les. *Skill with People.* Hohokus, NJ: *self published*, 1968.
Gleick, James, *Chaos - Making a New Science*, New York: Penguin Books, 1988
Glynn, Patrick. *GOD The Evidence*. Rocklin CA: Prima Publishing, 1997.
Hawkins, David R. *Power vs. Force*. Carlsbad CA: Hay House Inc., 1995.
Hawkins, David R. *The Eye of the Eye.* W. Sedona AZ: Veritas Publishing, 2002.
Hawkins, David R. *I, Reality and Subjectivity*. W. Sedona AZ: Veritas Publishing, 2003.

Hawkins, David R. *Truth vs. Falsehood.* Toronto: Axial Publishing Co., 2005.
Hill, Napoleon. *Think and Grow Rich.* New York: Fawcett/Random House Publishing, 1960.
Hoyle, Fred. *The Origins of the Universe and the Origin of Religion.* Wakefield RI: Moyer Bell, 1993.
Huebner, Solomon S. *The Economics of Life Insurance.* Appleton, Century, Crofts, 1929.
Huxley, Aldous. *Introduction to the* Bhagavad Gita. Translated by Swami Prabhavananda & Christopher Isherwood. New York: Signet/Mentor Classics, 1944.
"Is God Dead?" *Time Magazine.* 4/8/66.
Jampolsky, Gerald G. and Diane V. Cirincione. *Change your Mind, Change your Life.* New York: Bantam Books, 1993.
Janis, Sharon. *Spirituality for Dummies.* Foster City CA: IDG Books Worldwide Inc., 2000.
Jeffers, Susan. *Feel the Fear and Do it Anyway.* New York: Fawcett/Random House Publishing, 1987.
Jenny, Hans. *Cymatics.* Switzerland: Basilius Presse, 1974.
Jung, Carl G. *Man and His Symbols.* New York: Dell/Random House, 1968.
Klingbeil, John, and Bruce Klingbeil. *The Spindrift Papers.* Self-published, 1993.
Klopfer, Bruno. "Psychological Variables in Human Cancer", *Journal of Prospective Techniques* 31, 1957 pp.331-40
Lamsa, George. *The Modern New Testament form the Aramaic.* Covington GA: The Aramaic Bible Society, 1933.
Leslie, John. *Universes.* London: Routledge, 1996.
Loomis, Carol J., A *Conversation with Warren Buffet*, Fortune Magazine, June 25, 2006
Lorenz, Edward, The Essence of Chaos, 1993, Seattle, WA, Washington University Press
Maharaj, Nisargadatta. *I Am That.* Bombay, India: Chetana Pvt. Ltd. USA: Acorn Press, 1973.
Maharshi, Ramana. *The Spiritual Teachings of Ramana Maharshi.* Boston MA: Shambhala/Boston & Shaftesbury, 1988.
"Many Flee Homes to Escape 'Gas Raid From Mars'--Phone Calls Swamp Police at Broadcast of Wells Fantasy." *New York Times.* 10/31/38.
Marquez, Jeremiah. "LA on edge after Freeway Shootings." 4/29/05 AP, *www.abcnews.go.com*.
Maslow, Abraham. *The Farther Reaches of Human Nature.* New York:

Penguin Books, 1976.
McCutcheon, Mark. *The Final Theory*. Boca Raton FL: Universal Publishers, 2004.
Murphy, Austin, The Next Stage, *article* in Sports Illustrated magazine, May 2006
Nash, Carroll. "Psychokinetic Control of Bacterial Growth." *Journal of the Society of Psychical Research* 51, 1982.
Parkinson, C. Northcote. *Parkinson's Law*. Cutchogue NY: Buccaneer Books, 1957.
Pert, Candice B. Ph.D. *Molecules of Emotion*. New York: Scribner, 1997.
Price, John Randolph. *The Abundance Book*. Carlsbad CA: Hay House, 1987.
Proctor, Bob. *You Were Born Rich*. Kansas City MO: Praxis International, 1996.
Ponder, Catherine, *Dynamic Laws of Prosperity*, Marina del Rey CA, DeVorss and Company, 1984
Renier, Leonard A., *Learning to Avoid Unintended Consequences*, Haverford PA, Infinity Publishing, 2003
Robbins, Tony. *Awaken the Giant Within*. New York: Simon and Schuster, 1991.
Roberts, M. Royston. *Serendipity: Accidental Discoveries in Science*. New York: John Wiley and Sons, 1989.
Rorscach, Hermann. *Psychodiagnostik*. Switzerland, self-published, 1921.
Rosecrance, John *"The Next Best Thing:" A Study of Problem Gambling..* The International Journal of the Addictions, 20(11&12), p1727-1739, 1985-86.
Rose, Charlie. *Dr. Ben Carson Interview* (TV program), 1/1/03, PBS
Salzburg, Sharon. *Faith*. New York: Riverhead Books, 2002.
Schucman, Helen, and William Thetford. *A Course In Miracles.* Mill Valley CA: Foundation For Inner Peace, 1992.
Selye, Hans. *The Stress of Life*. New York: McGraw-Hill, 1978.
Shearer, Alistair. *The Yoga Sutras of Patanjali.* New York: Random House, 1882.
Sheldrake, Rupert. *A New Science of Life*. Rochester VT: Park St. Press, 1995.
Shinn, Florence Scovel. *The Game of Life and How to Play It*. Carlsbad CA: Hay House, 1925.
Sicher, Fred *et al.* "Randomized double-blind study of the effects of distant healing in a population with advanced AIDS" (Subtle Energies) www.wholistichealingresearch.com
Silva, Jose. *The Silva Mind Control Method*, New York: Pocket book/Simon & Schuster Inc., 1977.

Skinner, B.F. *Science and Human Behavior.* New York: Simon and Schuster, 1953.

Talbot, Michael. *The Holographic Universe.* New York: HarperCollins Publishing, 1991.

Tracy, Brian. *The 100 Absolutely Unbreakable Laws of Business Success.* San Francisco: Berrett-Koehler Publishing, 2000.

Walsch, Neale Donald. *Conversations with God Book I.* New York: G.P. Putnam's Sons, 1995.

Watkins, Graham K. and ArleneWatkins. "Possible PK Influence on the resuscitation of anesthetized mice," *Journal of Parapsychology* 35 (1971)

"What Money Can Buy." *The New Yorker (magazine).* 10/24/05.

Williamson, Marianne. *A Return to Love.* New York: Harper-Collins Publishers Inc., 1992.

Woods, Tiger. *How I Play Golf.* New York: Time Warner Books Inc., 2001.

Yogananda, Paramahansa. *Autobiography of a Yogi.* Los Angeles:
Self- Realization Fellowship, 1974.

Young-Sowers, Meredith. *Agartha.* Walpole NH: Stillpoint Publishing, 1995.